Hymes (w)

SO-AIR-329

LANGUAGE, SCIENCE, AND ACTION

Recent titles in
Contributions in Intercultural
and Comparative Studies
Series Editor: Ann M. Pescatello

Power and Pawn: The Female in Iberian Families, Societies,
and Cultures
Ann M. Pescatello

Tegotomono: Music for the Japanese Koto
Bonnie C. Wade

Historical Archaeology: A Structural Approach in an African Culture
Peter R. Schmidt

Sacred Words: A Study of Navajo Religion and Prayer
Sam D. Gill

Liberalism in an Illiberal Age: New Culture Liberals in
Republican China, 1919-1937
Eugene Lubot

Revolution and Counterrevolution: Mozambique's War of
Independence, 1964-1974
Thomas H. Henriksen

Flying Dragons, Flowing Streams
Ronald Riddle

Communicating with Quotes: The Igbo Case
Joyce Penfield

Ideology on a Frontier: The Theological Foundation of Afrikaner
Nationalism, 1652-1910
J. Alton Templin

CONTENTS

Preface   vii

Introduction: The Word and the World   3

1. The Polish Intellectual Milieu, 1890-1914   11

2. Between Poland and America, 1914-1933   25

3. Science and Sanity: A Historical Critique   45

4. Ideology and Praxis: General Semantics and Analytical
   Philosophy in America and Poland, 1930s-1960s   65

Conclusion   81

Notes   93

Bibliographic Essay   145

Index   157

PREFACE

In any project spanning several decades one incurs many intellectual debts and obligations to people who have helped along the
way. Space precludes mentioning all by name, so a few must stand
for all. My longest standing obligations for this monograph are
to Gordon Wiseman and Tom Ludlum of Ohio University, who introduced me to general semantics and the criticisms of it; to H.
Stuart Hughes and David Thomas of Harvard University, who whetted
my appetite for European intellectual history; and to Paul Conkin
and Don Dennis, who read the manuscript with critical eyes during
a National Endowment for the Humanities summer seminar at
Vanderbilt University. I began writing this monograph during a
sabbatical at Augustana College in the spring of 1974; explored
some of the issues further in a Lilly honors seminar at Augustana
in 1976; returned to it after a stint of departmental administration, completing the final version during a second sabbatical in
the spring of 1981; and polished up the final draft while serving
as a University House Fellow at the University of Iowa during the
summer of 1981. The preparation of the publisher's copy was
supported by a grant from the Faculty Research Committee of
Augustana College. My thanks to President Thomas Tredway and Dean
Harold Sundelius of Augustana College, to Douglas Nelson of the
Lilly Fund Committee of Augustana College, and to Jay Semel of the
University House program at the University of Iowa for their
support of these opportunities to engage in research, writing, and
creative thinking.

Many colleagues and experts have helped over the years in the
preparation of this monograph. Richard and Anna Wartman were my
guides to Polish civilization and culture. Richard generously
translated material from Polish; visiting lecturer F. Adamski of
Poland stimulated my interest in Polish sociology; Nicholas Ellig

and Ben Nefzger suggested sources in sociological literature; Harold Sjursen supplied guidance in the area of analytical philosophy; and Don Erickson, Harry Stelling, and John Lang mused with me over questions of language and meaning. Ralph Waldo Hanson criticized the sections on verbal therapies and generously loaned many key books in the area of psychology. Charlotte Schuchardt Read, Korzybski's literary executor, graciously and carefully responded to the request for permission to quote copyrighted material in the Korzybski estate. John Caldwell of the Denkman Library of Augustana College and his staff of librarians kept the flow of interlibrary loan books and articles coming across my desk and did not hesitate to purchase the highly specialized (and expensive) books and journals that I needed. Student research assistant Caryl Taylor helped find material on Mira Edgerly Korzybska. Student typists Kathy Eyster and Cathy Windheim labored valiantly over the peculiarities of Polish orthography in the first draft while Sue Amacher and Alice Dailing of the History Department served above and beyond the call of duty in typing the revised and final versions. Any errors of fact or interpretation in the final version are, of course, my responsibility.

For editorial assistance, special thanks are due to Ann M. Pescatello, of the Council on Intercultural and Comparative Studies, University of California, Berkeley, and to Louise Hatem, production editor, Greenwood Press.

LANGUAGE, SCIENCE, AND ACTION

INTRODUCTION: THE WORD AND THE WORLD _____

Edward Rothstein in a review of a marvelously innovative book, Godel, Escher, Bach: An Eternal Golden Braid by Douglas R. Hofstadter, has succinctly captured a moment in Western intellectual history:

> During the nineteenth century, mathematics, the acknowledged foundation of all the sciences, began to turn its attention to its own foundations. With the work of Boole, De Morgan, Frege, Peano, Russell, and others, a great project began to take shape: mathematics would examine its own structure with all the rigor it had brought to other explorations. The goal was a system that would be unquestionable and secure; a mathematical language would be developed whose simplicity and clarity would dispel all doubts, reveal all mathematical truths.[1]

This great project was, Rothstein noted, part of a larger tradition stretching back to the seventeenth century when certain men dreamed of creating or discovering a universal language. "Its structure would be so tied to the structure of the universe that the language itself could be used to discover truths. Its syntax would prevent falsity. There would be no ambiguous meanings."[2] Science would lift from mankind, once and for all, the curse that had followed the failure of the tower of Babel--the curse of misunderstanding. Henceforth, the mind would be like a machine, endlessly creating and recreating its universe by rigorously following the logical rules of its mathematical model.

Intertwined with the dream of a truth-generating mathematico-logical language was another tradition reaching far back into the history of the Western psyche: the hope of the word that would heal. Not only would language, including mathematics, reveal truth about the world, it would yield a _gnosis_, a secret wisdom, a curative for sick souls, minds, and bodies. The ancient world's belief in the power of oaths and incantations; the Jewish Kabbalist's notion of "a single primal language, an Ur-Sprache" that mimed creation; and the Christian doctrine of the divine Logos--all these intellectual traditions kept alive this hope.

In the nineteenth century, while some linguists searched for the evidence of a unified, naturalistic Ur-Sprache underneath or behind the apparent diversity of linguistic forms, another group of "scientists" searched for the clue to unravel the primal language of dreams, speech acts ("slips of the tongue"), and pathological utterances. Freud and a host of others sought not simply to understand the secrets of the mind but to unlock it, to set it free from the mental shackles that bound it. Psychoanalysis, the "talking cure," and a host of rival therapies sought to manipulate the symbolic language of the patient, the lost logic of the unconscious, in such a way as to produce healing, restoration of social relationships, or a philosophic resignation which would allow one to function in society. The poet, the playwright, and the publicist shared the hope of a primal language that would unleash the creative energy of the psyche, reorder social relationships, and restore genuine community to industrial civilization.[3]

The point at which the search for a mathematically pure and logical language that would reveal a "true" structure of "reality" intersected with the search for a "scientific"/humanistic and primal language that would restore the "true" dimensions of social existence lay within the bounds of the problem of meaning. That is, both the theory of language and the therapy of language raised anew the question of "semantics," the possibility of a science of meaning. Does a sparse, axiomatic, mathematical logic "map" a multifarious world teeming with objects, events, and intentions? How does a socially conditioned, culturally bound, finite natural language enable a speaker to think about, and talk about, an infinity of possible worlds? What is meaning? Meaning for whom? How can the clarity of one person's conception of the world be conveyed to another across time through the medium of language, through words, when languages and words, like species of animals and plants, change over time? How can the living present understand the meaning of past utterances when the language in which they were spoken has become "a dead letter"?

In the late nineteenth century, a host of commentators attacked these problems. Michel Bréal coined the term semantics for this new science of signification, to distinguish it from comparative grammar, phonology, and traditional philology. "The goal of Language is to be understood," he proclaimed, not to be self-consistent, perfectly logical, or in tune with some law of historical necessity. To be in harmony with the world, to live in peace and concord with one's neighbors, to be at ease with oneself, one must accept the limitations of language to insure comprehension. Thus, by the end of the nineteenth century, the faith in science, the yearning for certitude, and the desire for restorative communication had all coalesced about the problem of meaning.[4]

American intellectuals in the nineteenth century had inherited
the diverse dreams of mathematical logic, linguistic psychotherapy, and semantic clarity and, in some instances, had contributed to them. For example, Josiah and Willard Gibbs, father-
and-son team of philologist/mathematician; W.D. Whitney, the
linguist; and Charles Sanders Peirce, the logician, had contributed significantly to the transatlantic dialogue about the
nature and function of language and logic, about the relationship
of the word and the world. On the whole, however, it was the
American theologians and poets more than the philosophers and
scientists who had wrestled with the issues of the nature of
language, the problems of hermeneutics (particularly of Biblical
language), and the therapeutic role of language in society.
Horace Bushnell, the theologian, rejected the Lockean, empiricist
understanding of religious language and the excessively ration-
alistic ways of New England theology and read a romantic,
Coleridgean understanding of language and its limits into the
structure of evangelical theology. Emerson and the transcendenta-
lists, for all their differences and eccentricities, were drawn to
the common notion of nature as a universal symbolic language.
The American public in the late nineteenth century seemed peculiarly drawn to "mind cure" religions, to speculations about "lost
tribes" speaking preBabel, Adamic languages, and to grandiloquent
attempts at universal, monosemantic languages or to esoteric
attempts to decode the grand "cryptograms" of literature or life.
The American educated public, by and large, seemed drawn more
toward the therapeutic aspects of language than to the theoretical
or scientific aspects.[5]

By the second decade of the twentieth century, America--with its
teeming, polyglot cities; its vague, officially idealistic public
philosophies; its democratic rhetorical excesses; its vapid educational philosophies; its timid cultural conventions and polite
social conventions masking racial, gender, and ethnic linguistic
subordination--seemed ill prepared to understand the great dreams
of the European mathematicians, logicians, linguists, and semanticists. Academic specialists in America might have kept abreast
of the latest intellectual developments from England and Europe,
but the public garnered only bits and pieces secondhand or relied
on popularizations in the press. Bertrand Russell, for example,
one of the key figures in the philosophical-logical enterprise,
was known to the American public primarily as a publicist of un-
popular causes, a witty lecturer on "hot" topics, and a mildly
"dangerous" radical. An educated public that regarded amiable and
disheveled old John Dewey as the archetypical philosopher and that
waded patiently through his turgid prose in search of gems of
philosophic wisdom or pedogogic insight would hardly be prepared
for the rigor and profundity of Wittgenstein's Tractatus. The
public in the 1920s doted on Coué and similar self-help psycholo-
gies, on popular Freudian literary analysis, and the antibourgeois
diatribes of Mencken and Lewis; they could hardly be expected to
wrestle seriously with Ogden and Richards, The Meaning of Meaning,
or with de Saussurean linguistics. Even philologists and academic
linguists paid scant attention to the problems of semantics.[6]

It took the profound cultural and political nightmare of the Great
Depression and the approach of another world war to make many
American intellectuals aware of, and receptive to, the ideas of
the European mathematicians, logicians, and psychoanalysts on
language. Ideas that had been debated decades earlier in Europe
were seized upon by those American intellectuals who were trying
to understand their world in order to change it. In the confusions
and alarms of economic collapse, political turmoil, and military
aggression, they longed for the words that would not only reveal
coherent world order but also for the words that would heal, restore calm, recreate communal solidarity, and revive the spirit.[7]
One thinker who responded to the crisis of the times and tried to
share his thoughts and intellectual discoveries with his fellow
citizens was Stuart Chase. In 1938, Chase published another of his
popular attempts at getting the American people to understand what
was happening to them in the Great Depression and, he hoped, to
utilize this awareness to help them out of the morass in which they
still seemed to be floundering. In an era that was increasingly
aware of the threat posed by the propaganda of totalitarian regimes,
the book possessed an apt and catchy title, The Tyranny of Words.
In it, Chase recounted his own unhappy experiences with the
language of social reform:

> Meanwhile, I had long been aware of the alarming futility of
> most of the literature dedicated to economic and social re-
> form. As a young reformer I had organized meetings, written
> pamphlets, prepared lectures, concocted programs, spread
> publicity with enthusiasm. Those already inclined to my
> point of view attended the meetings, read the pamphlets,
> listened to the lectures, adopted the programs, but the apathy
> of the unconverted was as colossal as it was baffling. As
> the years went by it became apparent that I was largely
> wasting my time. The message--and I still believe it was a
> human and kindly message--had not got through; communication
> was blocked.[8]

The problem, he decided, was in the nature of language itself.
"Was there a way to make language a better vehicle for communicating ideas?" he asked.

Chase wrote with the passion of a recent convert. He wanted to
share the answer that he had found with his audience. He revealed
that Count Alfred Korzybski, a Polish mathematician living in the
United States, had published a book in 1933 titled Science and
Sanity. This book unraveled the secret of the identification of
words with things and the abuse of the abstracting power of words.
The solution, Chase believed, lay in the new science of semantics.
With homely examples, plenty of metaphors and analogies, Chase
summarized the discipline of semantics and applied its insights to
current economic, ideological, and political problems. "Good
language alone will not save mankind," he concluded. "But seeing
the things behind the names will help us to understand the structure
of the world we live in. Good language will help us to communicate

with one another about the realities of our environment, where now we speak darkly, in alien tongues."[9]

An experience that was to be repeated over and over during the next thirty years was typified by an industrial research chemist who picked up a copy of Chase's The Tyranny of Words that his wife had brought home from the lending library. "For some reason, I also read it," he remembered later, "probably to make sure we got our money's worth. Chase had been inspired to write the book by his reading of Science and Sanity by Alfred Korzybski. I bought this book and haven't been the same since."[10] Through popularized books and articles; through lectures in speech, psychology, or English classes; through Korzybski's seminars at the Institute of General Semantics; through psychiatric or speech correctional therapy; through the journal ETC.: A Review of General Semantics, people with problems "discovered" Korzybski and became disciples of his cause--general semantics. Yet, on the thirtieth anniversary of the publication of his classic text, some of his followers sadly and reluctantly concluded that, while there had been endless applications of Korzybski's ideas, there had been little fundamental rethinking or extending of his premises.[11]

And the world was in as great a mess in the 1960s as it had been in the 1930s. The problem, one of his critics charged, was that Korzybski's "general semantics is substantively a hygienic discipline, not a scientific one." That is, Korzybski had confused a therapy of language with a theory of language. He had created a closed system of "truths" that could only be accepted, not disproved by experiments for the sake of an ongoing theory.[12] Regardless of such criticism, Korzybski had been like a prism through which many Americans had caught brief glimpses of intellectual developments from European scientific thought, philosophical speculation, and literary experimentation. The story of the origins and fate of Korzybski's general semantics thus provides a microcosm of the general problem in comparative intellectual history of the transfer of ideas from one culture to another and their acculturation. In order to understand Korzybski and his contribution to American thought, as well as to criticize his system, it is first necessary to restore his ideas to their historical contexts.

Specifically, this monograph is organized in four parts around selected questions:

1. What was the influence of Korzybski's European, and specifically Polish, background on the initial formulation of his philosophical and semantic theories?

2. What was the influence of the American context on the articulation of his theories in the 1920s? What was the impact of renewed contact with the Polish logical school on the classic formulation of Korzybski's general semantic ideas in his Science and Sanity (1933)?

3. Was Korzybski's critique of Aristotelian logic and traditional semantics valid in the light of contemporary European, particularly Polish, studies in science, logic, and linguistics?

4. What happened to general semantic ideas and those who advocated them in the United States from the 1930s to 1960s? What happened to similar movements and analytical philosophy in Poland during the same time period? What does the comparative fate of these patterns of ideas and action tell us about the role of intellectuals in their respective societies?

What follows in this monograph is neither a definitive study nor an "official" biography of Alfred Korzybski, for which the available records present unique difficulties.[13] Whereas Robert P. Pula has recently attempted to derive some of Korzybski's particular doctrines from a psychohistory of certain general characteristics of Polish cultural life during the late nineteenth and early twentieth centuries, I have attempted, on the other hand, to understand the general structure of Korzybski's system by an analysis of particular intellectual influences in Central European and Polish thought during the period 1890 to 1914. I have taken what sketchy biographical information does exist and have tried to recreate by historical inference the context surrounding these bare facts. For the purposes of this comparative essay, I have relied on the published versions of Korzybski's works as a guide to his ideas rather than attempt to reconstruct the private dynamics of their creation. The focus throughout the preparation of this monograph has been on the public reception of, and the public debate among intellectuals on, the ideas contained in the historical texts associated with Korzybski and his contemporaries.[14]

Neither is this monograph a comprehensive history of the general semantics movement in America nor is it a contemporary account of analytical philosophy in Poland. For these developments I have relied on published records, journals, and scholarly studies by experts rather than embarking on extensive personal interviews or examining private correspondence to determine the "behind the scenes" life of these intellectual movements. The comparative story in this monograph is carried only up to the early 1960s. After that period, the story in Poland becomes too complicated and the general semantics movement in America too fragmented for concise comparisons. In Poland, the purge of liberals among intellectuals and students in 1968-1969, the suppression of the Gdansk workers' strike in 1970, and the consolidation of power by the Edvard Gierek regime in 1970-1971 laid the ground work for the emergence of Solidarity and recent tragic events. In the United States, the Chomskian "revolution" in linguistics once again put the question of meaning, of a systematic theory of semantics, into academic limbo. And in the emotionally charged intellectual atmosphere of the anti-Viet Nam war era, "semantics" as a psychosocial therapy no longer seemed relevant or very effective to many cultural critics. Intellectuals who experienced the "breakdown in communications" with those in power, or the "generation gap," did not, by and large, stop to engage in an analysis of communication; rather, they engaged in revolutionary praxis, the street theater of protest, or in verbal invective.[15]

This monograph, then, is an essay in comparative intellectual history, a first sketch of an answer to a larger set of questions concerning meaning in language and history. It focuses on Korzybski's general semantics as a way of controlling the data and providing a coherent framework for the narrative and analysis. If it is a biography of sorts, it is an intellectual biography of a cluster of ideas that were associated in America with Korzybski's system but that maintained their separate identities in Europe, particularly in Poland. It is, in one sense, but a chapter in the long story of a dream and a hope, of the rational dream and the emotional hope of once again uniting the Word and the World.

1

THE POLISH INTELLECTUAL MILIEU, 1890-1914

Alfred Habdank Skarbek Korzybski was born in 1879 in Warsaw, at that time the center of Russian-dominated Congress Poland. He came from an old Polish family, which he once described as being composed "of agriculturalists, mathematicians, soldiers, jurists, and engineers, etc."[1] In the aftermath of the unsuccessful insurrection of 1863, many Poles gave up on the political romanticism of the past and turned their energies to economic and educational pursuits. "Business and industry in Central Poland were flourishing as never before. The sons of the dispossessed landowners--in so far as they did not languish in Siberia--were now to be found in the professions, notably that of engineering."[2] Alfred's father, Ladislas Korzybski, was an engineer in the ministry of communication with the rank of general. Far from being dispossessed, the family owned a large estate, Korzybie, near Warsaw where they experimented with new agricultural techniques. The family also owned an apartment building at 66 Wilcza Street in Warsaw.[3]

In attempting to appreciate Korzybski's family's position in Polish society at that time, one must understand the concept of the "intelligentsia," that peculiarly Eastern European status group which came neither from the peasantry nor from the bourgeoisie but from the ranks of the frequently impecunious lesser nobility. Alfred Korzybski's title of count, which seemingly impressed so many of his American followers, was simply the badge of his class. As the Polish literary historian Czesław Miłosz has noted:

> Not so very long ago, it was customary for an Eastern
> European, newly arrived in the West and desirous of
> building up an image, to flaunt a title and tell stories

> of mythical riches. A cliché type was born, and
> innumerable novels and films cast every Russian as
> a prince or every Pole as a count. Basically, this
> was a case of mistaken sociology. In no matter what
> Carpathia, where towns and industry began to develop
> late, a title of nobility, conferring the right to
> use de or von, was a perfectly common thing: streetcar
> conductors, workers, cobblers or petty officials could
> own one.[4]

Alfred was taught mathematics at an early age by his father. He
was instructed in French and German by governesses and learned
Russian and Polish in school, from his household, and from the
civic surroundings. He grew up in the ethos of the multilingual
intelligentsia.[5]

Alfred Korzybski was trained as a chemical engineer at the Poly-
technical Institute in Warsaw and also studied mathematics,
physics, and law. At one point, he taught briefly in a gymnasium
in Warsaw (mathematics, physics, French, and German). Like many
of the educated youths of the day, he travelled in Germany, spent
some time in Rome, and read "the philosophies of the day, and in
history, history of cultures and of science, comparative religions,
the literatures of Poland, Russia, France, and Germany."[6] In
other words, he led the life of a free intellectual in the decade
prior to World War I.

The free intellectual is another feature of Eastern European life
that is frequently misunderstood in the West. Czesław Miłosz
has noted on this point that "a society that clearly distinguishes
an individual's social status from the amount of money he is
worth . . . is applying a scale of values that is, in one sense or
another, aristocratic. Thus, for the Eastern European the drive
to gain recognition in the sphere of literature, science, or art
has all the earmarks of a search for identity formerly conferred
by a coat of arms." The government, recognizing the role of the
intellectuals in the society, would attempt to subjugate them by
bribing them with fame and position. Therefore, in Polish intellectual life "the struggle, often going on within the same
man, between the artist (or scholar) and the bureaucrat reflects
to a great degree the structure of a hierarchical society that
has never lived under the reign of money and never fully accepted
it as a gauge of worth."[7] Korzybski wrote at times as if he belonged to that aristocracy of intellect which could neither be
bought nor bureaucratized.

There was another aspect of Polish history and society that is
significant for understanding the intellectual milieu in which
Korzybski matured. Polish Catholicism had all the characteristics
of a frontier religion. "This meant, especially in the nineteenth
century, resistance to Protestant Prussia and Orthodox Russia.
Polish culture developed entirely within the orbit of the Vatican."
This meant, particularly after the partition of Poland, that "the

notions of 'Pole' and 'Catholic' came to be equated."[8]   The relationship between Polish culture and Catholicism was not without
its tensions, particularly in the late nineteenth century infat-
uation with science and positivism, which happened to coincide
with the pontificate of Leo XIII (1878-1903).   Although Leo XIII
was not a liberal by conviction, he had pursued a policy of
apparent conciliation with the forces of modernism.   He made the
English theologian John Henry Newman a cardinal, encouraged historical research, and opened the Vatican Archives.   His policy
"encouraged a new and younger generation of Catholic scholars to
hope that a synthesis of Catholic theology with biblical criticism
and with the advancing tide of human knowledge was worth attempting."   Some writers were attracted to Catholic modernism before it
was condemned by the papacy in 1907.   Korzybski had visited Rome
during the last years of Leo XIII's reign and had made a speech
criticizing the clergy for their treatment of Polish youths.   How
much he was influenced (if at all) by Catholic modernism is unclear.   But among Polish intellectuals, the dream of a synthesis
of Catholicism and modern thought persisted.[9]   Alfred Korzybski
came to intellectual maturity, then, as a scientifically oriented
free intellectual during the period 1890 to 1914.

The period 1890 to 1914 in European intellectual history has been
characterized as one of a "revolt against positivism" and of the
creation of new modes of consciousness.   It was an era in which
artists and intellectuals challenged the previous generations'
confidence in objective scientific empiricism and called attention
instead to the subjectivity of consciousness and of social
actions.[10]   At the heart of this intellectual turmoil lay the
problem of language.   The mathematically pure, empirically based
language of science claimed a monopoly on description of physical
or natural reality.   What was left for the imprecise, subjectively
motivated language of poetry, literature, or religion--myths,
fleeting images, narcissistic epigrams, illusions, dreams, silence?
Reality seemed to be breaking apart; the realms of fact and of
value were separating.[11]

In Poland, the groups that struggled with these questions have
been labelled the "Positivists" and "Young Poland" (Młoda Polska).
The term Positivist meant anyone who believed in science, evolution, education, and laissez-faire capitalism.   "A strong moralis-
tic current permeated their publicism; they attacked obscurantism,
clericalism, class barriers and advocated equal rights for the
downtrodden--not only for peasants, but also for Jews and for
women.   The followers of the new trend were, to a large extent,
inheritors of eighteenth-century Polish rationalism, and like their
predecessors, they devised a program to spread literacy and popularize science, convinced that knowledge would automatically lift
the moral level of the masses."   In the context of Polish opinion,
the Positivists represented a liberal and progressive but cautious
ideology.[12]

European positivism had owed much of its initial formulation to the Frenchman Auguste Comte (1798-1857) who bequeathed a four-part legacy to his followers: (1) anthropomorphism (the cult of man); (2) belief in the scientific "laws of history" (including the Law of Three Stages: theological stage, metaphysical stage, and positive or scientific stage); (3) authoritarianism (rule by a sociological elite); and (4) belief in a religion of humanity. Comte believed that by the application of the methods of natural science to the subject matter of the social sciences he could create a new "queen of the sciences"--sociology. Underpinning the whole system was the philosophical belief that all one can know of reality is what can be observed or legitimately deduced from what one observes. Exported to England, positivism was tamed to fit the utilitarian temper of its chief English advocates, John Stuart Mill, Harriet Martineau, and Herbert Spencer.[13]

In France, the sociological inheritors of Comte's positivism had secured their niche in the Parisian university structure by the time of World War I via the sociology of Émile Durkheim,[14] but in Poland "between 1869 and 1914 there was no Polish university in Warsaw, only the Russian Imperial University. Thus sociology in Warsaw in those times was centred not in the university, but in the periodicals, which nevertheless encountered tremendous difficulties because of the Russian censorship and the russification of the country." Furthermore, the Polish positivists were influenced more by the Englishman Herbert Spencer than by the Frenchman Auguste Comte.[15] Three people were primarily responsible for the popularity of Spencer's version of positivistic sociology in Poland: Ludwik Krzywicki (1859-1941), Eliza Orzeszkowa (1842-1910), and Ludwig Gumplowicz (1838-1909).

Ludwik Krzywicki was a private scholar, a writer who existed outside the university system. He had graduated from the Russian Imperial University in Warsaw in 1889 in mathematics but had studied anthropology and social sciences in Germany, Switzerland, and France. Krzywicki was influenced not only by positivism but also by the social evolutionary ideas of Engels and Lewis Henry Morgan. He wrote portions of a series of home study guides for students, which were published in Warsaw in 1898. By these guides he helped spread Spencer's ideas in Poland, but Krzywicki also criticized Spencer's penchant for a priori principles, his lack of empirical research, and his neglect of economic factors in social evolution.[16]

Eliza Orzeszkowa was a self-taught provincial writer of the gentry class who was forced to support herself by writing when Russian policies led to the confiscation of her husband's estates. In 1866, she published an enthusiastic review of the Polish version of Henry Thomas Buckle's History of English Civilization. Buckle's exposition of positivistic "laws" of history enabled man to see, she wrote, "in magnificent perspective everything that he can create by the strength of his own thought, will, and work." By the 1880s she had fallen under the spell of Spencer's sociology. She nevertheless recast it into a Polish conception by emphasizing

the moral unity of the nation. "Orzeszkowa used Spencer's theory
of the social organism and evolution to support her views not only
on the natural character of the nation and its importance in the
history of her own country and of mankind generally, but also on
the evolutionary, not revolutionary character of social change."[17]
Her novels could be regarded as socio-literary studies of provincial life with positivist, didactic themes. "Her central motif
was a human being's fulfillment of himself in spite of the obstacles
thrown up by social conditions--which make out of a woman, a man's
toy; out of a Jew, a prisoner of ghetto superstitions; out of a
peasant, a prisoner of village superstitions; out of a landowner,
a prisoner of established mores."[18]

If Krzywicki and Orzeszkowa helped to introduce positivist
sociology to Polish readers from outside the university setting,
Ludwig Gumplowicz, at least, operated from within the university--
but outside of Poland. Gumplowicz had been born in Cracow and
had studied law in Vienna. Having been forced out of an academic
career in the Jagiellonian University in Cracow by antisemitism,
he practiced law and edited a journal. Eventually, he was
appointed to a Chair of Law in the University of Graz in Austria
where he wrote and taught in German. In 1883, Gumplowicz published his first sociological investigations, Der Rassenkampf (The
Racial Struggle); and in 1885, published Grundriss der Soziologie
(Outlines of Sociology), reportedly the first German work to
contain the word sociology in the title. While crediting Comte
and Spencer with recognizing the methodological foundations of
sociology (the positive nature of social science knowledge and
the "law of continuous human development, representing the
existing evolution as the necessary result of the gradual series
of former transformations"), Gumplowicz nevertheless criticized
them for utilizing biological analogies and for excessive paro-
chialism and individualism.[19] "In Gumplowicz's sociology the
group is the basic, primary 'social element.' Gumplowicz looked
on the 'struggle between races' as the mainspring of history."
By "races" he did not mean Gobineau's biological races but rather
ethnic communities and nations that struggled for mastery.
"Unlike Orzeszkowa, Gumplowicz saw in history an eternal, undimin-
ishing conflict between the races, not a progressive evolutionary
approach to international harmony."[20]

Gumplowicz's career served as a reminder of how much Polish intellectuals depended upon the less restrictive atmosphere of
Austria (and of the Austrian-administered areas in partitioned
Poland)[21] to keep alive some freedom of expression. Vienna, in
particular, acted as a window on the rest of Europe through which
Polish intellectuals could keep an eye on the latest intellectual
developments.

In Vienna, a unique synthesis of positivism and impressionism had
emerged in the period 1890 to 1914. One of its leading exponents
was the mathematician-physicist Ernst Mach (1838-1916) who occupied
the chair of the history and theory of inductive sciences at

Vienna from 1895 to 1901. Mach made important contributions to
physics (air-flow studies), psychology (sensation and stimuli research), and scientific theorizing (reduction of variables and
the rejection of mental images in favor of precise measurement).
Above all, along with Richard Avenarius (1843-1896), he was known
for the theory of empirio-criticism. Mach held that sensations
are the sole elements of experience, hence the basis of knowledge.
"The ego Mach dismissed as a useless hypothesis. Consciousness
consists of sensations coming in an orderly, continuous flow,
while memory involves reawakening a previous constellation of
sensations. Although our sensory apparatus necessarily distorts
what it perceives, we lack any means of differentiating impressions
from reality."[22] Thus, even before Henri Bergson's philosophy,
Mach "pointed out that if reality is a constantly moving process
of 'becoming,' the function of our intelligence is to immobilize
it through words and concepts that seize only what is permanent
and identical in the flow of phenomena." Knowledge, even scientific knowledge, is based on convenient fictions or conventional
hypotheses that serve a pragmatic function.[23]

Ernest Mach's empirio-criticism provoked a number of responses
from critical philosophers of language, including Fritz Mauthner
(1849-1923). Mauthner was born in Bohemia, raised in Prague, and
worked in Berlin (1876-1905) as a novelist, satirist, and un-
official philosopher-critic of word superstition and language
mysticism. He was particularly critical of the tendency of German
thought toward reification (the treating of abstract words as if
they were things) and the treatment of language itself as a
reified structure. "For Mauthner, then, language is an activity,
not some sort of entity." Above all, it is a human activity.
A critique of language usage was, therefore, a critique of society
itself.[24]

Mach's empiricism provided the basis from which Mauthner attempted
to build a nonreified theory of language and knowledge. "Like the
British empiricists, Mauthner wanted to root all knowledge firmly
in the sensations of the individual; however, he also wished to
retain the viewpoint of Völkerpsychologie--that is, the insight
that language is a social phenomenon. Sensations, as such, can
never partake of the social character of language; while language,
as such, can never partake of the private character of sensations."
The way out of this dilemma was provided by Mach's theory that
language was a part of man's biological survival mechanisms, that
meaning in language is a matter not of images called forth but of
actions prompted or prohibited. Thus, in the end the positivism
of Mach--the belief that only the empirical methods of natural
science could provide true knowledge--had become the "impossiblism"
of Mauthner--the belief that true knowledge is impossible, that
"men can never succeed in getting beyond a metaphorical description
of the world," and that all such metaphorical descriptions are but
convenient social fictions essential for survival. Beyond this,
there was only silence--and mysticism.[25]

If, in the Austrian context, positivism in the hands of Mach and

Mauthner led to epistemology, in the Polish context positivism
continually reverted to a theory of praxis (action). The theory
of praxis had been articulated in the 1830s and 1840s by the
Polish philosopher Count August von Cieszkowski as a critique of
Hegel. In his Prolegomena zur Historiosophie (Prolegomena to
History, 1838) Cieszkowski announced his theme: "Mankind has
finally reached a stage of consciousness that can now perceive the
laws of its own proper progress and development as the essentially
real determinations of God's absolute thought, as the manifestation
of objective reason in world history . . . ." He criticized Hegel
for only passively contemplating the past; rather, the task of
the scholar was to comprehend the essence of the future to change
the present. Where Hegel had divided history into four epochs--
Oriental, Greek, Roman, and Christian-German or modern--Cieszkowski
divided history into three periods: (1) Ancient, based on feeling;
(2) Christian-German or modern, based on thought; and (3) the
Future, which would be based on will or concrete activity. In a
subsequent work, Ojcze-Nasz (Our Father) Cieszkowski attempted to
unite the Hegelian Spirit (Geist) with the Christian Word (Logos)
through his philosophy of action.[27]

For the Polish Positivists, the way to change the future was
through the practice of education and literature. They held,
therefore, that the primary functions of language in literature
were descriptive and didactic. Somewhat influenced by the literary
naturalism of Zola and Flaubert, the positivist novelists indulged
in careful observations, dispassionate compilations of detail, and
realistic prose. Art was relegated to the role of illustrating
the truths of science; poetry was subordinated to prose. "Poetry
could be tolerated only if it was clear, understandable, logically
analyzable, and of educational value."[28] Positivist novelists
such as Bolesław Prus (1845-1912) and Henryk Sienkiewicz
(1846-1916) favored historical novels to inculcate an evolutionary
philosophy of civilization and a sense of historical continuity
with Poland's glorious past to provide a bridge to a nationalistic
future. Through the use of archaic words, naturalistic descriptions, and thinly veiled parallels with the present, Sienkiewicz
(the world-famous author of Quo Vadis?) conveyed a basic message:
"Man passes like a traveller through the world, so should not care
for himself, but only for the {mythic} Republic which is, and is
to be, everlasting."[29]

In summary, the party that bore the label Positivist in the Polish
cultural and intellectual debate of the period 1890 to 1914 was
characterized by a belief that the natural sciences provided a
basis for all true knowledge; a faith in cultural evolution and
historical continuity; and a faith in education, unrestricted capitalism, and equal rights within an ultimate respublica. Unlike
French sociologists, the Polish positivist sociologists stood
largely outside the university structure (except for Gumplowicz)
and worked in journalism, literature, and popular education. Unlike
the Austrian philosophers of science, the Polish were enthusiastic
popularizers of science, rather than practitioners of it. Unlike

the critical philosophers of language who retreated ultimately
into silence, the Polish positivistic novelists approached
Cieszkowski's concept of praxis through a direct, descriptive, and
didactic language.

The group that revolted against the smug materialism and empiricism of the Positivists has been labeled Young Poland (Młoda
Polska) and identified with the generation of writers that emerged
from adolescense around 1890. Young Poland rebelled against the
Positivists' dedication to utilitarian ethics and overweening confidence in progress. However, Young Poland members were also
"people imbued with a scientific, evolutionist Weltanschauung,
and their revolt against it did not spell their rejection of its
basic tenets. Yet science could not give them any foundation for
Value. Although their religious beliefs were undermined, they
could not renounce the search for the meaning of life and death."
They sought some hope in the philosophies of Schopenhauer,
Nietzsche, Stirner, Bergson, Kierkegaard, and Marx. They created
their own myth of the redeeming (but detached) artist. Above all,
they experimented with language.[30]

In the face of political division, the Polish people struggled to
maintain cultural unity. Learning or teaching Polish became a
nationalistic, revolutionary gesture of defiance. Intellectually,
"partitioned Poland was submitted to three different rhythms
emanating from three different capitals: Vienna, St. Petersburg,
and Berlin. Yet in literature she succeeded in blending cosmopolitan influences with her own literary past and in producing,
thus, something specific and original." In their reaction against
positivism and "realistic" fiction, the writers of Young Poland
turned to French symbolism, to Nietzschean subjectivity, to
historic Polish romanticism, and to existentialism. "Linguistically, it was a period of chaos. The subjectivism of indefinite
moods was an invitation to license both in poetry and in prose,
. . . {since } the Polish language had never been as rigidly
disciplined as, for instance, French; . . . ."[31]

In poetry, these developments are seen most clearly in Bolesław
Leśmian (1878-1937). Leśmian could be called a pure symbolist,
yet his poetic symbols did not correspond to natural or social
facts. Rather they were "myth-creating images." His works are
almost untranslatable because he "took advantage of the extremely
flexible Slavic morphology, inventing . . . verbs out of nouns, and
nouns out of verbs. Since, for him, rhythmical incantation and
rhyme were features that distinguished the 'lyrical language' { of
poetry } from what he called the 'scientific language' (of prose,
of everyday communication), he employed metrical patterns borrowed
from folk songs and ballads." As late as 1937, he still deplored
the fact that the poetic medium depended on the impurity of words,
which are both content-oriented (or contextual) and rhythm-oriented
(or colloquial). For Leśmian, words are both bound and free.[32]

Along with such poets as Leśmian, Young Poland prized the

nineteenth-century poet Cyprian Norwid (1821-1883) whose works
were rediscovered and published between 1911 and 1914. Norwid,
possessing an Augustinian view of history and time, saw reality as
allegorical and perceived "a world full of images of the Cruci-
fixion, the sign of the cross." In one poem he wrote:

> Above all your charms
> **You**! Poetry, and you, Rhetoric,
> One--will be eternally high:
> To <u>give</u> the <u>thing</u> the <u>appropriate</u>--<u>word</u>![33]

Thus it is the poet (as rhetor) who gives to the "thing"--history
--its appropriate word (logo) or symbol--the cross.

But Norwid, also influenced by Cieszkowski and his theory of praxis
(action), saw history as existing at two levels, each with its own
symbolic cross.

> Norwid's contrast of the words "czyn" (deed) and
> "čin" (rank--in Russian),... rests precisely on
> the two divergent orders of history, the first
> moving toward the fulfillment of history through
> mediation of Christ, "the Cross of history," while
> the second is a power limited to an historical
> movement outside of the plans of Providence {the
> stigma of the past, "stygmat przeszłości" }.[34]

Therefore, while the poet (as actor) must "change word into deed"
in history, he does so knowing that not all suffering is redemp-
tive. There is the hypocrisy of those who seek holiness through
suffering without accepting responsibility for relieving the
distress of others (a form of selfishness). Thus, "human suffering
itself, which should be vestige and fulfillment of Christ's
sacrifice, becomes a sign with no referent, a hieroglyph pointing
nowhere, as contrasted to the sign of the Cross in history pointing
to the fulfillment of history, the formation of the City of God."[35]
As Norwid wrote in his poem "Meditation {II}":

> And to see tears, and sorrow: here dainty hands,
> Clasped sweetly in prayer, in liturgical happiness,
> And there to see not a single hand,
> Which would bring help to grievous distress;
> And only hieroglyphs of mute sufferings . . . fists.[36]

The only way to change the hieroglyph of suffering into the sign
of the Cross is through the holy sacrifice of the mass--and
through art. For art, the fusion of matter and spirit reflecting
ideal forms, bears witness to the eternal Word (the Logos) in the
world. Thus, words are allegorical, not metaphorical, because
they participate <u>in</u> the temporal dimension of reality. They are
deeds of love for others; they are revolutionary fists shaken in
anger at distant tyrants.

While poets such as Leśmian and Norwid focused on the nature of words themselves, the literary critic and novelist Karol Irzykowski (1873-1944) "focused on the web of words in which his characters embroil themselves." His characters are shams, mere products of their culture. "They are prisoners of such concepts as love, fidelity, poetry, beauty, etc., which in fact are simply masks assumed by their subconscious, for the unavowable, which exists deep inside them, cannot come to the surface except in forms borrowed from the society of a specific time and place." Although this sounds like a pre-Freudian intuition on the role of the subconscious, Irzykowski was more influenced by the empirio-criticism of Ernst Mach and had engaged in a kind of semantic exploration of his characters' lives as a counterpart to Mach's procedures.[37]

If the work of Karol Irzykowski represented a psychological-semantic deviation from an earlier positivistic tradition of historically truthful, linguistically precise, realistic novels, the novels of Stefan Żeromski (1864-1925), W. S. Reymont (1867-1925), and Wacław Berent (1873-1940) represented a stylistic-symbolic aberration from the same realistic tradition. As Danuta Irena Bieńkowska has observed:

> The novelty of Żeromski's, Reymont's and Berent's prose is perhaps most clearly discernible in the field of language . . . Reymont's prose in Chłopi {The Peasants} (1902-1909) is a stylized peasant dialect. Berent's prose is made striking through the use of archaic expressions ... Żeromski enriched his prose through the use of colloquialisms, dialects, archaic expressions and neologisms. As a result, their prose is rich in unexpected turns of speech, very elaborate and ornamental. Its striking feature is its visual aspect. Żeromski, Reymont and Berent are impressionists... They paint nature in all its splendour, but their attitude to nature is symbolical, not objective (as in the writers of the preceding generation).[38]

Like Irzykowski, Żeromski, Reymont, and Berent explored the irrational in psychology and the pathological in language. (Berent translated Nietzche and published a widely admired version of Thus Spake Zarathrustra.) In their novels, through their use of allegories and figurative language, through their expressionistic and poetic styles, and through their characterizations of the relationship between art and life, one can see the influence of Schopenhauer, Kierkegaard, Nietzsche, and neo-romanticism.[39]

Stanisław Brzozowski (1878-1911) was another novelist, literary critic, and social theorist who helped shape the intellectual world of Young Poland. Romanticism, he argued, had created a split in the consciousness of Western man between an interior world of values (subject) and an exterior world of facts (object).

The Positivists, who worshipped the methods of science, and the Marxists, who believed in immutable laws of historical development, were both indifferent to the place of human values in society. The professors, who were preoccupied with questions of epistemology (the nature of knowledge), and the aesthetes, who were sunk in the miasmas of their own subjectivism (the source of knowledge), had both lost sight of an important fact: "the problem of subject versus object is solved exclusively through human praxis {action}." Thus, in dialectical fashion, Brzozowski attempted a reevaluation of European romanticism in general and of Polish romanticism in particular by returning to the ideas of Hegel and the young Marx. On the one hand, Brzozowski held to a kind of sociology of knowledge; he said that "the social element shapes what is the most personal in us; our physical and mental physiology {that is, our thought}." On the other hand, according to Czesław Miłosz, he believed that "man is a maker; he makes and incarnates values . . . ."[40] Man earns his freedom by labor which subdues Nature (the realm of necessity) and preserves his values by incarnating them in society (the realm of freedom). Thus, "history is shaped and freedom upheld by human action."[41]

While Brzozowski attempted to deal with the tensions inherent in the thought of Young Poland by a dialectical resolution of thought and language (which are socially conditioned) into historical action (which, in turn, conditioned society), he recognized that one of his contemporaries, Stanisław Wyspiański (1869-1907), had attempted a similar resolution in another cultural area. Wyspiański--a painter, poet, a theatrical genius--was the chief exponent of symbolist drama who "took the resources of the symbolist poetics, drove them to their very limits and finally overcame and discarded them."[42] Brzozowski once wrote that "the thought of Wyspiański never expressed itself through words; he did not think in words, he thought with tensions of his will and with emotions expressed in color, movement, and sound. He thought in theatrical terms."[43]

Wyspiański attempted to bridge the gap between the written word of the dramatic text and the sensory, auditory, visual and kinesthetic action of the dramatic event.[44] Janusz Degler has noted that Wyspiański combined conventional punctuation marks into new combinations to which he assigned specific functions. Thus, a multidotted elipsis "apart from its basic function of indicating the tempo of an utterance, also imparts a sense of indecisiveness; suggests silence, omission, and lack of confidence on the part of the speaker." Multiple exclamation points and question marks "indicate the dynamics of expression, the voice tension, and the severity or mildness of articulation." Dashes alone preceding an utterance may indicate the place where a gesture is performed or combinations of marks may indicate silence or mime. For example, in Act II of Liberation a character holds a conversation with a mask and the expressive marks suggest mimic actions to the actor who manipulates the mask.

Konrad:	Our people have lost their faith in the word.
Mask:	?!!
Konrad:	Do you really know what the Word means?
Mask:	?
Konrad:	You have indeed abused it.
Mask:	?!?
Konrad:	Yes, because this is an abuse, abuse, deceit, crime, lies, falsehood, falsehood. You're lying!
Mask:	!!
Konrad:	What do you think about yourself! About your soul!
Mask:	?
Konrad:	You do not understand a single word. Nothing, nothing.
Mask:	?

Overall, Wyspiański attempted "to expose the musical quality of the spoken word" and to convey "his belief that the tonality of expression reflects in an extremely subtle way even the most minute changes in feeling which accompany the recitation of a certain text." In short, Wyspiański carried out the dictum of the nineteenth-century Polish literary hero, Mickiewicz, that drama is but poetry (a special kind of language) carried into action before an audience.[45]

In summary, these then were some of the literary, linguistic, and philosophical themes that characterized the leading figures of the Young Poland era. For the poet Leśmian, words are both bound and free. Brzozowski was in partial agreement with the novelist Irzykowski that man is bound in a web of words and that his thought is shaped by cultural conditions; and he was in partial agreement with the insights of the poet Norwid that the artist must change words into deeds by an "incarnation" of values, the creation of life-giving, myth-sustaining symbols. In their revolt against scientific positivism, novelists such as Żeromski, Reymont, and Berent looked at nature and saw symbols, not facts. Language, therefore, could be allegorical, figurative, poetic, impression-istic, and idiosyncratic instead of merely descriptive. In the drama of Wyspiański, mere words became theatrical deeds, deeds became symbolic acts, symbolic acts became moods, sound became silence (mime). In Wyspiański's drama, Brzozowski's man the maker and shaper of values was shown in a Nietzschean "shift from the protagonist-victim of destiny, the man-puppet, to the tragic hero of will; the shift from passivism . . . to an activist attitude, to a richly moving action . . . what Nietzsche himself called 'the energy of greatness.'"[46]

The themes of Young Poland were but parts, too, of broader issues troubling the intellectual life of Central Europe. Norwid was regarded by Young Poland as a precusor of French symbolism. Leśmian's experiments with poetic myth-language echoed symbolist poetics. Wyspiański carried the symbolist poetic into drama.[47]

Irzykowski's attack on the impoverished and imprisoning language
that masked and entrapped the subconscious was similar to the
Viennese critique of the morally debasing nature of much linguistic
usage. Where Irzykowski was influenced by the empirio-criticism
of Ernst Mach, Mauthner was more sympathetic to the British
empiricists. Language was based on the sensations of the individual, Mauthner believed, but it was also a social phenomenon.
Above all, Mauthner saw that language was not a "thing," but an
activity.[48]

Such then were the intellectual currents whirling about Poland
when Alfred Korzybski came to intellectual maturity during the
period 1890 to 1914. By training and family situation he was
closer to the Positivists with their emphasis on science, evolution, and education. His biographer, Charlotte Schuchardt Read,
has recorded a telling incident:

> When he returned from Rome he was shocked with the
> realization that his former playmate, the gardener's
> son, as well as all the other peasants, could neither
> read nor write, yet their labor had for generations
> earned the money for the education and the freedom
> of travel of their landowners. He built a small
> schoolhouse for the peasants on the country estate,
> for which he was sentenced to Siberia by the Russian govern-
> ment, but his father managed to have the sentence suspended.[49]

It was a characteristic positivist act: one must turn theory
into praxis, but one must be practical.

For Alfred Korzybski, the central intellectual issues of the
day--the nature of language, the formation of consciousness, the
relation of facts and values, the articulation of a scientific
substitute for outmoded religious dogmatism--had to be confronted
from a position somewhat independent of the literary rebels of the
Young Poland. With his strong background in mathematics, physics,
and philosophy, he could not seek the same aesthetic or merely
literary resolutions as some of his Polish compatriots. In this
respect he was more like his Viennese contemporary, Ludwig
Wittgenstein, who also approached the question of language from a
background in engineering and philosophy.[50] Yet the themes and
problems with which the Young Poland writers and other Central
European intellectuals had wrestled in the years prior to World
War I found echoes and attempted answers in the works that
Korzybski wrote after the war. But by then he was subjected to
two sets of influences: the American intellectual climate of
the 1920s and his Polish intellectual heritage. Separating these
strands of influence is the next task at hand.

2

BETWEEN POLAND AND AMERICA, 1914-1933

With the onslaught of war in 1914, Poles in German-,Austrian-, and Russian-dominated areas were confronted with personal and political dilemmas. Should they heed the call to arms of their imperial overlords; would participation in the fighting serve the nationalistic aspirations of their divided nation? For the imperial authorities, "the Polish question" also posed serious problems. As Richard M. Watt has observed in his recent history of Poland, the Germans, Austrians, and Russians all mistrusted the Poles and "spent most of the war issuing a series of calculatedly vague pronouncements in which they half-promised future independence to the Poles. But none of these powers intended to fulfill these promises. Their object was simply to win the loyalty of the Poles and, more importantly, the military manpower that could be raised in the Polish provinces." The Russians pioneered the tactic when Grand Duke Nicholas, commander-in-chief of the Russian army and uncle to the Tsar, issued a manifesto on August 14, 1914, that seemed to promise reunification and autonomy for Poland, perhaps even eventual independence. The response of the Polish people, both individually and through the leading nationalistic political parties, was enthusiastic. The Poles in Congress Poland cooperated with the Russians, but for their own ends.[1]

Alfred Korzybski volunteered in Warsaw for military duty and was assigned to the Second Russian army with a special cavalry detachment of the general staff intelligence department. He took his favorite horse, a white Arabian, and reported to the front. During an artillery barrage he attempted to save the animal; both horse and rider fell into a steep ravine. Korzybski suffered a severely dislocated hip. On another occasion he was wounded in the knee. During the panic following the Battle of Lodz in November 1914, he sustained internal injuries amidst scenes of the destruction of the Second Russian army that have been so graphically described by

Alexander Solzhenitsyn in his famous book, <u>August, 1914</u>. In July
1915, Korzybski was placed "at the disposal of the Minister of
War" and sent to Petrograd. Thus he avoided another disaster as
Warsaw fell to the invading Germans and Austrians in August 1915.
Perhaps because of his background in mathematics and engineering,
Korzybski was sent as an artillery expert to Canada in December
1915 as a member of a commission to expedite the flow of supplies
to the Allies. Riots and "revolutionary" assemblages had already
occurred in Petrograd; the future looked bleak for both Russia and
Poland.[2]

By 1917, against the backdrop of the Russian revolution and the
collapse of the Russian armies, the Allies were ready to play the
game of supporting Polish nationalistic ambitions in exchange for
access to Polish military manpower. On July 4, 1917, "the French
Cabinet issued a decree dealing with the formation of a Polish
army on French soil"; a month later Polish nationalists formed a
government in exile, which "won not only <u>de facto</u> recognition from
the Allied Governments but also political control of the Polish
army being formed in France."[3] By October, the U.S. War Department
had endorsed the plan to allow recruitment for the Polish army in
France among Polish-American immigrants in the United States.
Alfred Korzybski, after a year in Canada, had come to the United
States where he supervised the loading of ammunition. Also he lectured for the American government and served as secretary for the
French-Polish Military Commission. He acted as recruitment officer
for the region including Ohio, Pennsylvania, and West Virginia
where there were large concentrations of Polish immigrants.[4] The
U.S. army also cast envious eyes on "the minority nationalities of
the Austro-Hungarian Empire, technically enemy aliens, but eager
to do battle against the Dual Monarchy for the sake of Polish or
Yugoslavian or Czechoslovakian independence." In July 1918,
Congress "authorized the formation of a 'Slavic Legion' in the
United States Army. The swift ending of the war in November,
however, cut that experiment short."[5]

The end of the war found Korzybski confronting a personal decision.
The Russian imperial government and its army, in which he had en-
listed at the outbreak of hostilities, no longer existed; the
Poland he had known had been devastated during the war. A new,
independent Poland had emerged phoenix-like from the ashes and had
immediately plunged into war with Russia to secure and extend its
borders. Should Korzybski stay in the United States, the fabled
land of opportunity, or return to Poland? In November 1918, he
had met the American artist Mira Edgerly, who specialized in
miniatures and portraits of wealthy and aristocratic clients from
England, France, and the United States. They were close in age
and of similar outlook. On January 17, 1919, they were married in
the chambers of the Supreme Court of the District of Columbia.
Korzybski had been in Washington promoting a number of military
inventions. His intention was to return to Poland within a few
months "to enlist in the reconstruction work in that country."[6]
But the economic situation in Poland was chaotic, the political
balance of power precarious, and the future of all aristocracies--

intellectual or otherwise--was uncertain in the light of socialist
sentiments and "bolshevik" uprisings in Central Europe. Korzybski
elected to stay in the United States.

Fate having cast him upon a foreign shore, Korzybski was befriended
by an American, Cassius J. Keyser, a professor of mathematics at
Columbia University, and by a fellow Pole, Dr. Julian Grove-Korski.
Korzybski labored over the manuscript of a book to be published in
a language he had only recently learned--English. The book was
published in 1921 under the title — Manhood of Humanity: The
Science and Art of Human Engineering. Korzybski later recalled:

> I wrote this book on a farm without any books at hand and
> I had been out of touch with the progress of science for
> the five years spent in the war service and war duties.
> My friend Dr. Grove-Korski, formerly at Berkeley Univer-
> sity, drew my attention to the books of Dr. Jacques Loeb.
> I found there a treasury of laboratory facts which
> illustrate as nothing better could, the correctness of
> my theory.[7]

Korzybski thus drew from his Polish background the ideas and con-
cerns of the pre-war era and mixed them with the new influences to
which he recently had been exposed in America, such as those of
the biologist Jacques Loeb.[8] Indeed, as Korzybski later acknowledged, "it was because of {Jacques Loeb's} urging me to stay in
this country and develop my work here, that I did not return to
Poland as I had intended after the First World War."[9]

The Manhood of Humanity was a typical example of the millenialist
books that appeared following the catastrophe of World War I.
Civilization--Western civilization, in particular--needed a new
base if mankind was to avoid another such disaster.[10] The solution,
Korzybski wrote, lay in applying the philosophical presuppositions
and methods of mathematics and the natural sciences to the problems
and procedures of the humanities and social sciences, including the
question of ethics, and in utilizing the skills of the new scientific elite, the engineers. It was, in short, Korzybski's reevaluation of the Positivist tradition and his answer to the question
that had haunted the Young Poland movement: How could one be
scientific, believe in evolution, and yet find a base for human
values?

Korzybski began with the question, "What is Man?" The traditional
answers--that man was an animal bound to an inexorable law (determinism) and that man contained a "spark of divinity" and could
transcend necessity (free will)--were both inadequate. "There can
be no doubt," he noted, "that humanity belongs to a class of life
which to a large extent determines its own destinies, establishes
its own rules of education and conduct, . . . But the power of
human beings to determine their own destinies is limited by natural
law, Nature's law. It is the counsel of wisdom to discover the
laws of nature, including the laws of human nature, and then to
live in accordance with them."[11]

To show that man was a part of nature, Korzybski used an essentially taxonomic approach and classified all forms of life according to their functions or transformational activities. Thus, plants, which transformed solar energy into organic chemical energy, were called the "chemistry-binding" class of life. Animals, which transformed the organic chemical energy into kinetic energy, the ability to move about in space, were called the "space-binding" class of life. Mankind, in addition, had the ability to transform past experience into present knowledge, to bind the past (time) to itself, and was called the "time-binding" class of life. Mankind had survived in the evolutionary process by its ability to learn from its past experience. The concept of time-binding was an intriguing extended analogy (man is like an energy-transforming organism) that threatened, at times, to become a primary metaphor (man is a time-binder). The logic of the analogy breaks down, however, in the step from animal to man. Whereas plants transform solar energy into chemical energy and animals transform chemical energy into kinetic energy (mobility), man does not simply transform kinetic energy (mobility) into some kind of mental energy. In ordinary terms, mobility ("space") is not transformed directly into past experience ("time"). Even if movement over space in time is regarded as the essence of past experience, there is still an intervening variable - language - before such past experience is passed from one generation to another. If time-binding was simply another way of talking about culture and acculturation through language acquisition, it nevertheless rested on a confusion of the psychologist's conception of time as duration with the cultural anthropoligist's conception of time as continuity and change of social institutions. Indeed, Korzybski's use of the notion of "class of life," to indicate the difference between animal and man, could have been made stronger if he had talked directly about man as a language user.[12]

Just as there are qualitative differences (dimensionality) in the transition from plane geometry to solid geometry to "non-Euclidean" geometry, so, Korzybski argued, there are qualitatively different laws of being for each class of life. The mistake of the older positivism was to treat man only as an animal and to undercut the basis for ethics; the mistake of the older "supernaturalistic" ethics had been to deny that man was a part of nature. According to Korzybski, "to live ethically, is to live in accordance with the laws of human nature; and when it is clearly seen that man is a natural being, a part of nature literally, then it will be seen that the laws of human nature--the only possible rules for ethical conduct--are no more supernatural and no more man-made than is the law of gravitation, . . . "[13] Freedom lies in the recognition of, and assent to, the iron realm of necessity.

If freedom lay in the recognition of the iron law of necessity, in obedience to natural law (or simply in the utilization of the wisdom of the past), how was mankind to transcend its fate? Having, in other words, redefined the Spencerian-Darwinian "survival of the fittest" for animals as survival in space, his definition of "survival of the fittest" for man as survival in time (or over time), as "intellectual or spiritual competition, struggle for excellence," rested on sheer assertion. It was simply the old confusion in Western thought between the "law of nature" (the statement of what "is") as a scientific description and the natural law (the statement of what "ought" to be) as a moral or ethical prescription.[14]

What were the immediate intellectual resources, in addition to his Polish background, upon which Korzybski drew for Manhood of Humanity? Three sources stand out: engineering millenialism, mechanistic biology and psychology, and mathematical philosophy.

Engineering millenialism had emerged briefly in the period 1915 to 1920 among the followers of efficiency expert Frederick Winslow Taylor; of engineering reformers such as Frederick Haynes Newell, Morris L. Cooke, and Henry L. Gantt; and of the radical economist Thorstein Veblen. They envisioned the organization of engineers as a prelude to the reorganization of society. Society was to be run by an engineering elite along the lines of "efficiency," "scientific management," and "human engineering." Agitation centered around the Taylor Society, the newly formed American Association of Engineers, Gantt's "New Machine" coterie, and, especially, the American Society of Mechanical Engineers (A.S.M.E.). It was at the annual meeting of the A.S.M.E. in New York in December 1920, that Korzybski rendered homage to Gantt and first disclosed publicly many of the ideas included in his Manhood of Humanity:

> My tribute to the memory of {Henry L.} Gantt will be, not only the homage of a friend and admirer, but the proof that his philosophy is scientifically true. A rigorous proof is necessary, because the word "service" belongs to that category of words, the meaning of which can be completely reversed by the verb, be it "give" or "take." Gantt took "rendering service" as an axiom; my observation . . . is that our civilization had quite another axiom, "we preach give, we practice take." The problem which interested me, was how to find a way out of this contradiction that would be irrefutable. If one of them is true and natural law for humans, then the other is not; if our words are true, then our deeds are not true, or if our deeds are true then the words are camouflage. I found the solution, by applying mathematically rigorous thinking.[15]

Gantt believed that the engineer could manage society because he "was the man of few opinions and many facts" who could promote production; Korzybski believed that "the minds of mathematicians and engineers are by education the first to see the far reaching importance of the facts disclosed" by mathematically rigorous definitions and that "just this realization will bring about the readjustment of values in life to a human dimension," a process he called Human Engineering.[16]

If the salvation of civilization depended upon correct thought
processes, how was it that thought per se operated? Since
Korzybski held that man was not simply an animal endowed with a
spark of divinity but rather a distinct class of life, he had to
confront the problem of the physiological and psychological origins
of that uniquely human attribute--"time binding" or historical/
cultural thinking--which was embodied in language acquisition and
usage. Having established contacts with intellectuals in America,
one might expect that he would be influenced by the controversial
psychological behaviorism of J. B. Watson; having lived the life
of a free intellectual in Eastern Europe in the pre-war years,
one could assume that he would be familiar with Freudian psychoanalysis, too. But an analysis of the sources used by Korzybski in
Manhood of Humanity indicates another story. Korzybski relied
heavily on the work of Jacques Loeb, whose books on comparative
physiology and "mechanistic" biology had been published between
1900 and 1918. "Scientific biology proves," Korzybski wrote, "that
life and all of its phenomena are the results of some special
physico-chemical processes, which manifest themselves in some
peculiar energies, of which the human mind is the highest known
form." These special processes he speculated might be related to
the "transformation of organic atoms" in a manner analogous to the
reversible change from chemical energy to electrical energy in
electrolysis and batteries.[17]

From Loeb, Korzybski borrowed the notion of "tropism," which was
defined as "forced movements" or reactions of the organism as a
whole to external stimuli of various types of energy (light, heat,
gravity, and so on). Whereas behaviorism studied the reflexes of
isolated parts or portions of the organism, Loeb's "mechanistic"
biology studied tropism of the organism as a whole. Whereas
psychoanalysis studied the influence of the unconscious on the
physiological or psychosomatic processes, Korzybski's version of
Loeb's biology studied the influence of the physiological on the
psychological. This notion even provided him with an explanation
of the power of words. "Every word has its energy and produces
some physico-chemical effects in the time-binding apparatus," he
wrote, "in accord with the idea which we associate with the sound
of the word. If we teach ideas which are untrue, then the physico-
chemical effects produced are not proper--in other words the human
mind does NOT WORK PROPERLY, that is, it does not work naturally
or normally or true to the human dimension."[18] But the implications of such a mechanistic conception of man for the question of
ethics were exceedingly deterministic. If man was an organism
made "sick" by "bad" words and responded with thinking only to
stimuli, how could he ever chose the right or be reconciled to
evil?

Korzybski thought that he had found the answer to this problem of
ethics in the mathematical philosophy of his friend Cassius J.
Keyser. Adrian professor of mathematics at Columbia University from
1904 to 1927, Keyser held that mathematics was "the science of the
forms of thought as forms." The application of modern logic to

mathematics had shown that the "self-evident truths" of classical
mathematics were simply assumptions rather than transcendent
truths. "The critical mathematician has abandoned the search for
truth," according to Keyser. "He no longer {believes his propositions are true}; and he contents himself with aiming at the
correct, or the consistent."[19] Coherence, or consistency, was the
real mathematical test of truth, not simply "correspondence" with
known or perceived reality. Since Whitehead and Russell in their
Principia Mathematica had demonstrated that mathematical doctrine
was deducible from a few basic ideas and propositions, the mathematician was free to explore any and all logically coherent
structures built upon them or to establish new basic ideas and
propositions. In short, while we have the freedom to choose our
assumptions, once chosen, the consequences follow from these
assumptions by logical necessity or what Keyser called "logical
fate." Free will and determinism could, therefore, be reconciled.[20]
But could Keyser's notion of the infinite creativity of man be reconciled with Korzybski's committment to mechanistic biology and
associationist psychology?

For Keyser, such a definition of mathematics meant that there were
many parallels between mathematical concepts and life experiences
(or conversely, that the goal of life was to approximate mathematical thinking). Thus, mathematical terms had equivalents in
life: limit/ideal; functionality/interdependence; transformation/
evolutionary transmutation; invariance and infinitude/permanence
amidst change and the presence of the infinite being in the
finite world.[21] But for Korzybski, since mathematical assumptions
rested on psychological convictions, then mathematics embraced
psychology. Therefore, mathematical laws must also apply to
psychological phenomena. "This new {philosophic} mathematics
would not only give correct results {that is, coherent or logical}
but also true results," he held. For Korzybski assumed that
"correct formulas will also be true formulas and will correspond
to psychological truths"; that is, a logically coherent axiom is
scientifically true and is simultaneously a corresponding psychological fact.[22]

This is what Korzybski took to be the spirit of modern mathematics.
"If there is to be a science of human engineering," he wrote in an
article in 1923, "it must be mathematical in spirit and in method
and if we do not possess methods to apply mathematical thinking to
human affairs, such methods must be discovered."[23] He was not
talking about how to apply inductive, statistical techniques to
social science methods; rather, he was talking about how to apply
the deductive, axiomatic procedures of mathematical logic to the
understanding of sociological structures of thought and action.
In light of his later writing on language, it is important to look
closely at this 1923 article. On the one hand, he noted that "our
language as a whole may be regarded as a vast system of assumptions
and potential doctrines with fixed logical boundaries." "No
matter where we start," Korzybski wrote, "we must start with some
undefined words which represent some assumptions or postulates . . .

Words written or spoken and mathematical symbols are like signs, labels, which we attach to ideas, concepts corresponding to our experience."[24] On the other hand, he said that "before a sign may acquire meaning and therefore become a symbol there must <u>exist</u> something for this sign to symbolize."[25] How could he reconcile this freedom to make assumptions with the necessity for signs to refer to something experiental?

The philosopher F. S. C. Northrop has attempted to clarify this aspect of Korzybski's thought by distinguishing between concepts by postulation and concepts by intuition. "<u>A concept by postulation is a concept whose meaning in whole or part is proposed for it imagelessly and syntactically by the axiomatically constructed postulates of a specific, deductively formulated theory</u>." Northrop has observed that "Korzybski's respect for scientists like Gibbs, Newton, Maxwell, Poincaré, and Einstein" showed "that he was aware of the axiomatically constructed, deductively formulated concepts of mathematical physics . . . ." For such concepts, a semantic analysis would involve relational thinking about axioms (that is, definition by reference to position in a coherent structure). On the other hand, "<u>a word is a concept by intuition if its entire meaning derives from something that can be immediately apprehended inductively</u>." This position is reminiscent of Ernst Mach's empirio-criticism or Mauthner's theories on language. For such concepts by intuition, a semantic analysis would involve a radically empirical process of reference back to particular images.[26]

The complexity of language arises, therefore, from the fact that a label or word can be attached to an object in experience and become a symbol with a referential meaning; or a label can be attached to a meaningless proposition (a noncoherent inference) and become a pseudo-symbol, a mere noise or blotch on the paper; or a label can be attached to a basic assumption and function like an axiom. Thus ordinary, colloquial language is a conglomeration of three types of labels: (1) assumptions that are true by definition or self-evidence (concepts by postulation in Northrop terms); (2) symbols that may be true or false by correspondence or reference to objects in experience (concepts by intuition in Northrop's terms); and (3) pseudo-symbols that are meaningless because they refer neither to objects or events in experience nor to "scientific" self-evident definitions but to anthropomorphized fictions. Korzybski attempted to support this last point by reference to the work of mathematical logicians in three-valued logical systems. "Not only do they distinguish between true and false propositions but also recognize the existence of statements which have the form of propositions, but which are neither true nor false, but are meaningless."[27] In practice, statements that Korzybski regarded as meaningless pseudo-symbols were those that violated his own positivistic assumptions.

From this brief discussion of Korzybski's 1923 treatise on language, it is evident that beneath the obvious, surface sources used in <u>Manhood of Humanity</u> there lay a substratum of assumptions and theories reaching back to pre-war Poland and Central Europe.

Although seldom mentioned or cited explicitly, there are many interesting parallels and echoes of the writers of the Positivist and Young Poland movements in Korzybski's English writings of the 1920s, particularly on the nature of language.

Like his positivistic predecessor Auguste Comte and the Polish philosopher Czieszkowski, Korzybski provided a three-stage historical foundation for his system in an article published in 1924. He divided the history of human thought into three stages: the Absolutist period, the Confused Absolutist-Relativist period, and the Relativist period. The first period, also called the Greek, Metaphysical, or Pre-Scientific Period, was characterized by an emphasis on the observer rather than the observed; by use of frequently erroneous but traditional subject-predicate, Aristotelian logic;and by an absolutism that led to blind, fanatical theories. The second period, also called the Classical or Semi-Scientific, was characterized by an emphasis on the observed rather than the observer; by the same Aristotelian logic;and by a confusing use of absolute and relative concepts and words that led to puzzles and paradoxes. The third period, also called the Mathematical or Scientific period, was dated from the publication in 1854 of George Boole's The Laws of Thought. It was characterized by the realization that knowledge is a joint product of the observer and the observed; by the use of a holistic, consistent logic;and by a consistent relativism. General truths about man could only be found in studying the unchanging "laws of thought" as discovered by modern, qualitative mathematics { that is, the mathematical logic of relations rather than the quantitative mathematics of static entities}.[28]

But inferring the nature of the human mind by using analogies borrowed from mathematical logic proved difficult and unconvincing to many. Korzybski had dropped the term human engineering and simply referred to his system as a general theory of time-binding or occasionally as humanology--the science of man. It was the old positivist dream of a science of society dressed up in a new garb of pseudo-mathematical profundity. "How to connect my own work with that of the psychologists became my next problem," he noted in 1925. "After much meditation I selected psychiatry for that purpose and not psychology, and that for serious reasons." He had concluded that a truly behavioral psychology was impossible at that time because it could not study "the behavior of man-as-a-whole and all the forms of his behavior."[29] During 1925 and 1926 he studied psychiatry at St. Elizabeth's hospital in Washington, D.C., and explored the boundary between psychiatry and mathematics. "There seems to be little doubt," he concluded, "that the 'scientific, or public unconscious' is a more fundamental, deeper level underlying the private unconscious. Perhaps the clarifications on the private level do not clear up the public, or scientific, level which represents the creeds of a certain epoch. . . ." Private, personal psychiatric therapy was not enough. What was needed was a public, interpersonal, prothetic "higher psychiatry" based upon mathematics, "a business of unraveling of unconscious assumptions."[30]

Korzybski returned once again to the problem of language but substituted the mathematical term <u>form of representation</u> for the common term <u>language</u>. In his clearest restatement to date of Keyser's principle, he said that "any form of representation has its own assumptions at the bottom, and when we <u>accept</u> a form of representation we <u>unconsciously</u> accept sets of silent assumptions of which we become victims in the long run." Like the Polish novelist Irzykowski, he saw men caught in a web of words, prisoners of abstract concepts that acted as masks of the unconscious; however, unlike Irzykowski, who found the origins of this situation in the sociological or cultural processes, Korzybski found that "fallacies and taboos can be manufactured unconsciously by logical processes, . . ."[31] Like the Polish literary critic Brzozowski, who held that the social element shapes our images of the world, Korzybski held that a baby, "having no knowledge of the past or future conditions," is from birth "under full dominance of the doctrinal set in which it happens to be born." Thus, he concluded, "there is no escape from the inherent structure of human knowledge; the choice is between having unconscious, unaccessible, unrevisable, and therefore extremely dangerous, creeds; or making these creeds, postulates, undefined terms conscious, and so giving one the liberty of analysing them or even of abandoning them."[32]

For the Polish poet Leśmian, words were both bound (contexual) and free (lyrical); for Brzozowski man was both bound by socio-cultural forms and free to incarnate values; for Korzybski, man was both bound in his thought by linguistic forms and free to choose alternate sets of assumptions. "All human knowledge is postulational in structure and therefore mathematical," Korzybski wrote, "in which { fact} we find the link between the conscious and the unconscious." Just as the mathematician must distinguish between the <u>intrinsic</u> characteristics of a set of postulates that do not depend upon the form of representation chosen (because they are the axiomatic characteristics that determine the structure or form of representation) and the <u>extrinsic</u> characteristics that are inherent in the form of representation, so the linguistic logician must distinguish between the <u>unconscious</u> facts, "which are the result of abstraction ('<u>not-all-ness</u>')" and the <u>conscious</u> labels or words used to describe those facts in a linguistic form of representation.[33]

His analysis proceeded at two levels, and needs to be considered carefully. First, like Ernst Mach, he held that we do not apprehend reality in its totality, but our consciousness or intelligence monitors the flow of sensations and immobilizes or fixes portions of it through the use of concepts. Thus we perceive in part by a process of selection or abstraction. In physicists' terms, we locate events by the objects in them. Second, like Fritz Mauthner, he criticized the tendency in uncritical thought to confuse the label or word with the object to which it referred. "Some call it 'hypostatisation' or 'reification' of the older philosophers," Korzybski noted; while others, "like Whitehead, use the term 'misplaced concreteness.' "[34] Korzybski called it a

confusion of the orders of abstraction because he believed that
abstractions are stratified by an evolutionary process in which
the unconscious embraces the individual's history, the race's
history, and species' history. Therefore, "the same question
can be answered sometimes both yes and no, depending on the order
of abstractions. . . ."35

As in Mauthner, a critique of language usage by Korzybski led to a
critique of society. The problem was that man's experience constantly moved to newer levels of abstraction, but his thinking
was hindered by older levels of abstraction that persisted in
daily language. All thought up to the present was but the childhood of humanity; ahead lay the manhood of humanity. Modern
physics and mathematical logic described a reality that was relative, dynamic, and asymmetrical; traditional language described
reality in terms that were absolute, static, and symmetrical.
Attempts to describe dynamic forms of representation in traditional
language ended up in the kinds of paradoxes discussed by Whitehead
and Russell. What was needed was a new set of assumptions and
new forms of representation. The root cause of the failure of
traditional language he traced to Aristotle and stated his
opposition to Aristotle succinctly:

> I reject { Aristotle's } postulate that man is an animal,
> the postulate of uniqueness of subject-predicate repre-
> sentation, the postulate of cause in the form he {used } it,
> the elementalism of "percept" and "concept," his theory of
> definitions, his postulates of cosmical validity of grammar,
> his predilection for intensional methods, . . .
> I accept man as a man, use functional representation whenever
> needed, expand the two-term relation cause-effect into a
> series, introduce organism-as-a-whole form of representation
> in the language of time-binding, orders of abstraction,
> accept postulational methods as the foundation for a theory
> of definitions and therefore of meaning, which bridges the
> conscious with the unconscious, introduce modern "logical
> existence," relations, differential and four dimensional
> methods, use the extensional methods, etc. . . .36

The new system of thought, therefore, must be non-Aristotelian in
its assumptions, mathematical in its rigor, and psychological in
its implications.

Like the Positivists of the late nineteenth century--Prus,
Sienkiewicz, Krzywicki, Orzeszkowa, or Gumplowicz--Korzybski
wanted to spread literacy and popularize science, to overturn old
dogmas, to create moral unity among nations, to strip language of
its obfuscations and turn it into a didactic tool, to establish a
science of man, to discover the laws of historical thought, to
foster social evolution, and perhaps to set free those captive to
superstition. Like the writers of Young Poland--Irzykowski,
Żeromski, Reymont, Berent--he appreciated the role of symbols and
the pathological in language, but, unlike them, he did not see

reality itself as symbolic, allegorical, impressionistic, or metaphorical. Korzybski approached reality as a mathematician-logician, not as an artist, poet, or dramatist. Different, too, in his system was the emphasis on praxis. Korzybski might agree with the poet Norwid that the rhetor gives to the thing its appropriate symbol or that there are mute hieroglyphs in the world, signs without referents, but there was little in Korzybski's thought that required the rhetor to change the word into deed. Brzozowski's resolution of the subject-object split in revolution-ary praxis or Wyspiański's idiosyncratic projection of words into dramatic deeds find few echoes in Korzybski's more aristocratic emphasis on realization or self-consciousness as a prelude to proper thought, mental health, and an acceptance of the world as embodied in natural law.

This note of aristocratic elitism, disdain for critics, and self-isolation of the intelligentsia was evident in Korzybski's papers of 1925 and 1926. The task of building a new, general, non-Aris-totelian system should be a group activity, he confessed; however, for the moment he must go it alone: "My main difficulty has seemed to be not with people who could not understand the { general theory of time-binding } at once, but with those who seemingly understood and approved it, but considered it a matter of 'platitudes.' "[37] If only people would realize that his system was not the same as Russell's theory of types; that portions of it were similar to Harry Stack Sullivan's idea of "preconcept"; and that it was, "among other things, a theory of what { Sir Arthur } Eddington, without formulating it, called the 'standpoint of relativity,' obviously a psychological affair."[38] Finally, Korzybski lamented: "My attempt is as yet without academic pigeon hole, academic sanction, chair, or bread and butter, blessed with all academic and non-academic prejudices, all of which is a serious handicap to the author and to future workers."[39] He wrote out the first draft of the definitive statement of his non-Aristotelian system, Science and Sanity, and laid it aside. (Significantly, he did not use the term semantics or semantic.)[40] In September 1929, he attended the Mathematical Congress of Slavic Countries in Warsaw, Poland, where he presented a paper. Most certainly this brought him back into personal touch with in-tellectual developments in Europe, especially in the areas of logic, the philosophy of science, and linguistic theory.

By the end of the 1920s, then, Korzybski had made a unique synthesis out of disparate elements: (1) the Positivist emphasis on the primacy of the natural sciences and their deduc-tive, postulational logical methods; the empirio-critical reduc-tion of consciousness or sense experience by concepts; the didactic approach to language usage; and the philosophical analysis of propositions; (2) Young Poland's aesthetic sensitivity to the sociological and psychological dimensions of language usage in particular social contexts; the masking of the private, unconscious psychological content in the publicly self-conscious cultural forms; and the need for a therapeutic critique of linguistic usage;

and (3) Americanized intellectual trends such as engineering
millenialism with its emphasis on a strategic elite; mechanistic
biology and clinical psychiatry with their search for holistic
explanations; and Keyser's mathematical philosophy with its
emphasis on logical fate and freedom of choice. The comparative
questions, therefore, intrude themselves with particular urgency:
What had happened to these intellectual traditions in Central
Europe and Poland during the same time period? How did Korzybski's
synthesis compare with contemporary syntheses by leading Central
European and Polish intellectuals? In short, how "Americanized"
had Korzybski become by the end of the 1920s? Could his synthesis
be enriched by renewed contact with his Polish and Central
European intellectual milieu?

In Central Europe, one of the most significant intellectual developments of the 1920s was the articulation of the set of doctrines
known as logical positivism or logical empiricism, popularly
associated with the group known as the "Vienna Circle."[41] The
Vienna Circle had evolved out of a seminar held by physicist Moritz
Schlick in 1923 and gradually came to involve mathematicians,
philosophers, sociologists, and logicians. "The discussions of
the Circle centered about the foundations of logic and mathematics,
the logic of empirical knowledge, and only occasional excursions
into the philosophy of the social sciences and ethics." By 1929,
the Circle had announced its programmatic goal: "The aim is to
form an Einheitswissenschaft, i.e., a unified science comprising
all knowledge of reality accessible to man without dividing it
into separate, unconnected special disciplines. . . . The way to
attain this is by the use of the logical method of analysis,
worked out by Peano, Frege, Whitehead, and Russell, which serves
to eliminate metaphysical problems and assertions as meaningless
as well as to clarify the meaning of concepts and sentences of
empirical science by showing their immediately observable con-
tent--'das Gegebene.' "[42] They claimed as their predecessors the
positivism and empiricism of Hume, Comte, Mill, Avenarius, and
Mach; the hypothetico-deductive scientific methods of Riemann,
Poincaré, Einstein, and others; the axiomatic and logistical
analysis of Peano, Frege, Whitehead, Russell, Wittgenstein, and
others; and the eudaemonistic ethics and positivistic sociology of
Bentham, Mill, Marx, Spencer, and contemporary figures such as
Müller-Lyer, Popper-Lynkeus, and Carl Menger.[43]

The Vienna Circle, in spite of its programatic aims and belief in
the unity of science, was divided within itself. One faction, represented by Rudolf Carnap, Hans Hahn, and Otto Neurath, put
primary stress on logical consistency. Carnap, who had studied
under Frege at Jena, first spelled out his views in Der Logische
Aufbau der Welt (The Logical Structure of the World, 1928),
Schein probleme in der Philosophie (Pseudoproblems in Philosophy,
1928), and Abriss der Logistik (Outline of Logistics, 1929). "A
scientific statement makes sense," he held, "only if the meaning
of the object names which it contains can be indicated" either by
perceptual, ostensive definitions ("That is Mont Blanc.") or by

definite descriptions of "as many characterizing properties as are required to recognize unequivocally the object which is meant within the object domain under discussion."[44]   There were four main kinds of objects with which the empirical sciences dealt— cultural objects, other minds, physical objects, and the experiental data of one's own mind — and statements about them were ultimately translatable into verifiable statements about "elementary experiences," the immediately given data of consciousness. Statements which could not be so constructed were empty or meaningless; philosophical theses built on them were pseudostatements, mere metaphysical nonsense.[45]   But, on the basis of verifiable statements about objects and their structural relationships, philosophers could, by the use of modern logic, construct a scientific view of the world. Ethical statements (statements of "ought") were excluded from such scientific construction (statements of "is") because they were beyond this principle of empirical verification.[46]

Moritz Schlick, in the other faction of the Vienna Circle, used the logical positivists' differentiation between knowledge (Erkenntnis) and experience (Erlebnis) to make room for "scientific" ethics. Basically, he accepted eudaemonism as a base for ethical experience. "In equating values with feelings of pleasure, Schlick defended neoutilitarianism with a subtlety of psychology rare in any philosopher." With the skill of a novelist, Schlick grounded the experience of pleasure in a prior torment of the soul or psyche and saw the fulfillment of pleasure in ecstacy. Thus, sorrow and joy motivate the whole person and move it to action. Concepts pertaining to the realm of nature and natural law (statements of "is") had erroneously been applied to the realm of society and the law of the state (statements of "ought"). "In disputes over freedom of the will philosophers have transposed terms from the two { realms }, confusing indeterminism { in the natural realm } with freedom from coercion { in the social realm } and universal validity with duty."[47]   In short, having separated knowledge from experience, Schlick grounded ethics not in knowledge but in experience, including the experience of youthful zest, rejuvenation, spontaneity, and choice.[48]

While the Vienna Circle of logical positivists were developing their systematic ideas on the unity of science and the priority of logical analysis and disagreeing among themselves on the possibility of a scientific basis for ethics, Polish logicians and mathematicians had been making significant advances in the very areas in which Korzybski had expressed an interest. As J. H. Woodger has noted, "the setting free of Poland after the First World War was followed by intensive activity in her Universities. In the departments of philosophy and mathematics this took the form, in a number of places, of new and powerful investigations in the fields of mathematical logic, the foundations of mathematics, and the methodology of the sciences. Prominent in this movement was the Warsaw school led by Łukasiewicz, Kotarbiński, and Leśniewski."[49]   The Warsaw school was preoccupied with the development of an algebra-like logic in which one proceeded by strict definitions (axioms) and rules of procedure to build up a coherent structure of logical "truths."

Jan Łukasiewicz (1878-1956) is best known for historical investigations in logic concerned with the principle of contradiction in Aristotle's logic; for a reevaluation of stoic logic, which he saw as an anticipation of modern propositional logic; and for a simplification of the axioms of Whitehead's and Russell's systems. "Thus prepared on all fronts, Łukasiewicz attacked his central problem, sketching, and elaborating as one of the first logicians ever, a system of three-valued propositional calculus," in which a proposition could be either true or false or possible. Łukasiewicz pointed out that it was Chrysippus, the stoic determinist, who had insisted on the "law of bivalence," which held that every proposition must be only true or false. Therefore, although Łukasiewicz called his three-valued logic "non-Aristotelian," a more accurate title would be "non-Chrysippian."[50] Such a multivalued system of logic, in Łukasiewicz's view, undercut traditional arguments supporting philosophical determinism and opened the door for an indeterminate ontology.[51]

Stanisław Leśniewski (1886-1939) was influenced not only by the logical studies of Łukasiewicz but also by the semantic aspects of Mill's System of Logic. Leśniewski constructed an innovative deductive system in which an object was simply a class of expressions and, as such, it functioned as a variable through the substitution of words belonging to the same semantic category.[52] Thus, "the conditions under which a word pattern, constituted of meaningful words, forms an expression which itself has a unified meaning" could be studied systematically using two-valued (true/false) systems, three-valued systems (true/false/possible), or multivalued systems. That is, a system of semantic categories could be worked out using the simplified hierarchy of logical types. It is important to note, however, "that any word of a language can be assigned to a certain semantic category by its meaning" and that all the deductive system of logic does is to determine the "truth" of the expression (truth being defined in terms of noncontradiction or coherence).[53] "So semantic disorder or nonsense occurs only when instead of a word of a given category, a word of a different, category is used."[54]

Tadeusz Kotarbiński (1886-), the third member of the Warsaw school, also used semantic analysis of philosophical concepts to build (or rebuild) a philosophical system called reism, later termed somatism or concretism. In Kotarbiński's reism, sentences asserting the relationship between objects or the possession of qualities by objects were analyzed in terms of certain nouns ("names") that acted as surrogates for more descriptive phrases. "In other words, certain nouns, although they may refer to objects, are not to be recognized as names unless {the} objects to which they apparently refer are concrete things located in space and time. Briefly, expressions which do not refer to concrete objects are not names, but pseudo-names or apparent names or onomatoids. Though they may stand as subjects or predicates in subject-predicate sentences, they ought not to be treated {as such}."[55] In subsequent versions of his system, Kotarbiński united his semantic reism with Leśniewski's ontology so that references to nonbodies were "reduced" to statements about bodies or objects (which were, in Leśniewski's system, simply classes of expressions), but not vice versa.[56] Kotarbiński thereby collapsed Cartesian dualism into a kind of monism; "in short, somatic reism identifies experiencing subjects with bodies." Thus, the final stage of Kotarbiński's system was similar to the Vienna Circle's position; his final dictum had a familiar ring: " . . . the principal rule of {concretism} may be formulated as follows: We should attempt to reduce every statement to a form which contains only concrete names."[57]

Another development in Polish logic in the 1920s can be seen by looking at the work of a Polish logician who was not a member of the Warsaw school. Leon Chwistek (1884-1944), who studied mathematical logic at the Jagiellonian University in Cracow, "saw for the first time that the notion of class may be replaced by the notion of function" and that the "theory of constructive types can be regarded as a system of rules concerning the ways in which signs and letters are put together and made into valid formulae of logic and mathematics."[58] He differed from both Kotarbiński's philosophical approach of dealing with spatio-temporal objects and Leśniewski's more verbal or syntactical approach of treating objects as symbolic expressions; rather, Chwistek dealt with objects, with classes of expressions, as logical constructions--products of the rules, so to speak. Thus, "by semantics Chwistek understands the set of rules and formulae by means of which the expressions of logic and mathematics can be constructed mechanically." Starting with a very restricted logical language, he constructed a hierarchy of languages, "each constituting the medium in terms of which the propositions of the consecutive languages are formulated." This, he believed, was necessary so that doubt and ambiguity could be banished, irrationalism confuted, and the limits of science clearly sketched.[59]

In contradistinction to Chwistek's restricted semantics, Korzybski called his system general semantics. What he meant by general semantics was evident in a paper read in 1931 before the American Mathematical Society. There, Korzybski drew his famous analogy between maps and languages:

A) A map may have a structure similar or dissimilar to the structure of the territory. {This is a restatement of the law of contradiction}.

A) Languages have structure {which is either similar or dissimilar to reality}.

B) Two similar structures have similar "logical" characteristics. Thus . . . in a correct map,. . . a similar relation is found in the actual territory. { A true map corresponds to the actual territory } .

B) If we use languages of a structure non-similar to the world and our nervous system, our verbal predictions are not verified empirically, . . .

C) A map is not the territory.

C) Words are not the things they represent.

D) An ideal map would contain the map of the map, the map of of the map of the map., endlessly. { That is, it would have self-reflexiveness } .[60]

D) Language also has self-reflexive characteristics.

Thus, by analogy, languages may have structures that correspond to or are similar to reality, or they may have structures that do not correspond to or are dissimilar to reality.

To this argument, he added another. First, he argued that the language of mathematics had a structure similar to reality. Secondly, he added that the language of ordinary communication had a structure dissimilar to reality. He called such languages elementalistic. Therefore, he concluded, the creation of a new language of communication with a structure similar to mathematics would give mankind a true description of reality. He proposed to call such a language a general semantic, nonelementalistic language. In sum, he argued that if mathematics corresponds to reality, and, if the new language corresponds to mathematics, then the new language would correspond to reality (since if A = C and B = A, then B = C).[61]

These parallels are never perfect, however, since even "mathematics appears as a very limited {case} but {nevertheless} the only language in existence, in the main similar in structure to the world around us and the nervous system." Therefore, Korzybski proceeded to draw a further parallel between contemporary mathematical logic as a language and a potential language:

Mathematical Level		Verbal Level
one-valued term	=	word as label for object
two-valued term	=	abstraction
three-valued term	=	inference
n-valued term	=	multiordinal term
propositional functions	=	statements about terms

Korzybski noted that multiordinal terms "apply to all verbal levels and in each particular case may have a different content or meanings," therefore, in general, they had no single content or meaning. They acquired a particular meaning only in a given context.[62]

As to theories of meaning--that is, systems of semantics per se--Korzybski was proposing primarily a contextual theory of meaning in which meaning is a function of position in a logical structure. "The realization of the inherent multiordinality of some of the most important terms we have," he noted, "gives us an enormous flexibility of language. It makes the number of our words indefinitely great. When both the writer and the reader recognize this multiordinality, and look for the meaning in the context and discriminate between the orders of abstractions, indicated by the context, confusion becomes impossible."[63] Only secondarily did he propose a referential theory of meaning in which meaning was determined by reference from a statement or word to an object and abstracting process in sense experience.

Korzybski, having based his analysis in part on an empirical, correspondence theory of truth, had to confront the problems inherent in it. If truth is correspondence with a natural order, does that order exist independently, or is it somehow a product of mind (objective or subjective empiricism)? How are we to know that order if we are dependent on sense data or linguistic conventions for our very perception of it? He tried to get around some of these by arguing that (mathematically) we deductively recreate reality by building axiomatic systems, but this introduced a coherence definition of truth that clashed with his insistence on empirical investigation.[64] As F. S. C. Northrop has observed, when Korzybski attacked Aristotelian thinking, he was attacking the confused notion "that the relatedness of axiomatically constructed scientific objects is the relatedness of inductively given, concept of intuition, sensed relations." The mathematical world of postulates is related to the experiential world of perception by "rules of correspondence," which are the epistemological relations between two semantically different worlds of discourse.

In summary, for the Polish logicians such as Leśniewski and Chwistek, a word's meaning determined its semantic category; for Korzybski, its semantic category (or context) determined, in most cases, its meaning.[65] For the Polish logicians such as Łukasiewicz or Kotarbiński, the truth of an expression was determined by its coherence, by its place in a logically deduced structure; for Korzybski, the truth of some expressions could also be determined by their correspondence to reality. Most broadly stated, Korzybski sought to combine the concepts by postulation of mathematical logic with the concepts by intuition of empirio-criticism and to hold the whole together with its inherent tensions by an analogical understanding of the nature of language and by a simplified version of the conditioned-reflex theories of physiological psychology.

Korzybski's 1931 paper thus represented a summation of all of his
writings since 1921. He had not repudiated any of it; he had
simply added layers of interpretation on top of his original
formulations. To his original use of Jacques Loeb's tropism, he
had added Pavlov's notions of reflexes; to Russell's and Keyser's
mathematical logic he had added reference to the ideas of
Łukasiewicz, Leśniewski, Kotarbiński, and Chwistek; and to his
studies in psychiatry he had added a nodding acquaintance with
Freud and psychotherapy. The net result was a unique, if re-
petitious, synthesis. Korzybski's renewed contact with the Polish
intellectual milieu in 1929 had sharpened his own ideas. He re-
worked the manuscript of his magnum opus, Science and Sanity,
developing the notions of general semantics in the manuscript.
Now his work was ready to stand the test of criticism--but in an
American context. Before looking at the effect of that American
context on its intellectual reception, it is necessary to examine
critically this final formulation of his ideas.

3

SCIENCE AND SANITY: A HISTORICAL CRITIQUE _____

Alfred Korzybski's Science and Sanity, published in 1933 in the
depths of the depression, was a classic example of the "leap of
negation" in intellectual history. This strategy of debate requires
simply that one isolate the basic assumptions of an argument or
system and then, instead of modifying them by evidence or redefining them, one leaps over to their negatives. This radical break
with the terms of the previous debate may provide a liberating
sense of intellectual or psychological freedom, but it leaves one,
paradoxically, still a prisoner of the past because the categories
of negation are a function of the categories of affirmation. In
a revealing passage, Korzybski indicated how this leap of negation
operated in his case (the material has been rearranged in parallel
columns to heighten the point):

In the present { non-Aristotelian }
system, I reject Aristotle's
assumed structure, usually called   and accept modern science (1933)
"metaphysics" (circa 350 B. C.),   as my "metaphysics."

I reject the following structur-   I base the { non-Aristotelian }-
ally and semantically important   system-function and system all
aspects of the {Aristotelian }   through on negative "is not,"
system, which I shall call postu-   premises which cannot be denied
lates, and which underlie the   without the production of im-
{Aristotelian}-system-function: possible data, and so accept
                                     "difference," "differentiation.,"
1) The postulate of the unique-   as fundamental.
ness of subject-predicate re-   I accept relations, structure,
presentation.   and order as fundamental.
                                     I accept the many-valued, more
2) The two-valued {elementalistic}   general, structurally more

"logic," as expressed in the law of "excluded third."

3) The necessary confusion through the lack of discrimination between the "is" of identity, which I reject completely, and the "is" of predication, the "is" of existence, and the "is" used as an auxiliary verb.

4) The elementalism, as exemplified by the assumed sharp division of "senses" and "mind," "percept" and "concept," "emotions" and "intellect,".

5) The { elementalistic } theory of "meaning."

6) The { elementalistic } postulate of two-valued "cause-effect."

7) The { elementalistic } theory of definitions, which disregards the undefined terms.

8) The three-dimensional theory of propositions and language.

9) The assumption of the cosmic validity of grammar.

10) The preference for intensional methods.

11) The additive and { elementalistic } definition of "man."

correct "logic of probability" of Łukasiewicz and Tarski, which in my { non-elementalistic } system becomes infinite-valued (∞ - valued) semantics. { I use the term infinite; or ∞-valued in the sense of Cantor as a variable finite.}

I accept functional representation whenever possible.

I introduce the principle of non-elementalism and apply it all through, which leads to:

(a) A { non-elementalistic } theory of meanings;

(b) A { non-elementalistic } theory of definitions based on undefined terms;

(c) A psychophysiological theory of semantic reactions.

I accept the absolute individuality of events on the unspeakable objective levels, which necessitates the conclusion that all statements about them are only probably in various degrees, introducing a general principle of uncertainty in all statements.

I accept "logical existence" as fundamental.

I introduce differential and four-dimensional methods.

I accept the propositional function of Russell. I accept the doctrinal function of Keyser, and generalize the system function of Sheffer. I introduce the four-dimensional theory of propositions and language.

I establish the multiordinality of terms. I introduce and apply psychophysiological considerations of { non-elementalistic } orders of abstractions.

I expand the two-term "cause-effect" relation into an ∞ - valued causality.

I accept the ∞-valued determinism of maximum probability instead of the less general two-valued one.

I base the { non-Aristotelian }

-system on extensional methods,
which necessitates the introduction of a new punctuation indicating the "etc." in a great many
statements.
I define "man" in{ non-elementa-
listic} and functional terms.[1]

The heart of Korzybski's argument by negation could be summed up
as follows: (1) If the traditional Aristotelian metaphysics says
that something (a word) is something else (a thing), then I say
that something (a word) is "nothing" (that is, not a thing); (2)
if Aristotelian grammar says that a word has a definite meaning
(that is, means what it means as a defined term), then I say that
a word has an indefinite range of meanings (that is, means what it
means as an undefined term in a particular context or structure);
and (3) if Aristotelian logic asserts that something cannot both
be and not be at the same time (that is, must be either one thing
or not be that one thing), then I say that, according to modern
quantum physics and relativity theory, something (light) can both
be one thing (matter) and not be that one thing (that is, it can
be a quantum of energy) at the same time.

The test of Korzybski's argument on this point must begin, therefore, with the question whether his assertions about the nature
of Aristotelian logic were valid. If so, did it necessarily follow
that the leap of negation was the only acceptable intellectual
strategy for dealing with the problem. Secondly, the underlying
empirio-criticism of his system, which has previously been traced
to its historic sources in European positivism, must be reexamined.
Thirdly, once his statements on Aristotelian logic have been
evaluated and his empirio-criticism scrutinized, then his theory
of language (including his doctrines of semantics per se) can be
judged and his therapy of language compared with contemporary
alternatives.

In matters of logic, Korzybski regarded himself as somewhat at
odds with all prevailing schools of mathematical logic. Although
he was indebted to a certain extent to the multivalued logics of
the Polish logicians, he still condemned them as being too "elementalistic." That is, most of the Western European and Polish schools
of logic still accepted the old "laws of thought" notion embodied
in the grammar of ordinary language. These laws of thought he
summarized as:

1. The law of identity. Whatever is, is.
      { A thing is what it is}.
2. The law of contradiction. Nothing can both be, and not be.
3. The law of excluded third {middle}. Everything must
      either be, or not be.

In short, they were still making the fatal error of falling back
on a two-valued, either/or logic of static categories to deal with

a many-valued, both/and logic of dynamic processes. "For structural reasons we must preserve determinism," Korzybski wrote, "but . . . the older two-valued determinism must be reformulated into the {infinite}-valued determinism of the maximum probability." Simply put, this means that mankind must take a radical leap of negation to the opposites of the law of identity, the law of contradiction, and the law of the excluded middle.[2] Some words (concepts by intuition) are only approximations of continuing processes at any given point in space - time; their meanings can only be indications of probabilities, rather than indicators or signs of static situations, and, therefore, require a logic of dynamic processes for their expression.

While Korzybski was attacking Aristotelian logic by the tactic of negation, the Polish logician Łukasiewicz was applying historical, textual criticism methods to the same problem in the 1930s. Łukasiewicz pointed out that while Aristotle had questioned the principle of bivalence (in the form that every statement is either true or false), he had accepted the law of the excluded middle (the formulation generally being given as "either P or not P," where P stands for a declarative sentence).[3]

Łukasiewicz also showed that the standard examples of the Aristotelian syllogism, as given in most textbooks, were not consistent with a close reading of Aristotle's texts. A famous example would be:

Major premise:	=	All men are mortal,
Minor premise:	=	Socrates is a man, therefore
Conclusion:	=	Socrates is mortal.

This was an erroneous example because Aristotle did not use singular premises or terms. A truer example of an Aristotelian syllogism would be the following:

Major premise:	=	{If } All men are mortal
Minor premise:	=	{And }All Greeks are men,
Conclusion:	=	{ Then} All Greeks are mortal.

Furthermore, Aristotle had divided premises into three types: Universalistic (all or no); Particular (some, not some, not all); and Indefinite (which are not used in the Aristotelian system of logic). These distinctions were important because "it is essential for the Aristotelian syllogism that the same term may be used as a subject and as a predicate without any restriction. In all three syllogistic figures known to Aristotle there exists one term which occurs once as a subject and then again as a predicate"[4] as in the following:

          predicate   subject
     If A is predicated of all B
     and B is predicated of all C,
     then A is predicated of all C.

In an illustration that cut to the heart of Korzybski's critique
of Aristotelian logic, Łukasiewicz showed that there were two laws
of identity in Aristotle:

> Besides the Aristotelian law of identity "A belongs to all A"
> or "All A is A," we have still another law of identity of
> the form "If p, then p." Let us compare these two, which are
> the simplest logical formulae:
>   All A is A   and   If p, then p.
> . . . In both formulae the arguments are variables, but
> of a different kind: the values which may be substituted
> for the variable A are terms, like "man" or "plant." . . .
> The values of the variable p are not terms but propositions,
> like "Dublin lies on the Liffey" or "Today is Friday;" . . . ,
> and, as propositions and terms belong to different semantical
> categories, the difference is a fundamental one.[5]

For convenience, these two laws of identity will be referred to as
the Law of Identity,[1] {the logic of terms or all A is A} and the
Law of Identity[2] {the logic of propositions, or if p, then p}.
Furthermore, there are two versions of the Law of Identity.[1] As
Łukasiewicz expressed it in another context: "The Aristotelian law
of identity Aaa, where A means 'every - is' and a is a variable
universal term, is different from the principle of identity $\mathcal{J}$xx,
where $\mathcal{J}$ means 'is identical with' and x is a variable individual
term." Because of certain "awkward consequences," Łukasiewicz
concluded that the formula $\mathcal{J}$xx should not be used.[6] The whole of
the Aristotelian logic does not stand or fall on one law of
identity, therefore, and Korzybski's leap of negation is not the
only way to deal with the problem of semantic traps and logical
quandaries. Nor was the law of the excluded middle so absolute as
to forbid further development of multivalued logic even with
Aristotelian means.[7]

Korzybski, following the tradition of George Boole, regarded the
Aristotelian syllogism as the "laws of thought"(that is, a description of how the mind works), whereas Łukasiewicz regarded the
syllogistic as simply the "rules of the game" of a particular
type of logic, the logic of terms, and also found in Aristotle
evidences of another type of logic, the logic of propositions.

Korzybski's denial of the law of identity rested heavily on
empirio-criticism and its analysis of perception. From the multi-
plicity of sense data the organism via its neural processes
selected out, "abstracted," certain patterns that became organized
into a perceptual object. The existent pattern of sense stimuli,
the "event," was therefore always greater than the selected perce-
putal pattern of sense data organized as the "object." Thus,
whatever "is" in perception is a portion of what "is" in reality
or, vice versa, the "object" of perception is not identical in all
respects with the "event" of temporal-spatial occurence.[8]

The same point had been made not only in Mach's empirio-criticism

but also in the early analytical tradition in philosophy in the
nineteenth century. For example, the German philosopher Otto
Friedrich Gruppe (1804-1876), "in a post-Kantian age," could not
"simply assume something given{in experience }with which human
cognition can start. The objects we take to be given . . . are
already products of a highly complicated cognitive process-- . . .
i.e., the result of human operations. Objects or things are thus
something like logical constructs rather than ontological entities
with substantival character." From this premise, Gruppe rejected
Locke's empiricism and with it all instrumentalist theories of
language as simply a means of denoting objects. Furthermore, he
had pointed out that Aristotle's logic was "dependent on and influenced by the structures of the Greek language. The occurence
of nouns allows for easy and illegitimate hypostatization of entities. The one word 'is' prevents men from realizing the
various functions it has (from the copula 'est' to the 'is' of
existence, the 'is' of equality, etc.)."[9]

Korzybski, likewise, called attention to the various functions of
the verb "is." As an auxiliary verb or as the "is" of existence,
he felt that its use was innocuous. But he rejected its use in
identification ("the rose is a flower"), unless one said "I
classify the rose as a flower." He also tended to reject the "is"
of predication ("the rose is red"), unless one said "we see the
rose as red." His rejection of the use of the verb "is" in its
identification and predication functions tended to carry over into
a rejection of the linking function, the copula "est," of
Aristotle's syllogistic logic as well.[10] That is, in rejecting
various versions of Łukasiewicz's Law of Identity,$_1$ he assumed
that the Law of Identity$_2$ was also invalid. That Korzybski's
critique of the "is" of identity was an example of Łukasiewicz's
Law of Identity$_1$ can be seen by substituting the following terms
for a in the formulas:

A belongs to All A	Roseness belongs to all roses.
All A is A	All roses are roses.
Aaa	Every rose is a rose.

Thus there would seem to be no logical reason to reject the "is"
of identification (unless it is asserted in the $\mathcal{J}$xx version, where
a rose "is identical with" itself would cause problems). The
grounds are rather psychological; he wanted to remind his readers
that they do the classifying. Similarly, that the "is" of predication was an example of Łukasiewicz's Law of Identity$_2$ can be
seen by substituting the following propositions for p in the
formulas:
    If p, then p.
    If the rose is red, then the rose is red.
Again, there seems to be no logical reason to reject the results.
Korzybski, however, would substitute the following propositions:
If we see the rose as red, then the rose is red. In the original
case, P=P, the rose is red=the rose is red. In the second case,
P≠P, the rose as red≠the rose is red. Again, the grounds for
rejection of the Law of Identity$_2$ are more psychological (we

see . . .) than strictly logical. Much of his criticism also
turned on his definition of identity as "absolute sameness in all
aspects." That is, he attacked identity in the sense of identical, overshadowing the sense of indicative or implicative.[11]

This psychological rejection of the logic of identity reflected
Korzybski's deep attachment to Ernst Mach's empirio-criticism.
For, given Mach's evolutionary, biological theory of knowledge,
"the uniformities of nature generate the uniformities of thought"
and "the tenacity of the associative links between the two ideas
constitute . . . the basis of logical necessity which is a subjective counterpart of the objective order of nature." What is
true in nature must (ideally) be true in thought and any linguistic
or "logical" convention that denies this state of affairs must, of
necessity, be false. Like the French mathematician Poincaré,
whom he also frequently cited, Korzybski conflated biological usefulness and logical simplicity and "stressed the importance not
only of individual, but of ancestral experience as well."[12]
Thus what one "learns" from experience is conditioned not only
by one's own sensory apparatus but also by the collective,
evolutionary experience of the race mediated through the language
of one's culture.

The link, then, between Korzybski's logical assumptions about the
structure of thought and his psychological assumptions about the
origins of empirical knowledge was found in his conception of the
role of language. Language provides the "forms of representation"
that enable the organism to move from the level of objectification
to the level of visualization, which is essential for "thought."
Thus, for the child and the childlike neurotic, language represented
a form of psychological determinism--the imposition of a logical
structure whose unvoiced assumptions (functioning as undefined
terms) created the matrix of semantic categories that established
the meaning of words, phrases, and propositions, and that shaped
the organism's reactions to them. But for the normal adult, and
for those who achieve self-reflexiveness, that is, consciousness
of their own abstracting processes, language could represent a
form of logical freedom--the choice of assumptions that would
create logical structures, evaluations, and semantic reactions more
adaptive to survival.[13] If the solution to the problem of in-
correct semantic evaluations was "consciousness of abstracting,"
what was the origin of such consciousness? Korzybski's definition
of consciousness was somewhat imprecise:

> From our daily experience, we are familiar with what we
> usually denote as being "conscious;" in other words, we are
> aware of something, be it an object, a process, an action,
> a "feeling," or an "idea." A reaction that is very habitual
> and semi-automatic is not necessarily "conscious." The
> term "consciousness," taken separately, is not a complete
> symbol; it lacks content, and one of the characteristics
> of "consciousness" is to have some content. Usually, the
> term "consciousness" is taken as undefined and undefinable,

because of its immediate character for every one of us.
Such a situation is not desirable, as it is always
semantically useful to try to define a complex term by
simpler terms. We may limit the general and undefined
term "consciousness" and make it a definite symbol by
the deliberate ascribing of some content to this term.
For this "consciousness of something" I take "consciousness
of abstracting" as fundamental. Perhaps the only type of
meanings the term "consciousness" has is covered by the
functional term "consciousness of abstracting," which
represents a general process going on in our nervous
system.[14]

A comment by the Russian psychologist Lev Semenovich Vygotsky on
Piaget's psychology may help to clarify Korzybski's concept of
consciousness. Vygotsky pointed out that Piaget used "the so-
called law of awareness, which states that an impediment or dis-
turbance in an automatic activity makes the actor aware of that
activity."[15] Such a notion would be in keeping with Korzybski's
reflex-oriented psychology and would correlate with his emphasis
on semantic blockages, impediments, and other pathologies of
sensory perception and linguistic labeling.

Simplified into a schematic representation of the relationship
between thought, language, and action, Korzybski's model saw
language shaping thought, which in turn led to action. Since
language was itself a form of reflexive behavior or action (hence
Korzybski's term semantic reaction), the process was circular
and self-reinforcing. In the second paper on his general theory,
(1925) Korzybski had relied on Smith Ely Jelliffe's phylogenetic
psychoanalytic model in which psychological development in the
child represented a gradual repression of egocentrism, a cultural
imposition so to speak, via the acquisition of language, doctrines,
and socialized semantic stages or characteristics. In Science and
Sanity, he added Pavlov's notions of conditioned reflexes to
strengthen the point.[16]

But was Pavlov's notion of conditioning compatible with Korzybski's
conceptualization of the process of language acquisition by the
child? Once again, one of Korzybski's key notions was being
undermined by contemporary research in Eastern Europe. Just as
Łukasiewicz's research on Aristotle's syllogistic undercut some
of Korzybski's assumptions about the law of identity, so research
in the period 1924-1934 by Vygotsky undercut the assumed link with
Pavlov.

Vygotsky started from a point similar to Korzybski's view of the
objectifying and labeling functions of language. "A word does
not refer to a single object," Vygotsky noted, "but to a group or
to a class of objects. Each word is therefore already a generalization." (He defined generalization as a verbal act of thought
that reflected reality in a more diffuse way than either sensation
or perception). "A word without meaning is an empty sound, no

longer a part of human speech"; but a word with meaning is not only a part of speech (that is, a "full" sound) but also a unit of thought. The crucial question, therefore, was whence arose this bond between word and meaning?[17]

Associational psychology had believed that the bond between a word's sound and its content was "established through the repeated simultaneous perception of a certain sound and a certain object." Later, this bond was generalized to include other experiences. Rather, Vygotsky discovered, "word meanings are dynamic rather than static formations. They change as the child develops; they change also with the various ways in which thought functions." Vygotsky assimilated Piaget's egocentric phase of development into his own theory of thought as "inner speech."[18]

While it was true, Vygotsky said, that "thought development is determined by language," and that a "child's intellectual growth is contingent on his mastering the social means of thought, that it, language," nevertheless, the important psychological point was that "the nature of the development itself changes, from biological to sociohistorical. Verbal thought is not an innate, natural form of behavior but is determined by a historical-cultural process and has specific properties and laws that cannot be found in the natural forms of thought and speech."[19] Therefore, the proper supplement to Jelliffe's biologically oriented ontogenetic theories of cognitive development in children was not more biology in the form of Pavlovian reflex conditioning (as Korzybski attempted), but rather a genuine social psychology in the form of a functional semantic analysis based on socio-historical foundations. Korzybski, in short, was building an elaborate psychological structure on the wrong foundations.

If Korzybski's theory of language could be criticized on the basis of logical and psychological studies in Central and Eastern European thought (in which he had been nurtured), what could be said of his therapy of language? Science and Sanity summarized, in part, Korzybski's studies in psychiatric therapy at St. Elizabeth's Hospital, Washington, D.C., during 1925 and 1926, under the influence of Dr. William Alanson White. St. Elizabeth's was a large government hospital specializing in psychiatric referral cases from other government agencies, particulary the Veterans Bureau. Dr. White was "a brilliant, experienced, charming psychiatrist of international reputation, who had a comprehensive knowledge of psychiatry and wrote and taught well. Although White was one of Freud's earliest exponents in the United States, he had strong reservations about many of Freud's concepts and felt they should be accepted only with modifications."[20]

One of White's principal contributions to psychiatric research was his interpretation of schizophrenia as a regressive psychosis. That is, normal thought and language undergo genetic or evolutionary development and "change from feeling, concreteness, and perception in the direction of reasoning, differentiation and

abstraction." Therefore, the language and thought of the
schizophrenic represent a reversion to an earlier, "infantile"
order of abstraction. White is remembered today, however, less as
an original researcher than as a great encourager of others. Two
of those whose work he encouraged were Alfred Korzybski and Harry
Stack Sullivan.[21]

Harry Stack Sullivan, remembered today primarily for his theory of
interpersonal relations, had worked at St. Elizabeth's Hospital in
1921-1922 as a liaison medical officer representing the Veterans
Bureau. He had little medical training and even less psychiatric
training. "He got his knowledge of psychiatry by working with
patients and by attending lectures, seminars, and case discussions
in the Washington-Baltimore area during the early and middle
1920s." Sullivan soon rose to prominence as a skillful practiti-
oner of psychiatric therapy, particularly with male schizophrenic
patients, and published innumerable articles on schizophrenia.[22]

Korzybski, in his Time-Binding: The General Theory (Second Paper)
published in 1926, noted at one point that his view was "similar
to the 'preconcept' of Dr. H. S. Sullivan, with which I became
acquainted recently, and whose work I respect highly." But, he
insisted, their views were "not as yet the same thing."[23] In
Science and Sanity, Korzybski included several of Sullivan's works
in his bibliography but did not cite any of them in the text or
notes and references section of the book. To what extent, then,
were their views on psycho-linguistic therapy similar? To what
extent were they different? What light do these similarities and
differences throw on an evaluation of Korzybski's ideas in Science
and Sanity?

Korzybski's therapy of language was based on the notion of levels
of abstractions or an evolutionary progression of abstracting
functions uniting the submicroscopic level of nervous energy with
the macroscopic level of behavioral or semantic reactions. Thus,
the natural processes of identification and abstraction related the
physiological and psychological aspects of the organism in an
ordered, sequential semantic reaction. This ordered, sequential
reaction he interpreted in terms of modern physics and relativity
theory as taking place in "a four-dimensional space-time manifold."
Therefore, he could sum up his basic principle "that organisms
which represent processes must develop in a certain natural
survival four-dimensional order, and that the reversal of that
order must lead to pathological (non-survival) developments."
Extensively citing William Alanson White's paper on "The Language
of Schizophrenia" and the psychotherapy of Philip S. Graven,
Korzybski observed that "in all human difficulties, 'mental' ills
included, a reversal of the natural order can be found" and that
"different primitive 'magic of words,' or modern 'hypostatizations,'
'reifications,' 'misplaced concreteness,' 'objectifications,' and
all semantic disturbances represent nothing else but a confusion
of orders of abstractions, or identifications in value of essentially different orders of abstractions."[24]

If a reversal of natural order was pathological, then the proper
therapy, or psychotherapy, consisted of training in the realization of natural order, a system based on the Pavlovian notions of
reflex and reinforcement.[25]   To achieve this therapy, Korzybski
had devised a little device he called a "structural differential,"
which the patient manipulated thus setting up a conditioning and
reinforcing situation.   Several pieces of pegboard were cut into
different shapes.   One, a portion of an ellipse or parabola
(broken off to indicate indefinite extension) stood for the
submicroscopic world, "a mad dance of 'electrons,' which is different every instant, which never repeats itself, which is known to
consist of extremely complex dynamic processes of very fine structure, acted upon by, and reacting upon, the rest of the universe,
inextricably connected with everything else and dependent on
everything else."[26]   This parabola stood for the event or object
as known to modern quantum physics; the holes in the pegboard represented the characteristics or states of the interaction processes.   These states or characteristics were, theoretically,
infinite.

From this infinite set of states or characteristics, the nervous
system (or senses) selected or abstracted a finite number that
constituted the identification of the object.   This was illustrated by a circular piece of pegboard (a finite closed space)
connected to the parabola by strings tied to pegs in certain holes
that represented the characteristics thus selected.   Thus the
object known to sense experience was not the totality or actuality
of the constantly changing, dynamic states of the "mad dance of
'electrons'," but rather a static representation of those states at
a given moment; hence, the object was not the event for which it
stood.

From this finite set of characteristics (indicated by the circle),
the mind selected a few that became the basis for linguistic
identification, the selection of a label for the object.   The
label was indicated by a rectangular piece of pegboard that was
suspended under the circle (object) by strings from pegs inserted
in the selected characteristics.   Thus, the label (word) was not
the object of sense experience but was, in fact, a selection or
abstraction from the set of characteristics identifying the object.
In addition, characteristics that were disregarded or not selected
were indicated by loose, unattached strings hanging from the pegs
like unkempt hair.   "The number of characteristics which we ascribe
by definition to the label is still smaller than the number of
characteristics the object has," Korzybski noted.[27]

It is important to note that, in addition to its identifying set
of characteristics (its label or definition), each configuration
(parabola, circle, rectangle) as a configuration had a characteristic (its uniquely parabolic feature, circle-ness, or rectangu-
larity, so to speak).   In F. S. C. Northrop's terms, each configuration as a configuration was a concept by postulation; each
object, or selected set of characteristics, was a concept by

intuition. A general semantic analysis or therapy, therefore,
would necessarily have to proceed at two levels: (1) a critique
of the axiomatic bases that determined the configuration as a
configuration (rather than as the sum of its characteristics),
and (2) a reference backward from the semantic label to its
referent or object. As a therapeutic device, however, the
structural differential was restricted to denoting objects (as
sets of characteristics) and illustrating the relationships between
levels (the structure of the structure) but could only show, not
criticize, the foundations of those levels. The device could show
the configuration visually - as a configuration - but could not
indicate the axioms that determined it. To parody Wittgensteinian
terms, what could not be shown, could only be said; that is, the
basis could be explained verbally and philosophically, but not
internalized or learned by a conditioned reflex.[28]

To what extent was Korzybski's psychotherapy with the use of the
structural differential true to its own philosophical foundations?
For example, what was the principle or criteria by which the
selection of characteristics was made to define the label? For
Korzybski, it was, apparently, immediate interest or usefulness to
the organism. "The lable, the importance of which lies in its
meanings to us, represents a still higher abstraction from the
event, and usually labels, also, a semantic reaction." Thus, the
label was attached to its meanings, which, in this case, were both
the object itself and the organism's reactions to it.[29] But,
mechanically, Korzybski's structural differential device had no
way of showing the reaction of the organism. What Korzybski's
device would show, mechanically and visually, was the process of
linguistic and logical abstraction by attaching additional re-
tangular pieces to the first label in a kite-tail fashion. He
described the process as follows:

> In our diagrams, the label (L) stands for the name which
> we assigned to the object. But we can also consider the
> level of the first label (L) as a descriptive level or
> statement. We know very well that {we} can always say
> something about a statement (L), on record. Neurologically
> considered, this next statement (L_1) about a statement (L)
> would be the nervous response to the former statement
> (L). . . . So { our} statement (L_1), about the former
> statement (L), is a new abstraction from the former
> abstraction.[30]

Strictly speaking, the new abstraction was a selection of characteristics from the set of characteristics that constituted the
reaction (the nervous response) to the previous abstraction.

As a therapy, use of the structural differential involved the
"childishly simple operation of the teacher pointing a finger to
the event and then to the object, saying 'This is not this' and
insisting on silence on the pupil's part."[31] The same procedure
was repeated at each step "up" the process of abstraction thus

illustrating, in Korzybski's mind at least, a non-Aristotelian system based on a denial of the "is" of identity. Furthermore, it provided him with an operational and behavioral definition of the key notion of "consciousness." For, if the whole purpose of therapy was to raise to consciousness the process of abstraction, then the nagging question had remained--What is consciousness? Consciousness, in this analysis, was simply the memory of the characteristics that had been "left out" in the process of selection and definition. The sight of those unconnected strings hanging from the pegs of the event (parabola) or of the object (circle) would be enough to remind the patient of (that is, bring into memory) this fact. The use of the structural differential device, in other words, bridged the gaps between the verbal level of teaching, of ordinary psychotherapy, and the nonverbal, affective level where, hithertofore, one had to rely on mime, gesture, and empathetic silence.[32]

As a therapy, how successful was Korzybski's technique? He did not give statistics on his experiences but in a cryptic passage in Science and Sanity he noted:

> In experiments with the "mentally" ill in whom the
> semantic disturbances were very strong, it took
> several months to train the patients in non-identity
> and in silence on the objective levels. But, as soon
> as this was achieved, either complete or partial relief
> followed.[33]

For the rest, for patients who were not "mentally" ill, he could only assert in 1933 that his techniques would (or should in theory) remove the blocks to communication and eliminate some of the sources of confusion and contention in society.

> To gain the full benefit involves the uprooting of old
> habits, taboos, "philosophies," and private doctrines,
> the worst being the structure of our primitive { Aristotelian }
> language with the "is" of identity, all of which are deeply
> rooted and work unconsciously. Only the semantic training
> with the {Structural} Differential in non-identity can affect
> the "habitual" and the "unconscious."[34]

The larger claims can not be judged historically at this point (being largely matters of faith or belief rather than practice at that time); however, the historian can ask how Korzybski's therapy compared with other therapies, in this case Harry Stack Sullivan's. Judged in terms of its own times, how valid was Korzybski's therapy for mental patients with linguistic disorders?

Like Korzybski, Harry Stack Sullivan was influenced by William Alanson White's notion of schizophrenia as a regressive psychosis. As Sullivan noted in one of his early papers:

> The tentative conclusions from our work are that the primary
> disorder in this illness is one of mental structure; . . . in

> turn reflected in the thought content and in the purposive
> activity--behavior. The mental structure is disassociated
> in such fashion that the disintegrated portions regress in
> function to earlier levels of mental ontology, without
> parallelism in individual depth of regression. This dis-
> parity of depths seems the essence of that which is
> schizophrenia. . . . [35]

In particular, Sullivan saw that "any problem in psychopathology
becomes a problem of symbol functioning, a matter of seeking to
understand and interpret eccentric symbol performances."[36] The
schizophrenic patients spoke a private, "primitive" language.
They heard "voices" or were abnormally sensitive to sound. It was
the duty of the therapist to decipher such symbol systems by
associational techniques and by questioning.

The psychotherapist, however, was not content to apply the term
symbol solely to words or other labels. Drawing on Korzybski's
discussion of abstraction, Sullivan concluded that "word-symbols
. . . are anything but simple psychobiological symbols. In so far
as they are used in thinking, they function as very high order
abstractions."[37] Thus, experiences, including prenatal experiences,
are summed up in, or abstracted into, mental structures or symbol
sets and "are structuralized into preconcepts, complexes, and
sentiments (partly accessible to awareness)."[38]

The task of the therapist, therefore, was to understand the meaning
that a particular symbol had for the patient. One way in which
this might be accomplished was through the use of the techniques of
Freudian psychoanalysis, which were in vogue in the 1920s and
1930s in psychiatric circles in the United States. But "it was
readily admitted that on-the-couch psychoanalytic techniques
could not be applied to most schizophrenics and other psychotic
patients."[39] Sullivan, accordingly, called for a modified psychoanalytic treatment of schizophrenia based on the notion that
the problem with the schizophrenic patient was not simply an
intrapersonal symbolic disorientation but also was an inability
to cope with interpersonal relationships, particularly as they
related to sexuality. Therefore, he combined a socio-psychiatric
group therapy with a psychoanalytically derived verbal analysis.[40]

Working in a small ward with his own specially trained assistants,
Sullivan developed a therapeutic procedure based on the notion
that the goal of psychotherapy was to change the patient's interpersonal orientations. "His aim was for the entire staff to form
comfortable interpersonal relationships with the patients to help
them come back from the psychotic worlds in which they had re-
tired; in the process the patients would develop capabilities for
sounder relationships with people and would gradually acquire
better contact with reality."[41] At the time, he claimed an
improvement rate of 80 percent; modern critics would question the
validity of the claim, although his procedures were institutionalized into the fabric of American psychiatric practice.

Sullivan went on to integrate his ideas on language development
into his more general theories of personality development. He
distinguished between "syntaxic thinking" and "consensual validation." Syntaxic thinking in the child's development was "the
capacity for logical, realistic thinking and sound appraisals of
himself, other people, and his relationships with them"; it also
included the ability "to think about material objects in logical
ways." By consensual validation Sullivan meant the process by
which "a person arrives at a healthy consensus (or agreement) with
one or more people about some aspect of his feelings and thoughts,
and this consensus is validated by repeated interpersonal experiences which emphasize its soundness." Language was crucial
because it helped the child "to crystallize to himself and others
the nature of his feelings and thoughts" and therefore "to resolve
his interpersonal problems and misconceptions."[42]

As a theory of semantics, as a way to determine the meaning of
language, Sullivan's ideas focused primarily on the meaning of the
symbol for the individual in terms of interpersonal relationships
and only secondarily on the socialized meaning of the symbol in
terms of syntactic relationships with perceived external objects.
As a theory about the nature of language and its relation to
thought, Sullivan's ideas developed along lines similar to
Vygotsky's notion of inner speech. In Sullivan's later views, as
in George Herbert Mead, thinking takes the form of an interior
dialogue with a "generalized other" who acts as "the carrier of a
socially derived logical apparatus {that } restricts and governs
the direction of that thought." Language is simply the socially
conditioned set of categories and meanings upon which communication depends; the laws of logic are simply a set of general
agreements within a universe of discourse. "They are the rules we
must follow if we would socialize our thought."[43]

The comparison between Korzybski's linguistic therapy and
Sullivan's psychotherapy of schizophrenic patients reveals a
basic difference in spite of their common adherence to William
Alanson White's regression theory. Korzybski's therapeutic use
of the structural differential device was designed initially to
reorient the patient toward the impersonal world of empiro-critical
reality; Sullivan's modified psychoanalytic procedures and group
setting were designed primarily to reorient the patient toward the
interpersonal world of psycho-social reality. The scientific
chapters in Korzybski's Science and Sanity--on Einstein's theory
of relativity, on Minkowski's four-dimensional space, and on the
structure of matter according to quantum mechanics--annoyed his
critics and overawed his disciples but they were essential to his
argument.[44] Korzybski's linguistic therapy was essentially a
philosophical reorientation, which might or might not have
psychological benefits for understanding the role of language in
communication; Sullivan's psychotherapy was essentially a
psychological reorientation, which might or might not have philosophical benefits for the understanding of the role of language in
personality development. In Sullivan's mature thought, there

lingered the ghostly echoes of his early schizophrenic patients
with their "peculiarities of thought," their other "voices," and
their desperate need to communicate.

If there was a ghost that haunted Korzybski's intellectual mansions,
on the other hand, it was the spirit of Bertrand Russell's work
in mathematical logic more than the memory of Korzybski's studies
at St. Elizabeth's Hospital. For all his emphasis on the psychobiological effects of confusions of level of abstractions,
Korzybski continually returned to the refrain that some such
confusions were inherent in the logical structure of ordinary
language itself. Language conceived as a structure of abstractions,
including statements about statements, approximated the logical
structure of mathematics. "Statements such as 'a proposition
about all propositions,'"Korzybski noted, "have been called by
Russell 'illegitimate totalities.' In such cases, it is necessary
to break up the set into smaller sets, each of which is capable of
having a totality. . . . In the language of the Principia
Mathematica, the principle which enables us to avoid the illegitimate totalities may be expressed as follows: 'Whatever involves
all of a collection must not be one of the collection' . . . "45
Or, "in the language of Wittgenstein: 'No proposition can say
anything about itself, because the propositional sign cannot be
contained in itself (that is the 'whole theory of types')."46
Thus, Korzybski attempted to incorporate Russell's theory of types
within his critique of language (although rejecting Russell's use
of the law of identity) and stated his own version of it: "In the
language of the present general semantics a statement about a
statement is not the 'same' statement, but represents, by structural and neurological necessity, a higher order of abstraction,
and should not be confused with the original statement."47

Korzybski also assimilated Russell's denoting theory of language
that Russell had outlined in his early writings. The meaning of
a name was identified with the object that it denoted. A name
that did not denote anything was meaningless. Furthermore,
"anything that could be mentioned was said to be a term; any term
could be the logical subject of a proposition; and anything that
could be the logical subject of a proposition could be named. It
followed that one could in principle use names to refer not only
to any particular thing that existed at any place and time, but
to abstract entities of all sorts, to non-existent things . . . ,
{ and} even to logically impossible entities like the greatest
prime number."48 This notion had been incorporated into
Korzybski's theory of language in the early 1920s under his
positivistic critique of pseudo-symbols.

Russell found, however, that his early formulation led to difficulties, particularly if one translated Frege's distinction
between Sinn (sense) and Bedeutung (reference) into Russell's
terms meaning and denotation. Then, "if one assumes with Frege
that every denoting phrase has both a sense and a reference, and
if one treats the sense as an object, the requisite connection

between sense and reference cannot be established." Russell, therefore, moved on to elaborate his theory of descriptions in which expressions classified either as indefinite or as definite descriptions were not used as names, "in as much as it is not necessary for them to denote anything in order to have a meaning." That is, they functioned as "incomplete symbols" that contributed to the meaning of the sentence even though they did not, strictly speaking, denote anything.[49]

Korzybski tried to follow Russell in this step but was hindered somewhat by his dedication to psychiatry. As F. S. C. Northrop has pointed out, Korzybski's "concepts by postulation" had "meaning" even if they did not have "reference" (in the sense of denoting an object) while his "concepts by intuition" had "meaning" by reference to an object in sense experience (that is, by denotion). This was the basis of Korzybski's acceptance of the notions of intensionality and extensionality. "'Intensional relations are relations of 'concepts,' " he noted, "extensional relations are relations of denoted facts.' "[50] To these logical definitions, Korzybski drew parallels to the psychological conditions of introversion and extroversion. The introvert concentrated on what was "going on inside his own skin"; the extrovert projected "all that { was } going on within himself upon the outside world, and { believed } that his personal projections have some kind of non-personal objective existence, and so have 'the same' validity and value for other observers."[51] While most people had some of both traits, nevertheless intensionality/introversion (the disease of philosophers) was a reversal of survival order and led to failure; extensionality/extroversion (the genius of mathematicians) was the natural survival order and led to successful adaptation.

Korzybski's psychological preference for extensionality obscured his logical commitment to concepts by postulation and rested on the idea that "extension recognized the uniqueness, with corresponding one-value, of the individual { event or object} by giving each individual a unique name, and so makes confusion impossible."[52] It was this logical problem of names that had led Russell on from his early denoting theory of names to elaborate his theory of descriptions. As A. J. Ayer has observed:

> Historically, . . . Russell's theory of descriptions is rooted in his assumption that the meaning of names is to be identified with the objects which they denote. We have, however, also seen that the theory, when logically developed, leads to the elimination of names, so that it is not in the end affected by the truth or falsehood of the assumption from which it originated. . . . In the case of ordinary proper names, the decisive objection to it is that the name makes the same contribution to the meaning of the sentences in which it occurs, whether the object which it purports to denote exists or not. In the case of the purely demonstrative signs which Russell called logically proper names, the main argument against

his original assumption is that it prevents them from having any constant meaning.[53]

Russell modified his denoting theory of language and moved on to elaborate his "logical atomism"; Wittgenstein renounced his Tractatus and elaborated a critique of all denoting theories; Korzybski, however, did not challenge his own assumptions.[54]

The main body of Korzybski's Science and Sanity ended with a revealing comment:

> In the process of formulating the above system a curious observation has been forced upon me; namely, that statements which are, for instance, quite legitimate for the English language, even though they probably apply in general to all Indo-european languages, do not apply in a similar degree.
>
> I am intimately acquainted with six languages, two Slavic, two Latin, and two Teutonic, and also with the psychological trends of these groups. I have been led to suspect strongly that the finer differences in the structure of these languages and their use are connected with the semantics of these national groups. An enquiry into this problem, in my opinion, presents great semantic possibilities and might be the foundation for the understanding of international psycho-logical differences. Once formulated, this would lead us to a better mutual understanding, particularly if a { non-Aristotelian} semantic revision of these different languages is undertaken.[55]

A little more self-reflection on this point might have led Korzybski to a reexamination of some of his assumptions. For example, the principle of nonidentity is awkward in English but quite natural in Polish, which has a special case (genitive) for such situations. With a negated verb in Polish, one uses a different form of the noun to indicate that it is no longer a subject but the object of an impersonal phrase. While Korzybski did acknowledge toward the end of his career that in some languages, including the Slavic, there was no "is" of identity, he had not carried this awareness into a thorough going critique of his system.[56]

There was, thus, a certain irony in Korzybski's position at the time he published Science and Sanity. He had started his intellectual journey with a rich Polish and Central European heritage of positivism, empirio-criticism, linguistic diversity, and an Anglo-French tradition of mathematical logic. In the United States in the early 1920s, he had been influenced by engineering millenialism, mechanistic biology, psychiatric theory and clinical experience, and by Cassius J. Keyser's mathematical philosophy of fate and logical freedom. To this mixture, he had added in the late 1920s and early 1930s an additional layer of ideas borrowed from Polish logicians (Łukasiewicz, Leśniewski, Chwistek, Kotarbiński) and from the Russian behavioral psychologist

Pavlov. But these later additions were used only as elaborations to or glosses on his text. By the time he published the final version of Science and Sanity in 1933, his ideas had long since hardened into their idiosyncratic form.

The irony of Korzybski was that, if he had stayed in closer touch with his intellectual sources or had vigorously pursued their arguments, he might have discovered that some of his fundamental assumptions were being overturned. Łukasiewicz's studies of Aristotle's texts showed that there were two laws of identity in Aristotelian logic. Korzybski's leap of negation in his theory of language to deny the law of identity was not as fatal to Aristotelian logic as he claimed. Vygotsky assimilated genetic developmental theory of language acquisition and influence into his own theory of thought as inner speech but showed that the process of development (including language manipulation) changed from a purely biological to a socio-historical one. This undercut Korzybski's union of Jelliffe's philogenetic structuralism with Pavlov's conditioned-reflex concept. Both Harry Stack Sullivan and Korzybski started from a similar point on the question of the linguistic pathology of schizophrenia; both drew on William Alanson White's hypothesis that schizophrenic language represented a regression to infantilism or primitivism, an earlier level of development. But Sullivan soon integrated his views into an interpersonal therapy of language and of personality. Korzybski's "therapy" of language turned out to be another way of inculcating his root philosophical position--a mixture of Mach's empirio-criticism, Polish positivism, and Russell's logical theory of types and his denotation theory of language. Portions of these intellectual systems were eroding away as Science and Sanity was published.

By 1933, Korzybski had used his intellectual freedom to choose assumptions from his cosmopolitan background, but the fate of his ideas would now be determined as much by the American intellectual environment as by their logical implications.

4

IDEOLOGY AND PRAXIS: GENERAL SEMANTICS AND ANALYTICAL PHILOSOPHY IN AMERICA AND POLAND, 1930s-1960s

Korzybski's Science and Sanity was published in 1933, a time that was both auspicious and disastrous for such a book. The descent into the depths of the Great Depression was both precipitous and frightening. Perhaps now people would be willing to listen to Korzybski and to recognize the need for the fundamental reorientation in thinking that he prescribed. But who could afford to buy books when confronted with a bank panic, the fact or threat of unemployment, and the bleak prospects of the future? Who had time to contemplate an intellectual revolution when confronted with the imperatives of individual survival or institutional reform?

Who, indeed? The task fell, partly by default and partly by desire, to the self-appointed class of intellectuals--both inside and outside academia--whose instinctual response to the crisis of the depression had been a frantic search for an adequate analysis of its causes as a necessary premise to the prescription of remedial solutions.

To such men and women fell the initial task of evaluating Korzybski's book. Ernst Nagel, the logician, published an uncomplimentary review in the New Republic and defended his position with the terse statement that "its main thesis rests on a misunderstanding of recent works on the foundations of logic."[1]

Sidney Hook, the philosopher, was in the throes of his attempt to reconcile the thought of the young Marx with the evolutionary naturalism and pragmatism of Dewey through the doctrine of revolutionary praxis.[2] Hook reviewed Korzybski's book for the Saturday Review of Literature and wrote: "I believe that Mr. Korzybski's fundamental position is sound and that his obiter dicta contain some seminal ideas which undoubtedly will bear fruit in the minds of others." What Hook prized most in Korzybski was precisely those logical and linguistic issues that had already been worked out by John Dewey in his Studies in Logical Theory and other early writings. "The author would be well advised to develop his views on logic and mathematics," Hook concluded, "and keep out of the fields of economics, history, and culture study in which he is obviously not at home."[3]

The lingering traces of Korzybski's Polish and European intellectual ambiance were thus rejected by Hook and his distinctive contributions were subsumed under the general rubric of American pragmatism. As Richard J. Bernstein has pointed out in his study of American philosophy, "many students of pragmatism were sympathetic to positivism and logical positivism { in the 1930s} and saw in this philosophic movement--especially in the centrality of the verifiability criterion of meaning--an attempt to state rigorously what the pragmatists were supposedly groping toward. What they failed to see," he has noted, was "that positivism harbored an atomistic epistemological doctrine which had consistently been one of the main targets of attack by the pragmatists."[4]

Korzybski was not a logical positivist (although he occasionally sounded like one) nor was he a consistent pragmatist. (His theories of truth, for instance, were closer to correspondence and coherence theories than to pragmatism). At best he might be described as a misplaced Polish positivist, a psychological positivist who had united Mach's empirio-criticism with Pavlov's behaviorism and cast it in an idiosyncratic idiom of mathematical terminology. But he had assimilated enough elements of American millenialism, reformism, and behavioral psychology and psychiatry by 1933 to make him acceptable to an American audience even if they did not always understand him correctly or completely. In 1935, Korzybski began to "conduct seminar courses in general semantics in schools, colleges and universities, and before various groups of educators, scientists, and physicians, including psychiatrists. In the same year a group of students of Science and Sanity organized the First American Congress on General Semantics at the Washington College of Education at Ellensburg, where a number of papers from various fields were presented." Also in 1935, Korzybski presented papers before the American Mathematics Society and the Psychology Section of the American Association for the Advancement of Science.[5]

While the logicians, philosophers, and mathematicians debated Korzybski's formal ideas in the context of analytical philosophy, the tendency among other readers was to reject or ignore the metaphysical foundations of Korzybski's theories and seize upon the more pragmatic aspects of his verbal therapy. This tendency was even found in his wife, Mira Edgerly-Korzybska. In a radio interview in 1936 on how the portrait painter uses language--that is, conversation--as a key to personality, Lady Edgerly-Korzybska said:

> . . . the world is beginning to see that the most highly
> regarded looks are those only we ourselves can create.
> We are continually having more worthwhile ideals of
> beauty. When we speak of beauty in connection with humans
> we must include the human brain. For the human brain is
> what distinguishes us from animals. Our features are but
> the instruments of expression.

Ideals were the real core of personality, and "everyone no matter
how dumb, dull, stupid, or even low in the scale of life they may
be, . . . has something which to them is an ideal." The happy
people were the ones who pursued their ideals and thus created
true beauty because "humans are creators," she said. "That is the
thrill of being human. There is that creative magic in our thoughts
and our words." Because humans had the unique capacity of language,
"that is carrying our world around in our heads, in a 'world of
words,' " they could affect their whole lives.[6] In her hands,
general semantics became a variant of the American mind-cure
religions where by positive thinking one could attain health,
wealth--and beauty.

Mira Edgerly-Korzybska's portrait of her husband, painted in the
early 1920s, showed a vigorous middle-aged man in profile in a
casual pose. His sleeves were rolled up exposing muscular arms.
His head was bald, and he stared into the distance through wire-
framed glasses. In one hand he held a long, aristocratic
cigarette holder in a European manner. The total effect was one of
youth, vigor--and a certain aura of mystique. It was the portrait
of a thinker who acts, a doer.

It was the pragmatic emphasis in much of the discussion of general
semantics that attracted many nonspecialists to it--including
Stuart Chase. R. Alan Lawson and other historians have shown in
their studies of "independent liberalism" in the 1930s that Chase
and those who had shared his faith in rational planning, regionalism,
and a renewal of spiritual and communal values had come to a
crisis point in 1936-1937. The failure of planning in the debacle
of the National Recovery Administration, the continuing strength
of individualism, the piecemeal approach of New Deal reform, and
the failure of third-party initiatives in the 1936 election had
left them stranded:

> The clear import of the situation was that many { independent
> liberals } had come to feel it was no longer sensible to
> promote radical alternatives to the New Deal. Reform thought
> was shifting from anticapitalist, collectivist reconstruction
> to advocacy of moderate change. . . .
> Adding greatly to the discouragement the unbreakable strength
> of the New Deal imposed on the hopes that collectivism
> would prove to be a practical reform approach, was the example
> of collectivism abroad running amuck. Were Americans really
> so different from Germans and Italians and Russians that
> they could establish collectivist social planning without
> power cliques forming at the center and the mass of the

people becoming abjectively subservient to propaganda
and terror?[7]

With demagogues at loose in the land, with sit-down strikes and
"memorial day" massacres, with Communist united front wordmonger-
ing, who could but wonder whether Americans really were immune to
the trends of the times. The tendency to downgrade ideology; to
celebrate the unique and particular in America's past and in its
present regional cultures; to seek workable, immediate solutions
--all these inclinations helped to reinforce the "pragmatic"
filter through which independent liberals viewed all current ideas.

Most important for intellectuals, all those who lived by independent thought, was the fate of ideas in the shifting kaleidoscope
of politics in the New Deal. Only certain ideas became institutionalized and survived the tests of time, the courts, and the
conservative bloc in Congress. The ideas that survived were
those that were taken up by interest groups or which provided a
rationale for the self-assertion and power hunger of some group
such as organized labor, commerical farmers, or retail merchants.
The Roosevelt administration might borrow a slogan here or there
(as it had lifted Chase's phrase, "a new deal"); it might en-
courage experimentation in consumerism, regionalism, subsistence
farming, cooperation, or collective art for a season; but, when
the administration needed key votes in Congress, when public
criticism got too hot, when the bureaucratic in-fighting created
intolerable tensions in the inner circles of the New Deal, then
ideas without constituencies would be shunted aside, allowed to
wither on the bureaucratic vine by underfunding, or would be
simply buried in a shuffle of the bureaucracy. Why were the
people so indifferent to the fate of independent ideas?

In November 1937, Stuart Chase published the first of a series of
three articles in Harpers magazine on the problems of communication and change. "The Tyranny of Words" introduced the general
reading public to some of Korzybski's ideas. Bernard De Voto, the
perennial critic, was generally favorable to Chase's intentions
but criticized his ideological bias against "conservatism" and his
ignoring of nonlinguistic factors in human problems. In spite of
the criticism, Chase had succeeded in doing for Korzybski what
Korzybski had been unable to do--popularize some basic concepts
of general semantics.[8]

By March 1938, a hostile review in the Christian Century condemned
"The Tyranny of Semantics" and detected a threat to religion in
the positivistic bent of semantics: "The catch in this rather too
pretentious 'science of semantics' is that it furnishes a gag
with which to stop the mouth of anyone who would speak of matters
other than the particular things which are present to the senses."
The Partisan Review also attacked semantics ("the opium of Stuart
Chase") on Marxist philosophical and political grounds. Thus,
semantics emerged in the public consciousness as a specie of
liberalism being attacked simultaneously by the Catholic right

and the Marxist left.[9] The distinction between the "Science of
Semantics" as a concern for better communications and Korzybski's
general semantics as a concern for better evaluations of
psychological reactions was not always apparent to the general
public.

The capstone on the newly won popularity of general semantics was
an article in Time magazine in November 1938, recounting the
opening of Korzybski's Institute of General Semantics in Chicago.
Located near the University of Chicago and funded by a grant from
Cornelius Crane of the Crane Company, the institute opened in
July 1938, "to teach General Semantics to educators and maladjusted
people." (Well-adjusted noneducators were presumably beyond the
pale of general semantics's and Time's concern.) The "theory of
General Semantics is exceedingly complex," the Time article noted,
"but its method of instruction is simple. . . ." After devoting
some attention to Korzybski's use of his little device, the
structural differential, the article credited general semantics
with raising points in intelligence scores for sophomores; helping
maladjusted students to gain weight, cure insomnia, and fight
mental depression; and curing alcoholism. "Whether General
Semantics will become a cult such as technocracy, or will rank in
historic importance with the work of Aristotle and Einstein," the
article concluded, "it is spreading rapidly in the U.S. Already
3,000 copies of Science and Sanity . . . have been sold."[10]

The few blocks that separated the Institute of General Semantics
from the University of Chicago campus were symbolic of a growing
rift in American culture between the "free intellectual" and the
academician, a gulf that would widen considerably in the next
two decades. In the 1930s, however, the free intellectual, unattached to any academic institution, occupied an important place
in the intellectual and cultural landscape. Edmund Wilson,
Bernard De Voto, Bertram D. Wolfe, Will Herberg, Reinhold Neibuhr,
Walter Lippmann, and Irving Howe participated in the partisan
acrimony of intellectual and ideological battles of the decade
without any sense of being outsiders or interlopers. Free-lance
writers, social workers, poets, and seers moved in and out of New
Deal agencies, bureaus, and programs all the while maintaining
their credentials in the larger "brain trust" of intellectuals and
avoiding the permanent stigma of the label "bureaucrat."[11]
Korzybski as a free intellectual, then, was not a unique phenomenon,
but Stuart Chase's popularization of general semantics provided him
with access to a larger audience.

Academicians, on the other hand, suffered severe setbacks during
the Great Depression from the economics of institutional budget
cutting and from the political pressures on academic freedom and
dissent. With demagogues and charlatans on every hand, with left-
wing internecine warfare rampant in some departments, and with
painful personal sacrifices to be endured for the love of one's
discipline, the academics were prepared to do battle to maintain
the standards and prerogatives of their craft. Scholarly reviews

of Korzybski's book sometimes hinted that the founder of general
semantics lacked the requisite academic "union card"--a Ph.D.   But
even in academia in 1938, Korzybski was not without his supporters
and popularizers, among them a young instructor named S. I. Hayakawa.[12]

Samuel Ichiyé Hayakawa, Canadian born of Japanese parents, was a
poet and aesthetician with a doctor of philosophy degree in
American and English literature.[13]   Stuart Chase readily admitted
that he did not understand all of Korzybski, particularly the
psychological aspects of his system; that he had conflated
Korzybski's epistemology with Ogden and Richards's symbol/referent/
reference triangle; and that he did not know whether posterity
would regard Korzybski "as a genius or as a man overstrained by an
idea too big to handle. . . ."[14]   Hayakawa, on the other hand, was
convinced that he did understand Korzybski and wasted no time in
setting Chase and all other critics of Korzybski aright.[15]   In
reviewing a book on the philosophy of language, Hayakawa objected
to the omission of a discussion of Korzybski's ideas "since it
makes it hard to avoid the conclusion that the author is either
unaware of or indifferent to the numerous practical and social
implications of his subject."[16]

It was precisely those "practical and social implications" of
Korzybski's thought that excited Hayakawa's pedagogical imagination
in 1939.   "Can we speed up the abolition of two-valued { either/or}
orientation, not only among the 'educated' classes, but also
among the masses of people?" he asked.[17]   Hayakawa regarded
Korzybski primarily as an educational innovator and applied his
general semantic ideas in an experimental freshman English course
taught in the extension division of the University of Wisconsin.
In 1939, Hayakawa published for his students a first-draft version
of a text based on general semantics principles. He called it
Language in Action. A second-draft version was published in 1940
by the Institute of General Semantics. It was designed to support
Hayakawa's conviction that "an enlightened public opinion can be
achieved only when the average citizen is, at least to some degree,
a semanticist."[18]

Korzybski was also impatient with the events of 1939, particularly
with the propaganda and the two-valued orientation of Hitler and
the Nazi regime. In September 1939, he wrote to several governments,
"urging the employment of permanent boards of neuro-psychiatrists,
psycho-logicians, and other specialists," to counteract these
abuses of "neuro-semantic and neuro-linguistic mechanisms" in the
world crisis. But the governments politely ignored his advice,
much to Korzybski's frustration, and the crisis developed inexorably
of its own momentum.[19]   A student who encountered Korzybski and his
ideas at the Institute in Chicago in the summer of 1940 remembered
years later that Korzybski "was a man of tremendous energy and
magnetic personality, dedicated to what appeared to be a great
cause, although there was at that time considerable mystery in the
heads of many of his followers as to exactly what the cause was."[20]

Korzybski moved through the turbulent events of the wartime and post-war period with a singleness of purpose and the imperturbability of an autocrat. In 1941, he addressed two hundred of his followers at a Second American Congress on General Semantics held at the University of Denver. Some of his devotees founded the International Society for General Semantics and, in 1943, launched a journal, ETC.: A Review of General Semantics, with headquarters in Chicago. In the summer of 1946 Korzybski's Institute moved to Lakeville, Connecticut, where he offered "what he termed his seminars, which really were lectures (one-way communication, for he brooked few interruptions)." The official connection between the Institute and the Society was ended in 1947 as Korzybski disapproved of the drift of the journal ETC.[21] When Korzybski issued a third edition of Science and Sanity in 1948, he noted:

> Lately the words "semantics" and "semantic" have become widely used, and generally misused, even by important writers, thus leading to hopeless confusion. "Semantics" is a name for an important branch of philology, as complex as life itself, couched in appropriate philological terms, and as such has no direct application to life problems. . . . My work was developed entirely independently of "semantics," "significs," "semiotic," "semasiology," etc. . . . Those works do not touch my field, and as my work progressed it has become obvious that a theory of "meaning" is impossible . . . and "significs," etc., are unworkable. . . .{ He called his own system "an empirical natural science of non-elementalistic evaluation" and a system of values }.
> The present theory of values involves a clear-cut, workable discipline, limited to its premises, a fact which is often disregarded by some readers and writers. They seem also often unaware of the core of the inherent difficulties in these age-old problems, and the solutions available through changing not the language, but the structure of language, achieved by the habitual use of the extensional devices in our evaluational reactions.[22]

In 1949 as an apogee to his career, Korzybski lectured at a seminar at Yale, and the Third Congress on General Semantics convened in Denver. Time magazine lauded the "success" of his movement, but Korzybski was pessimistic of the future of civilization. He died unexpectedly in 1950. He left a canon of authoritative texts, a host of disciples, and an ambiguous legacy.[23]

The irony of Korzybski was that, for all of his celebration of three-valued and infinitely-valued logic, he sometimes utilized the same two-valued, either/or logic that he had warned others about. This was graphically illustrated in the 1941 introduction to the second edition of Science and Sanity where his charts of the opposition of Aristotelian and non-Aristotelian orientations ran over two pages.[24] But such an approach was congenial to popular modes of thought that have characterized Americans since the time of the Puritans. American intellectual history has been characterized by an implicit set of either/or categories that have changed slowly over time:

Either one is _____	/ Or one is _____ .
good	/ bad
virtuous	/ full of vice
saved	/ damned
Whig	/ Tory
Federalist	/ anti-Federalist
Democrat	/ Republican
slave	/ free
Yankee	/ Rebel
Liberal	/ Conservative
Progressive	/ Reactionary
American	/ un-American
Communist	/ anti-Communist
establishment	/ dissent [25]

As Korzybski seemed at times to be saying, either you had communication or you had chaos; either you had an Aristotelian system
(unsane) or you had a non-Aristotelian system (sane).

The imprisonment of many general semantics advocates within the
two-valued categories of American intellectual history was facili-
tated by events after World War II, particularly the growth of
higher education and the disintegration of the free intelligentsia
during the McCarthy red scare. Above all, they were caught up in
the coils of the emerging cold-war ideology of anti-Communism and
the pervasive self-help or "positive thinking" movements of the
1950s.

The separation of the "academics" from the "free intellectuals" in
the late 1930s and 1940s was accelerated by government assistance
to higher education. The subsidizing of higher education during
the New Deal, particularly with the National Youth Administration
program; the wartime manpower training grants, science and engineering research grants, and the V-12 officer-training program; and
the underwriting of post-war educational benefits in the famous
"GI Bill"--all these laid the foundations for a spectacular post-war
increase in enrollments. "From 1940 to 1949 enrollments nearly
doubled in institutions of higher education"; the academic year
1946-1947 alone saw the greatest increase ever recorded in one
year.[26]

The balance of power in intellectual matters gradually shifted.
The free intellectual became the "outsider"; academia swallowed
the poet, the writer, the playwright, the philosopher. The left-wing
radicals of the 1930s--writers, publicists, and political theorists
--had become, in many cases, the anti-Communist radicals of the
right in the post-war era or endorsed a quasi-official cold-war
cultural ideology. A pervasive anti-intellectualism made the very
notion of the free, unattached and critical individual seem somehow
subversive. The free intellectual survived, if at all, as an exile,
a supplicant for foundation grants and fellowships or as a

foundation executive or expert.[27]

The fate of general semantics ideas in the changing balance of power among intellectuals can be seen in the activities of Stuart Chase and S. I. Hayakawa. Chase had spent the war years writing a series of studies for the Twentieth Century Fund to aid in post-war planning.[28] In 1948, he shifted his focus somewhat and published The Proper Study of Mankind in praise of cultural anthropology and offered the liberal arts as an ideological foundation for resolving tensions in society. It was "an attempt to map the social sciences, and establish interconnections and lines of progress in the study of human relations." This book was followed in 1951 with Roads to Agreement: Successful Methods in the Science of Human Relations. Chase included a chapter in Roads to Agreement called "Danger: Men Talking: Semantics as a Useful Tool." In Chase's hands, the science of semantics was reduced to a series of eight practical rules.[29]

Chase still honored Korzybski's contributions to his thought. "As I knew him in his later years," Chase recounted of Korzybski, "he had the general aspect of an amiable Buddha, bald as a newel post, with kindly, intelligent eyes behind vast, round spectacles, and a rich, rolling Polish accent. He was rude, formidable, over-verbalized, and strangely appealing--for all I knew an authentic genius."[30] But clearly Chase's mind and interest had moved on to other issues and visions. The science of semantics, including in Chase's mind Korzybski's general semantics, was but part of the larger search for a scientific means of improving communication and resolving conflicts, something he called human relations.

Hayakawa, like Chase, was concerned with the fact that communication per se could lead to either conflict or cooperation. He, too, firmly believed that "the basic ethical assumption of semantics, analogous to the medical assumption that health is preferable to illness, is that cooperation is preferable to conflict. This assumption, implicit in Language in Action, was made explicit as a central and unifying theme in Language in Thought and Action, an expansion of { Hayakawa's} earlier work, published in 1949."[31] Whereas Chase, the free intellectual and generalist, subsumed Korzybski's ideas into broader developments in the social sciences, S. I. Hayakawa, the academic specialist, subsumed these developments into the framework established by Korzybski.

Following Korzybski's sudden death in March 1950, Hayakawa was one of a host of disciples and claimants for the mantle of leadership of the general semantics movement--and also confronted a host of rival self-help and self-awareness movements--all within a climate of cold-war conservatism. Scientist-semanticist Anatol Rapoport complained in 1952 that "many academic semanticists { were } inclined to dismiss Korzybski's work as unsound and to view his 'lay following' as a cult" and that there was "resistance both among the 'academicians' and among the { cultic } Korzybski-ites against treating as part of the same intellectual current both the semantics of Whitehead, Russell, Tarski, Carnap, etc., on the one

hand and the general semantics of Korzybski on the other."
Rapoport also observed:

> "The accusations of cultism leveled against Korzybski's
> followers are not altogether unfounded. In the United
> States there is a large floating population of 'truth-
> seekers.' Many of them lack the capacity for the strenuous
> intellectual effort required in a fruitful pursuit of
> knowledge and wisdom; others lack the power of critical
> evaluation, which would enable them to tell the genuine
> from the false. . . . Moreover, the seminars conducted by
> Korzybski at the Institute of General Semantics emphasized
> problems of personal integrations, of human relations, etc.,
> and so attracted considerable numbers of people without
> sufficient background to understand the philosophical
> implications of Korzybski's ideas. As often happens, many
> of these people came out of those seminars happier than
> they went in. Whether they were actually helped by general
> semantics or by other factors cannot be determined without
> sufficient controls. But they went about spreading the
> faith, thus giving a cultist flavor to the 'movement.' "[32]

In his role as editor of ETC., the International Society's journal,
Hayakawa was in a strategic position to try to shape the post-
Korzybskian image of general semantics. In his hands, the popular
image of general semantics emerged in the 1950s as a mildly liberal
critique of America's consumer-oriented civilization, a rival to
Norman Vincent Peale's "positive-thinking" religion, an effective
antidote to Soviet two-valued propaganda and ideology, and an
eminently sane approach to improving communications and interpersonal relations. The Institute of General Semantics tried to
remain faithful to the Korzybski canon by republishing his writings,
continuing his training sessions, sponsoring lectures, and publishing a bulletin. Others tried to extend or modify Korzybski's
system by combining some of his ideas with various intellectual
trends. For example, Irving J. Lee blended group dynamics and
communications theory; Wendell Johnson combined cybernetics
ideas borrowed from the philosophy of science; Theodore Longabaugh
included Whorfian anthropology; Bess Sondel worked in Ogden and
Richards's semantics and Morris's semiotics; and J. Samuel Bois
recast Korzybskian formulas with awareness psychology and systems
analysis.[33]

The irony of these adaptations of Korzybski's general semantics to
the prevailing intellectual temper in the United States is
heightened by a comparison with the fate of Polish analytical
philosophy in its post-war clash with Marxism. As Henryk
Skolimowski has shown in his study of recent Polish intellectual
history, the collision between Marxism and analytical-linguistic
philosophy went through several phases. In the period 1951 to
1955, the analytical philosophers turned the tables on their
Marxist critics by pointing out the idealistic elements in Polish
Marxism and by emphasizing their own "materialistic" orientation.
Also Marxists and analytical philosophers clashed, particularly

because the Marxists said that formal logic was only an empty game, that dialectical logic was supreme, and, therefore, that the law of contradiction was irrelevant and not binding. Analytical philosophers, on the other hand, considered that ignoring the law of contradiction meant that their opponents were no longer engaged in rational and critical scholarship.[34] Gradually, the leading Marxist critic Adam Schaff abandoned the position of Engels and Lenin, who had questioned the universal validity of the law of contradiction, and acknowledge Kazimierz Ajdukiewicz's reinterpretation of Zeno's paradox: " . . . although reality can be seen as contradictory in itself, the logical law of contradiction must be unconditionally observed."[35] Adam Schaff's position reflected his belief that, while dialectical logic applied to the development of nature and society and encompassed "contradictions," formal logic applied to the verbal expressions that described aspects of these developments and included the law of contradiction.

While analytical philosophers such as Ajdukiewicz dealt with the logical issues, the novelist-philosopher Leszek Kołakowski raised again the ethical question of freedom and determinism. As Skolimowski summarized his argument, Kołakowski held that: "The recognition of historical inevitability does not release us from having to make decisions in particular instances, . . . Inevitability is an attribute of past events; with respect to future events, inevitability appears less certain and the room for free choice and independent decisions much larger."[36] By thus arguing that moral responsibility was compatible with determinism, Kołakowski undercut the grounds for Marxist indifference to ethics. The semantic game of hiding behind inevitability (that is, the acceptance of the unethical as necessary for the sake of the greater good of the revolution) was exposed. As Kołakowski said in 1957: "No one is released from the moral responsibility of condemning a crime because of his theoretical conviction about the inevitability of the crime."[37]

During the Polish "thaw" and into the 1960s, Adam Schaff initiated his "philosophy of man" as a new area of Marxist analysis. Schaff saw the fatal flaw in Sartre's accommodation of Marxism and existentialism: "For existentialism, the individual is autonomous and is the starting point; for Marxism, the individual is a product of society, created by society, the 'totality of social relationships,' in a sense the end product of social determinants. The existentialist concept of the individual implies indeterminism and the negation of historical materialism."[38] Schaff, on the other hand, wanted to supplement Marxism not with such existentialism but with an analytical-linguistic philosophy, "socialist humanism," and semantics.

In his pioneering Marxist text, Introduction to Semantics (1960), Schaff examined semantics as a branch of linguistics, a branch of logic, a philosophy, and included a discussion of Korzybski's general semantics. He discussed the Sapir-Whorf principle of linguistic relativity at length and even claimed that it provided

a materialistic interpretation of primitive languages, an extension
rather than a strict reading of Whorfian ideas. As a Marxist,
Schaff believed that it was not possible to solve the problem of
communication without reference to the Marxist notions of base and
superstructure, that is, to the premise that social being determined consciousness.[39]

Adam Schaff devoted an entire chapter in his Introduction to
Semantics to general semantics and chided Marxist critics who dealt
only with a caricature of Korzybski's ideas. "It is difficult to
escape the impression," he wrote, "that probably none of those who
in our literature have written about Korzybski has read his book
thoroughly." After a brief summary of Science and Sanity, Schaff
noted that the concept of the role of symbols in social life was
taken from behaviorism and Pavlovian theory; that the idea of a
non-Aristotelian language was "taken from Łukasiewicz and his theory
of many-valued logic;" that the idea of the separability of the
label and the object, the map and the territory, was derived from
neopositivism and Gestaltpsychologie; and that the multiordinality
of symbols and the hierarchy of languages was borrowed from
Russell's theory of types. In all cases, however, Schaff charged
that Korzybski either misunderstood or misused his sources and
denigrated Science and Sanity as "a specifically American product, a
sect rather than a school." Nevertheless, "for all its oddity and
its simply maniacal traits, Korzybski's conception includes
something which cannot be dismissed lightly." This something turned
out to be the notion that the structure of language must be similar
to the structure of reality for language to fulfill its proper
function. Furthermore, by having a dynamic, rather than static,
view of reality, Korzybski came close to dialectics; and by using
Pavlov's theory of conditioned responses and secondary signals
(words), he had opened the way to "the study of language from the
point of view of the producers of language signs." Thus, while
Schaff interpreted Korzybski as being too American, too pragmatic,
he nevertheless valued certain European influences that he found
in Science and Sanity and regarded general semantics as a useful
antedote to some of the rigidities and crudities of pseudo-Marxist
criticism.

In his next work, Language and Cognition (1964), Schaff went beyond
the Sapir-Whorf hypothesis in an attempt to "rescue" Lenin's copy
theory of truth. "Marxist philosophers have known for a long time,"
he wrote, "that the process of cognition is the unity of the
objective and subjective factors. That knowledge has enabled us to
disassociate ourselves in epistemological research from both
idealism and mechanistic materialism. In practice, however, this
has not prevented us from transforming the copy theory of cognition
into a mechanistic theory."[40] The book then took up the question
of what role language played in the social conditioning of individual cognition. On the crucial "thought and language" question,
Schaff adopted de Saussure's distinction between "speech" and
"language," assumed as a hypothesis that thinking was always
thinking in some language, and sided with Vygotsky's critique of
Piaget's developmental psychology. Schaff also endorsed the work of

Kurt Goldstein on aphasia, particularly his distinction between concrete thinking and abstracting, and applied it to language: "Words acquire meaning, in the strict sense of the term, only within the framework of the abstracting approach." Nevertheless, Schaff concluded that "neither research in developmental psychology nor research on aphasia provide the philosopher with a well-documented answer to his questions about the interrelationship between speech and thinking."[41]

He turned instead to the work of the psychologist G. Révész which Schaff interpreted to mean that "since language is the unity of the material vehicle, i.e., sign system, and the semantic aspect of the signs involved (without which the signs cease to be a language), speech cannot exist without thought." In the end, Schaff held to the unity of language and thinking as they had developed together in social evolution. This linking of semiotics, semantics, and the communication situation was characteristic of Polish structuralism in the post-war period and of its interaction with Marxist philosophy, historicism, and sociology.[42] Henryk Skolimowski has concluded that the conflict between Polish Marxism and analytical philosophy had two consequences. Most importantly, in addition to the impact of World War II on Polish philosophy, the encounter with Marxism had greatly reduced the productivity and prominence of the analytical school. However, secondly, the Marxists themselves were, perhaps unintentionally, influenced by the style of analysis and incorporated semantics into their problematic and philosophical procedures. One of the main themes of Polish analytical philosophy, of course, had always been semantics.[43]

The role of semantics in Polish thought after World War II could also be seen in trends in poetry and drama. While the older poets of the pre-war period were "trying to maintain an equilibrium between the sense of tragedy and an approval of life" based on their humanistic background, post-war poets such as Tadeusz Różewicz /1921-) "arrived at a negation of literature because it seemed to be no more than a lie covering up the horror of man's brutality to his fellow man. Thus, if poetry could be practiced at all, it should seek to destroy all literary conventions. Różewicz's opposition to metrics, rhyme, and even metaphor had a moral meaning." He stripped his poetry naked, built his verse nonsyntactically with simple words in a primer-like fashion. His irony, pessimism, and paradoxical stance as an "antipoet" made him a pillar of the Polish theater of the absurd. "Realistic 'action' was abandoned for the metaphorical structure of the fable, the parable, or the morality play."[44] Such developments culminated a decade later in the work of Jerzy Grotowski, the theoretician of the Polish theater. For Grotowski, the actor is a priest who, through dramatic action, breaks down the psychological defenses of the audience and makes them confront their hidden, collective reality: "The actor . . . must be able to construct his own psychoanalytic language of sounds and gestures in the same way that a great poet creates his own language of words."[45]

Poets also explored the complex nature of their language. "To
expose language as a very imperfect tool of communication between
human beings became the fad of the day; thus, it is not suprising
that 'semantic poetry' with its exploding of grammatical syntax
received much attention." The leading "semantic poets" were Miron
Białoszewski (1922-), in whose "antipoetry" everyday reality dis-
appeared, "supplanted by language as the only cosmos accessible to
man"; Zbigniew Bieńkowski (1913-), who was "obsessed with the
superabundance of meaning in words and with the resulting ambiguity
in language"; and Tymoteusz Karpowicz (1921-), who excelled at
"transforming objects into metaphors through tongue-in-cheek
descriptions."[46] Karol Wojtyla, the future Pope John Paul II,
published poems during the period 1950 to 1966 that exhibited a
sensitivity to drama, poetic language, and the poetry of Cyprian
Norwid. According to his recent translator, Wojtyla's "language
is often charged with unusual metaphors, and his way of describing
physical detail is reminiscent of Gerard Manley Hopkins' inscape."
Particularly important was his 1956 poem, "The Quarry." Where
Cyprian Norwid, in "Meditation II," had seen hands as "hieroglyphs
of mute sufferings . . . fists," Wojtyla in "The Quarry" saw hands
as the landscape of the heart where man learns to achieve an
equilibrium of love and anger expressed in a simple language that
is beyond words. Some hands perform acts of service or toil; others
submit to deeds of love or sacrifice.[47]

In all these experiments and modifications of thought and cultural
forms in the clash with official Marxism, Polish intellectuals
played a key role. Although divided among themselves into Catholic
and Marxist factions and within each faction into "orthodox" and
"revisionist" tendencies, the intellectuals had a recognized role
in Polish society even under the Communist regime. As early as
1955, "the weakening of the terror apparatus emboldened the Polish
writers, who began to openly criticize various aspects of the
Communist political system. In August 1955 Adam Ważyk's celebrated
'Poem for Adults,' bitterly denouncing the grim reality of life in
Poland, was published in Nowa Kultura, climaxing the early phase
of intellectual discontent. Spokesman for the Communist Party
severely admonished Ważyk, but no other sanctions against him
followed. The Communist regime failed to silence the Polish
writers."[48]

Thereafter, the intellectuals, particularly philosophers such as
Leszek Kołakowski, associated with the weekly Po prostu (Speaking
Frankly) ran ahead of the regime and demanded further reforms.
This outspoken criticism upset the Russians who accused the Polish
intellectuals of deviation. "In the spring { of 1957 } Po prostu
was ordered to suspend its publication for the summer; Kołakowski's
writings were singled out by { Polish Communist leader } Gomułka for
public criticism as an example of attempted revisionism. These
measures neither silenced the Polish critics nor appeased the
Russians, however."[49] The end of 1956 and the beginning of 1957
thus marked a high water mark in Polish reform within the Communist
system; thereafter, the regime retreated slowly from the promises
of the "Polish October." Unrest among intellectuals surfaced again

in 1961–1962 with public speeches by Kotarbiński, Adam Schaff, and other leading figures. The result in June 1963 was a renewed attack by the Gomułka government on the intellectuals whose leading journals were closed. The estrangement of the intellectuals from the party establishment led to another cycle of dissent and suppression in 1964.[50]

Thus, a double irony attended the fate of the ideas that had been born in Poland's "revolt against positivism," 1890–1914, and the era of Young Poland. Some of these ideas had been transplanted in the United States by Korzybski, Alfred Tarski, Bronislaw Malinowski, the anthropologist, and others.[51] In the two decades after World War II, Korzybski's general semantics had been subsumed by some of his followers in the United States into the ruling ideology of pragmatism, liberalism, and self-help psychology within a rigid framework of cold-war dichotomies. The division in the United States between free intellectuals and academics had contributed to this process of accommodation. Reintroduced into the Polish and Central European intellectual landscape in the 1950s and 1960s Korzybski and his ideas were not treated as repentant prodical sons but as a wayward immigrants returned after too long a time – too Americanized, too popular, and too rich in unacknowledged cultural debts – to be embraced with any enthusiasm. In Poland the intellec- tual inheritors of the positivist tradition, of analytical philoso- phy, of "logicistic" semantics, and of the "Young Poland" poetics, with their strong institutional and cultural roles, had helped to modify the ruling ideology of Marxism–Leninism and to engage in significant cultural experiments. However brief and temporary their achievements, they had demonstrated the ability of the living word to change their world. They had also left a legacy to the future in the premise that, in matters of human freedom, there is no sub- stitute for praxis.

CONCLUSION _____

Count Alfred Korzybski, 1879-1950, was born in Russian-dominated
Poland, the son of an engineer who belonged to the intelligentsia
and the nobility. He was trained as a chemical engineer but read
and studied widely in the humanities and the social sciences. He
came of age intellectually during the period of debate in Polish
intellectual circles between the Positivists and Young Poland over
the nature of language and its role in healing the breach between
the objective sciences and the subjective arts.

The Positivists had faith in natural science, education, capitalism,
and cultural evolution; they saw language as essentially descriptive
and didactic in nature. Whereas positivism in France was integrated
into the university system, in Poland, for political reasons,
positivism existed among writers such as Ludwig Krzywicki, Eliza
Orzeszkowa, Henryk Sienkiewicz, and Bołeslaw Prus or among exiled
intellectuals such as Ludwig Gumplowicz, the sociologist, in
Austria. Through contacts with Austria, Polish intellectuals kept
abreast of such developments as Ernst Mach and Richard Avenarius's
synthesis of positivism and impressionism, called empirio-criticism,
and Fritz Mauthner and Karl Kraus's critiques of reification in
language and the metaphorical nature of linguistic descriptions.
While in Austria positivism thus led to a critical epistemology, in
Poland it also led to a revival of August von Cieszkowski's theory
of praxis as a means of overcoming the subject-object split in
values.

The Young Poland group, on the other hand, reacted against the
reigning positivism and realistic fiction and turned instead to
French symbolism, to Nietzschean subjectivity, to historic Polish
romanticism, and to contemporary existentialism. They looked to
the nineteenth-century poet Cyprian Norwid for a symbolic view of
the world as a multipicity of hieroglyphs. Bołeslaw Leśmian

experimented with poetic symbolism, while novelists Karol
Irzykowski, Stefan Żeromski, and Wacław Berent explored the
psycho-semantic in the subconscious, the irrational in psychology,
and the pathological in language. In the protean figures of
Stanisław Brzozowski, the literary critic, and Stanisław Wyspiański,
the symbolist dramatist, Young Poland contributed to the broader
currents of European intellectual life. Young Poland saw language
as symbolic, psycho-semantic, and impressionistic in nature.

Alfred Korzybski, with his strong background in mathematics, physics,
and philosophy, was closer to the Positivists camp and did not seek
to engage in aesthetic or literary solutions to the problems of
the day. Yet there were similarities between Korzybski's later
pronouncements on language and some of the themes and techniques
of Young Poland. The questions debated in pre-war Poland found
echoes and answers in Korzybski's post-war writings. By then,
however, he was subject to a number of American influences. Having
come to the United States via Canada during World War I as a
representative of the Russian army general staff to expedite
munitions shipments and to help in artillery training, he came in
contact with the American "engineering millennialism" of Frederick
Winslow Taylor, Frederick Haynes Newell, Morris L. Cooke, Henry L.
Gantt, and Thorstein Veblen. He established contact with emigré
European intellectuals in America and was influenced by the
mechanistic biology and "behaviorist" psychology of Jacques Loeb
of the Rockefeller Institute for Medical Research. He was also
influenced by the American mathematician Cassius J. Keyser and his
doctrine of "logical fate."

Korzybski blended these various influences in his first book,
Manhood of Humanity, published in 1921, and in numerous articles
published in the 1920s. Mankind, he said, was a "time-binding"
class of life; it had survived in evolution by its ability to
learn from past experiences and to pass this knowledge on from
one generation to another through language. While current language
might preserve earlier assumptions and, thus, no longer accurately
describe reality, it was possible to reconstruct language, following the model of Bertrand Russell's mathematical logic, so that a
more consistent or coherent view of reality was possible. This
was important because man's true freedom and ethical dignity lay
in recognition of the law of nature and obedience to it. While
mankind had the freedom to choose its intellectual and logical
postulates, it must accept the consequences that followed by the
iron law of logical necessity (Keyser's "logical fate").

In the 1920s, Korzybski attempted to add to these philosophical,
mathematical, and logical notions about the theory of language
some practical training in psychiatry as an acceptable therapy of
language. His studies at St. Elizabeth's Hospital, where he came
in contact with the ideas of William A. White and Harry Stack
Sullivan, led Korzybski to embrace views on psycho-semantic
difficulties that were similar to those of the Polish novelist
Irzykowski, the literary critic Brzozowski, and the poet Leśmian.

Korzybski's attempted reconciliation of the "unconscious" facts
of experience with the "conscious" words or labels used to describe
them represented a blending of Mach's empirio-criticism on perception, Mauthner's linguistic critique of reification, and Loeb's
mechanistic biology and "behaviorism."

On the basis of his theory of language and his therapy of language,
Korzybski outlined a tentative system of semantics. As the philosopher F. S. C. Northrup has observed, Korzybski's system rested
on two different sets of concepts: (1) concepts by postulation,
which were axiomatically constructed, deductively formulated concepts relative to particular scientific or mathematical-logical
theories; and (2) concepts by intuition, which were the immediately
apprehended, inductively formulated "facts" of sensory experience.
Therefore, semantic analysis of language would have to proceed at
two different levels. For concepts by postulation, semantic
analysis would involve a philosophical critique of axioms and relational assumptions. For concepts by intuition, semantic analysis
would involve a psychological critique, a radically empirical process of reference back to the particular images behind the named
objects of language. In the late 1920s, Korzybski sketched out a
preliminary version of his ideas on philosophy, psychiatry, and a
language and set it aside.

In September 1929, Korzybski returned to Poland to attend the
Mathematical Congress of the Slavic Countries held in Warsaw.
There, he came into renewed contact with the innovative work being
done in mathematical logic, scientific methodology, and formal
semantics by such Polish intellectuals as Jan Łukasiewicz, Tadeusz
Kotarbiński, Stanisław Leśniewski, and Leon Chwistek. Łukasiewicz
had developed a three-valued propositional logic, Kotarbiński had
combined Russell's logical calculus of propositions with a calculus
of names developed by Leśniewski, and Chwistek had created a restricted formal semantics based on sets of rules and classes of
expressions. The Polish logicians saw such deductive, logical, and
linguistic structures as being constitutive of reality itself;
logical and philosophical analysis led to an ontology as well as
an epistemology. For Korzybski, on the other hand, the ontological
objects of reality were revealed by the psychological process of
abstracting from sense perception through the use of concepts.
Mathematical logic, he assumed, had a structure most similar to
such reality. If ordinary language, which had a structure dissimilar to reality as understood by modern science, could be restruc-
tured along the lines of mathematical logic, then people could
reorient themselves and escape the psychological and communicational
pathologies of ordinary language. Partly rejecting the Polish
school, partly assimilating some of its logical doctrines, Korzybski
created a synthesis of his ideas in his magnum opus, Science and
Sanity, published in 1933. He called his system non-Aristotelian
and referred to it as general semantics.

In Science and Sanity, Korzybski sought to combine the concepts by
postulation of mathematical logic with the concepts by intuition of

empirio-criticism and a simplified version of the conditional
reflex theory of physiological psychology and to hold the whole
structure together by an analogous understanding of language as the
system of "rules of correspondence" or epistemic correlates between
the separate semantic realms. His theories of meaning were, thus,
primarily contextual and only secondarily referential. Furthermore,
the meaning of language for the organism as a whole was not simply
the syntactic category created by the axiomatic foundations of the
language as a system of implicit logic nor yet the referent "object"
of sensory experience but meaning was also the reaction of the
organism to changes in its linguistic and affective environment.

Korzybski's Science and Sanity was an example of the "leap of negation" in intellectual history. He attempted to isolate certain
basic assumptions of traditional theories and then, instead of
modifying them or redefining them, he leaped over to their negatives.
Paradoxically, this left him a prisoner of the traditional theories
because the categories of negation are a function of the categories
of affirmation. In particular, Korzybski believed that all forms
of Western logic, derived from Aristotle, rested on false
premises--the law of identity, the law of bivalence, and the law
of the excluded middle. Mankind, he believed, must make the leap
of negation to the opposite of these three premises. In the midst
of the Great Depression, it seemed a radical intellectual proposal.

How is the historian to judge Korzybski's synthesis of ideas and
the status of the larger intellectual trends of which his ideas
were but parts? What was happening to these intellectual trends
during the period of history, 1930s-1960s, when his ideas were being
spread and institutionalized in American society? How did the
fate of his general semantic ideas in America compare with the fate
of analytical philosophy in Poland during the same time period?
For convenience, the various aspects of Korzybski's thought and
the broader intellectual trends that they reflected will be
summarized under three headings: (1) the theory of language derived
from mathematical logic and the dream of a consistent, universal
lingua mathematica; (2) the therapy of language derived from
psychiatry and physiological psychology and the hope for a healing
Logos; and (3) the system of general semantics and its relationship
to the science of semantics within recent philosophical, logical,
and linguistic developments.

What, then, must be the judgment of history on those who, like
Alfred Korzybski, shared the late-nineteenth-century dream of a
mathematically sound, logically consistent theory of language and
the hope for a psychologically valid, linguistically coherent therapy
of language united in human action or praxis both to reveal and
reorder the world? What is the perspective of the late twentieth
century on this hundred-year-old effort? What light does the story
of Korzybski and his general semantics, and the comparable story
of the Polish analytical philosophers and semantic poets, litera-
teurs and logicians, and neo-Machists and Marxists, throw on this
dark corridor of time and intellectual effort? Where in an America
that has institutionalized its academics, trivialized its education,

debased its public discourse, and denied its free intellectuals the dignity of secure status--where in such a culture is one to look for the word that will not only hurt but heal, not only command but bring communion, not only deceive the mass audience but decipher the mysteries of human destiny?

From the perspective of the present, it is now clear that "the dream of producing . . . a {mathematically precise, logically consistent } language was shattered in 1931 by a twenty-five-year-old Austrian mathematician, Kurt Gödel." At a sufficiently high level of abstraction and performance in any mathematical system, he showed that "consistency could not be proven" simply by manipulating mathematical signs according to certain rules of logic, "and more importantly, that such systems were incomplete: there are true statements in mathematics that the system will not produce, true statements, that is, that cannot be proven." Thus, gradually, the educated public has become aware, however dimly and inadequately, of Gödel's proof and its challenge to all systematic approaches to problems. "This result has since taken its place among the other metaphorically powerful scientific results of our century--{Einstein's} Theory of Relativity and { Heisenberg's } Uncertainty Principle. Gödel's result is known as the Incompleteness Theorem."[1]

Even without the devastating impact of Gödel's proof on the whole mathematical logical enterprise, it is clear that Korzybski's critique of Aristotelian logic was being undercut at the very time that he was proclaiming it by research in Poland. Łukasiewicz showed that there were two laws of identity in Aristotle. The values that could be substituted for one were terms, while the values that could be substituted for the other were propositions. Since terms and propositions belong to different semantic categories, Aristotelian logic did not stand or fall on any one law of identity. Korzybski's denial of the law of identity in its identification and predication functions had rested on the empirio-critical theory of perception as a process of abstraction; that is, the "object" of perception was not identical to the "event" of temporal-spatial occurrence. But, as Otto Friedrich Gruppe had noted in the nineteenth century, the verb is had performed various functions in Aristotelian and Greek logic: existence, equality, linkage, and so forth. Korzybski's rejection or negation of the "is" of identification and predication need not be extended to include the "is" of equality or logical inclusion; that is, rejecting the law of identity on psychological grounds did not necessarily entail rejecting it on logical grounds.[2] Nor was the law of the excluded middle so rigidly interpreted in Aristotelian logic, according to Łukasiewicz, as to forbid the development of multivalued logical systems. Korzybski's leap of negation was not the only way to deal with the limitations of traditional Aristotelian logic.

On the hope for a therapy of the word, too, history has not dealt kindly with the dreams of Korzybski's generation. The contributions of Freud and his rivals, the whole development of psychiatry and psychoanalysis, which seemed to the generations that experienced

the dual traumas of world war and worldwide depression to be a
great liberation of the human spirit, now seem suspect. The
psychoanalysts are regarded by some intellectuals as tragic heros
at best, as slightly comic cultural stereotypes or as positive
barriers to human liberation by women who do not share Freud's
views on female sexuality. Freud himself is regarded more as an
artist or moralist in recent scholarship than as a scientist in
the older empirical sense. Practioners have questioned the therapeutic effectiveness of the once sacrosanct psychotherapeutic
techniques of psychoanalysis with their excruciating dynamic of
transference and countertransference. Popular therapy has embraced a number of nonverbal techniques, particularly of a group
nature, or has sanctioned aggressive behavior modification. The
theories and therapeutic practices of William A. White and Harry
Stack Sullivan are seen as inadequate or out of date. Schizophrenia
is not regarded as simply a regressive psychosis; indeed, even the
definition and diagnostic categories of schizophrenia are constantly
changing.[3]

The link between Korzybski's logical assumptions about the structure
of thought and his empirio-critical assumptions about the origins
of knowledge had been his conception of the role of language, which,
in turn, had provided the basis for his therapeutic techniques.
On the one hand, he borrowed from Jelliffe a form of psycho-linguistic determinism. The acquisition of a language by a child was
the imposition of a cultural and logical structure whose unvoiced
assumptions created the matrix of semantic categories that established meaning. On the other hand, self-reflexiveness, consciousness of one's abstracting processes in language usage, represented a form of logical freedom: the choice of assumptions
could create logical structures and semantic categories more
adaptive to survival. This was the basis of Korzybski's therapeutic
approach. Borrowing from Pavlov the notion of language as a form
of reflexive behavior or reaction, Korzybski then tried to reinforce the therapeutic insight with a physical stimulus through the
use of his structural differential device. Korzybski's model saw
language shaping thought, which, in turn, led to action; the whole
process was circular and, through greater awareness or consciousness of one's assumptions, self-reinforcing.

Just as in the case of Łukasiewicz's critique of Aristotelian logic,
so research in Europe was undercutting Korzybski's therapeutic
assumptions. Vygotsky, the Russian psychologist, challenged the
assumed link between Jelliffe and Pavlov. Vygotsky had assimilated
Piaget's egocentric phase of child development into his own notion
of thought as inner speech and saw language as a socio-historical
rather than biological process. The proper supplement to Jelliffe's
ontogenetic studies of cognitive development was not more biology
in the form of Pavlovian reflex conditioning but rather something
closer to Mauthner or Kraus's critique of reification and socio-
linguistic usages. Korzybski's therapy of linguistic "pathologies"
was essentially a philosophical reorientation, an introspective
awareness of the process of abstraction and identification, that
might or might not have psychologically beneficial results.

On the narrower grounds of semantics per se, and the quest for a
science of meaning, it is clear that developments in philosophy
and linguistics were redefining the field and dividing it into a
series of narrowly specialized inquiries at the very time that
Korzybski's followers were proclaiming his more general approach.
Korzybski's general semantics "fell through the cracks" between
these newly defined specialties and tended to get pushed to the
fringes of academic respectability. Thus, the transplantation of
the center of logical positivism from Europe to America as a con-
sequence of World War II, the analytical turn in Anglo-American
philosophy, the persistence of socialist humanism in Europe, and
the predominance of "structuralism" in linguistics reshaped the
science of semantics during the period from the 1930s to the 1960s.
In the process, Korzybski, the free intellectual, the nonacademic
"outsider," lost out in the intellectual struggle for power.

In philosophy, for example, Professor Max Black of Cornell gave a
devastating critique of Korzybski's general semantics in 1946. He
was not so much trying to read Korzybski out of the philosopher's
camp as he was attempting to delimit the area of semantics to a
set of problems and procedures within which analytically oriented
philosophers were prepared to talk about the issues.[4] The logical
positivists and their disciples dominated the academy, but the
oft-repeated jibe that Korzybski's general semantics was "really
the poor man's logical positivism"[5] missed the point. As a theory
of semantics, the early logical positivists' verification principle
as applied to meaning was actually narrower than Korzybski's com-
bination of meaning by context for concepts by postulation (the
axiomatic "auxilliary concepts" and fictional "as if" conceptions
necessary for scientific theories) and meaning by reference for
concepts by intuition (the empirio-critical reduction of perception).
As George Steiner has recently argued (contra the logical positivists), it is precisely the counter-factual capacity of language
that gives it its flexibility, semantic creativity, and survival
value.[6] Korzybski's emphasis on postulational knowledge and consciousness of abstracting could potentially accommodate the
counter-factual usages more readily than the strict logical
positivist position.

The period when Korzybski's general semantics movement flourished
in America, the 1940s and 1950s, was also a period in which linguistics as an academic discipline was undergoing a paradigm shift.
Both the increasing dissatisfaction with the Bloomfield descriptive
legacy and the initial articulation of Noam Chomsky's program of
"generative grammar" downplayed the field of semantics.[7] As
William Labov has recently noted:

> In the course of the last thirty years or so, the field
> of linquistics has undergone a remarkable series of
> oscillations in the amount of attention paid to meaning,
> and the status of semantics in the discipline as a whole.
> It is difficult for those who began the study of language
> in the 1970's to appreciate the strength of the bias against
> semantics that held sway a decade or two before they arrived

on the scene. The notion of an autonomous syntax,
cleanly cut away from all semantic entanglements, lost
its attractiveness for many linguists as early as 1968,
when Kiparsky and Kiparsky published their demonstration
that the choice of sentential complementizers was
semantically motivated.[8]

While this neglect of the area of semantics by the linguists left
the field open for the general semanticists to hold sway, it also
gave them few people to talk to for the kind of fruitful inter-
change that keeps a body of ideas alive and vital. There were
endless repetitions and applications of general semantic principles
and a few critical exchanges in the pages of ETC. and the General
Semantics Bulletin; but, like Stuart Chase's enthusiastic young
reformer, advocates of general semantics were increasingly
speaking only to those already convinced or to each other.

It could be argued that, after all, Korzybski's general semantics
owed more to European philosophy (in particular positivism,
symbolism, and empirio-criticism) than to American linguistics
and that his contributions should be judged accordingly. But,
even on these criteria, it is evident that the ground was shifting
out from under the edifice of European positivism. The predominence
and popularity of existentialism, structuralism, Marxism, and
phenomenology created alternate ways of defining semantics and of
understanding language. The socialist humanists, for example, had
gone back beyond classic nineteenth-century positivism to the
phenomenology of the young Hegel and his analysis of alienated
consciousness, the role of language in overcoming such alienation,
and the ontological understanding of logic to criticize contemporary
Marxism and to undercut its self-serving rhetoric.[9] Polish logicians criticized Marxists for holding that formal logic was an
"empty game" and for not respecting the law of noncontradiction
under the guise of dialectical necessity. Adam Schaff, the leading
Marxist theoretician, acknowledged the validity of Ajdukiewicz's
defense of the law of noncontradiction and opened the way for a
Marxist accommodation with analytical philosophy and formal
semantics. Yet in his own work on semantics, Schaff did not regard
Korzybski as an inheritor of the Polish positivist position;
rather, he subsumed him under the heading of American pragmatism
(although he considered him as having raised significant questions
for Marxist analysis). Polish free intellectuals who were interested in semantics, formal logic, and ethical voluntarism thus
played an important role in modifying the position of official
Marxist academicians and in keeping alive the tradition of
humanist values.[10]

There was, thus, irony in Korzybski's intellectual development and
the subsequent fate of his ideas in America. He had been nurtured
in the rich Central European intellectual tradition, he was
exposed to both the Positivist and Young Poland movements in his
native Poland, and he inherited the dreams of the Anglo-French
mathematical schools of Russell and Poincare and the Polish school

of logicians. Yet by the time he came to proclaim his grand
synthesis in the 1930s and to preside over a movement in the 1930s
and 1940s, he was seemingly losing touch with these living traditions; his own basic synthesis was frozen in a particular moment.
Ironically, research in Central Europe, Poland, and Russia--
Łukasiewicz on Aristotelian logic, Vygotsky on developmental
psychology, and socialist-humanists on language and consciousness--
was undercutting the basis of many of his assumptions. Gödel's
proof in mathematical logic, criticism of psychotherapeutic
techniques in psychoanalysis and psychiatry, and the increasingly
specialized definitions of semantics as a field of inquiry further
undermined the larger intellectual traditions of which he was a
part.

Seen against the background of his European heritage, Korzybski
must be viewed as an inheritor of the educational mission of
European positivism. Science would set people free from the dogmas
and false doctrines of the past, aid social and cultural evolution,
and turn theory into praxis. European positivism in the nineteenth
century had had an intellectual rigor and vitality because it had
confronted entrenched aristocracies, officially sanctioned religious establishments, and slowly changing social structures.
But in America, positivism in the early twentieth century had confronted only a beleaguered "aristocracy" of wealth struggling with
a politically assertive middle-class progressivism, an amorphous
religious situation, and a constantly shifting struggle of groups
for social status, political power, and economic advantage. In
short, the "sting" was taken out of European-style positivism in
the American context.

With no compulsory religious indoctrination to be denounced, with
no encrusted privileged order hiding behind obscurantist rhetoric
to be overthrown, with little immemorial peasant wisdom and
superstition to be enlightened, with little proletarian class
consciousness to be challenged, positivism in America was rendered
innocuous. The ultimate recipient of Korzybski's positivist
message in America was the individual: confused, isolated, vaguely
unhappy, seeking solace from the stains of living in a complex
industrial society, yet, pragmatic, eager to "solve problems," to
find answers. The program of the Institute of General Semantics
seemed to appeal largely to the educated, middle-class or professional citizen of good will who wanted to "do something" about the
problems that beset society and, at the same time, find some
personal comfort and companionship in the effort.[11]

American recipients of Korzybski's positivist message, lacking his
European presuppositions, tended to assimilate his ideas into their
own pragmatic frameworks. The free intellectuals of the 1930s--such
as Stuart Chase--and the academic advocates--such as S. I. Hayakawa
--who took up Korzybski's cause did so on their own terms. In the
conflict for power between the free intellectuals and the academics
in the 1940s and 1950s, the balance of power in intellectual matters
gradually shifted in favor of the academics. Free intellectuals

such as Korzybski became the outsiders; his few supporters within
academia struggled to establish and maintain the legitimacy of
his approach against hostile criticism from philosophers or
studied indifference from linguists. Popular general semantic
rhetoric became trapped in the familiar two-valued categories of
American intellectual history and the emerging cold-war ideology
of anti-Communism and the pervasive ethos of self-help or positive-
thinking movements of the 1950s. Korzybski's own ideas were institutionalized in the program of the Institute of General
Semantics, which severed its ties with the journal ETC. in
1946-1947. Following Korzybski's death in 1950, the general
semantics cause struggled on with a host of claimants for the role
of popularizer of the Korzybski canon. In his strategic role as
editor of ETC., S. I. Hayakawa helped to present general semantics
to the public in the 1950s as a mildly liberal critique of
America's consumer-oriented civilization, an effective antidote
to Soviet propaganda and ideology, a rival to Norman Vincent
Peale's positive-thinking religion, and a safe way to improve
communications and interpersonal relations. Stuart Chase and others
attempted to subsume Korzybski's general semantics into their
search for a science of human relations, a synthesis of cybernetics
and information theory, and to buttress it with material drawn
from cultural anthropology, linguistic relativism, or systems
theory.

Buried in Korzybski's views on language there had been an ethic
that reflected his European presuppositions. In Manhood of
Humanity he had attempted to ground ethics (the "ought" of
morality) in an acceptance of natural law, in recognition of the
given (the "is" of reality). This reflected the characteristically
European notion that freedom lies in the recognition of necessity;
that is, one is truly free when one fulfills a duty or obeys a
superior authority.[12] But many Americans, particularly reform-
minded liberals such as Stuart Chase or S. I. Hayakawa, instinc-
tively rejected the premise. They had been influenced by the more
characteristically American intellectual assumption that freedom
lies in the overcoming of necessity; that is, one is free when one
can overcome a handicap or obstacle and assert authority over a
situation. This instrumentalist attitude toward ethics turned
Korzybski's general semantics away from its function as an
orientation toward reality and toward a new function as a means
toward reform.[13]

When S. I. Hayakawa said that his approach to general semantics was
based upon the assumption that just as health is preferable to
sickness, so cooperation is more socially desirable than competition, he was shifting the ethical foundation of general semantics
from the "is" of accepting necessity to the "ought" of overcoming
necessity. Hence, the gradual shift from Korzybski's emphasis on
awareness of abstracting, having a "correct" perception and
description of reality, to the more pragmatic one of having a
"right" attitude or self-fulfilling idea that could change reality.
Korzybski had wanted to cut through the "false" verbal worlds in
which people lived and reorient them to an acceptance of what

"really is" (or "is-not," to be strictly Korzybskian); some of his American followers, on the other hand, wanted to cut away the verbal justifications of the status quo (what "really is") to achieve the "ought," to create a new reality. This they believed would be both therapeutic and prophetic; but, once cut from its philosophical grounds in positivism or empirio-criticism and natural-law doctrine, there was no way to prevent misuse of semantic and general semantic techniques by unscrupulous advertising agents, ambitious politicians, or pseudo-scientific "saviors" of mankind.[14]

In summary, by the 1960s the intellectual threads that Korzybski had woven together in his classic Science and Sanity had come unraveled. However correct or prescient he might have been in details, in understanding scientific insights, the intellectual whole no longer held together.[15] The mathematician and the logician, the philosopher and the psychologist, the linguist and the psychiatrist, the poet and the playwright, the novelist and the polemicist, the ethicist and activist--each have gone their separate ways. The "glue" of assertion could no longer hold together the disparate elements of mathematical logic, linguistic analysis, and behavioral psychology. The appeal of Korzybski's synthesis had been precisely its holistic approach, its claim to deal with the whole organism in its environmental setting and as a psychosomatic unity. However much Korzybski's followers might have fallen victim to "scientism," to use of the trappings and claims of "scientific" status for essentially ideological beliefs,[16] they reflected the widespread feeling that science ought to have something to say about the very real problems that afflicted people in society. If the older humanistic disciplines--philosophy, literature, religion, psychology, and so on--no longer spoke in a language intelligible to "laymen" or even were directed to them, where were they to hear the authoritative truth that would "set them free" except in the realms of science?

Of the many "gods that have failed" twentieth-century Western civilization, such "science" has been but the latest. Yet the yearning has persisted for the word that would be scientifically grounded in the nature of the world, unambiguous in its syntax, and humane in its impact. But, as the poets had said earlier in the century, the center no longer holds. We have come full circle on the issue of language. And we are left alone--with only words and wonder, sounds and silence.[17]

NOTES

INTRODUCTION: THE WORD AND THE WORLD

1. Edward Rothstein, review of Douglas R. Hofstadter, Gödel,
Escher, Bach: An Eternal Golden Braid (New York: Basic Books,
1979), New York Review of Books (December 6, 1979): 34.

2. Ibid. On the seventeenth-century quest for a universal language, see George Steiner, After Babel: Aspects of Language and
Translation (London: Oxford University Press, 1975), pp. 70-76.

3. Steiner, After Babel, pp. 58 (quotation), 59-63, 81-85, and
176-93; Isaiah Berlin, Vico and Herder,(New York: Vintage Books,
1976), pp. 166-67. See also Pedro Laín Entralgo, The Therapy of
the Word in Classical Antiquity (New Haven: Yale University Press,
1970); Stefan Zweig, Mental Healers: Franz Anton Mesmer, Mary
Baker Eddy, Sigmund Freud, trans. Eden and Cedar Paul (New York:
Viking Press, 1932, reprint, 1962), pp. xix-xxv.
For the origins of linguistic relativity and the question of
language universals, see Roger Langham Brown, Wilhelm von Humboldt's
Conception of Linguistic Relativity (The Hague: Mouton, 1967),
chapter 7.

4. Stephen Ullman, The Principles of Semantics (Glasgow: Jackson,
Son and Co., 1951); Michel Bréal, Semantics: Studies in the Science
of Meaning, trans. Mrs. Henry Cust (New York: Dover Books, 1964),
pp. 7 (quotation) and 251; Edward Stankiewicz, ed. and trans., A
Boudouin de Courtney Anthology: The Beginnings of Structural
Linguistics (Bloomington: Indiana University Press, 1972), pp. 5-7,
12-14, and 20-30.
On the interdisciplinary nature of the problem of meaning and its
status in linguistics, see Geoffrey Leech, Semantics (Middlesex,
England: Penguin Books, 1974), pp. x-xii and chapters 1 and 5.

For the eighteenth-century background of semantics, see Stephen
K. Land, From Signs to Propositions: The Concept of Form in
Eighteenth-Century Semantic Theory (London: Longman Group, Ltd.,
1974).

5. Muriel Rukeyser, Willard Gibbs (New York: E. P. Dutton, 1964),
chapters 6 and 13; Ferdinand de Saussure, Course in General
Linguistics, trans. Wade Baskin (New York: Philosophical Library,
1959), pp. 4-5; Gay Wilson Allen, Waldo Emerson: A Biography
(New York: Viking Press, 1981), pp. 259-61; John James Fitzgerald,
Peirce's Theory of Signs as Foundations for Pragmatism (The Hague:
Mouton, 1966); Donald A. Crosby, Horace Bushnell's Theory of Lan-
guage; In the Context of Other Nineteenth-Century Philosophies of
Language (The Hague: Mouton, 1975); and Donald B. Meyer, The
Positive Thinkers: A Study of the American Quest for Health, Wealth,
and Personal Power from Mary Baker Eddy to Norman Vincent Peale
(Garden City, N.Y.: Doubleday, 1965).
For transatlantic influences, see Michael Silverstein, ed.,Whitney
on Language (Cambridge: MIT Press, 1971); William Dwight Whitney,
The Life and Growth of Language (New York: Appleton, 1876); and
Charles S. Hartwick, ed.,Semiotics and Significs: The correspon-
dence between Charles S. Peirce and Lady Victoria Welby (Blooming-
ton: Indiana University Press, 1977).

6. Barry Feinberg and Ronald Kasrils, Bertrand Russell's America:
1896-1945, vol. 1. (New York: Viking Press, 1973), chapters 7-9.
For the relative neglect of semantics by American linguists in the
1920s, see Geoffrey Sampson, Schools of Linguistics (Stanford:
Stanford University Press, 1980), chapter 3. Even H. L. Mencken,
who first published his famous The American Language in 1919, was
more of a philologian than a semanticist. That is, he was more
concerned with the meaning of particular words than with the problem of meaning per se. Whereas the grammarians in the 1920s were
concerned with correct usage, primarily of literary language,
Mencken was fascinated with the current usage, primarily of ordinary speech. See H. L. Mencken, The American Language: An Inquiry
into the Development of English in the United States, 4th ed., ed.
Raven I. McDavid, Jr. (New York: Alfred A. Knopf, 1963), pp. 97,
509, 518, and 570; and Charles A. Fecher, Mencken: A Study of His
Thought (New York: Alfred A. Knopf, 1978), chapter 5.
Leonard Bloomfield's classic work in American linguistics, Language,
published in 1933, adopted a behavioristic model that identified
meaning with particular acts or practical events. "The statement
of meanings is therefore the weak point in language-study," he
concluded, "and will remain so until human knowledge advances very
far beyond its present state. In practice, we define the meaning
of a linguistic form, wherever we can, in terms of some other
science." Leonard Bloomfield, Language (New York: Holt, Rinehart,
and Winston, 1933), p. 140.
The problem with Bloomfield's approach to semantics was that he
was trying to find a determinate mechanism to account for the indeterminate freedom of language users to change forms, meanings,
and linguistic structures over time. Having ruled out a priori

"mentalistic" psychology (that is, intentional acts), he could only deal with reactions that, paradoxically, made all learning depend on past experience. Hence, only an infinite description of conditioning factors (or stimuli) could account for the infinite variety of "meanings" (or responses). See the criticism of Bloomfield's semantics in Leech, Semantics, pp. 2-4. Ogden and Richard's referent theory of meaning and interest in language, on the other hand, had grown out of (and partly in reaction to) the philosophical influence of G. E. Moore at Cambridge prior to World War I. See the interview with I. A. Richards published in Reuben Brower, Helen Vendler, and John Hollander, eds., I. A. Richards: Essays in His Honor (New York: Oxford University Press, 1973), pp. 19-26.

7. Edward A. Purcell, Jr., The Crisis of Democratic Theory: Scientific Naturalism and the Problem of Value (Lexington: University Press of Kentucky, 1973), chapter 4.
By treating the twenties and thirties as a unit, Purcell somewhat obscured the slow diffusion of Ogden and Richards's ideas in America. A survey of articles in both popular and scholarly journals and indexes revealed that scholarly discussions of meaning (or semantics) developed slowly among American philosophers in the twenties and centered on C. I. Lewis's theory of meaning in the early thirties. I. A. Richards was best known in the United States for his Principles of Literary Criticism, and Ogden for his work in psychology. Not until the depression did the issue of a theory of meaning per se become a critical intellectual issue for nonspecialists. As Kenneth Burke summarized the problem in a 1934 article on C. K. Ogden: "If language is the fundamental instrument of human coöperation, and if there is an 'organic flaw' in the nature of language, we may well expect to find this organic flaw revealing itself throughout the texture of society." Therefore, "for such reasons, a thoroughly documented technique of linguistic skepticism might be considered as essential to human welfare as any single line of inquiry." Kenneth Burke, "The Meaning of C. K. Ogden," The New Republic, 78 (May 2, 1934): 330. As shall be shown later in this monograph, many intellectuals did not worry about a theory of communication and meaning until after they had experienced a "breakdown" of communication and the "corruption" of meaning in the thirties.

8. Stuart Chase, The Tyranny of Words (New York: Harcourt, Brace and Company, 1938), pp. 5-6.

9. Ibid., p. 361. For Chase's summary of semantics, see chapters 6 (Korzybski), 7 (Ogden and Richards), 10 (general summary), and 11 (example).
For background and analysis of Chase, see R. Alan Lawson, The Failure of Independent Liberalism, 1930-1941 (New York: G. P. Putnam's Sons, 1971), pp. 75-84 and 226.

10. Harry L. Weinberg, Levels of Knowing and Existence: Studies in General Semantics (New York: Harper and Row, Publishers, 1959), p. xi.

11.   Dean C. Barnland, "Is There Any New Business?" foreword to the Bibliography of General Semantics by John C. Condon, ETC., 20 (May 1963): 82-83.

12.   Lee Thayer, ed., "Editor's Preface," in Communication: General Semantics Perspectives (New York: Spartan Books, 1970), p. ix.

13.   According to Korzybski's literary executor, Charlotte Schuchardt Read, "records concerning Korzybski's life prior to his coming to this country in 1915 are . . . practically non-existent." Charlotte Schuchardt Read, "Alfred Habdank Skarbek Korzybski: A Biographical Sketch," General Semantics Bulletin, no. 3 (Spring 1950): 33-40. (Quotation on p. 40). A few pictures from the Polish period of Korzybski's life are reprinted in General Semantics Bulletin, no. 3 (Spring 1950): 23. For the period after 1915, the problem in reconstructing Korzybski's life and thought is just the opposite. Again, according to Read, there were in 1959 "thousands of . . . letters and documents, throwing light upon the origin and development of his theory, the writing of Manhood of Humanity and the first edition of Science and Sanity, etc.," some of which were deteriorating rapidly. See Charlotte Schuchardt Read, "The Korzybski Archives, circa 1914-1938," General Semantics Bulletin, nos. 24-25 (1959): 134.

14.   Robert P. Pula, "Korzybski's Polish Matrix," General Semantics Bulletin, no. 47 (1980): 38-54. Pula relied particularly upon an oral autobiographical statement by Korzybski recorded in 1947, the so-called Keyes document. While useful, I believe that the Keyes document, as is so often the case in oral history, reflected Korzybski's attitudes late in his life and must be used with caution in interpreting the earlier phases of his life, especially on the question of Tarski and the Polish logicians.

15.   For developments in Poland, see the analysis by Andrzej Korbonski in Teresa Rakowska-Harmstone and Andrew Gyorgy, eds., Communism in Eastern Europe (Bloomington: Indiana University Press, 1979), pp. 37-70; and Lawrence Weschler, Solidarity: Poland in the Season of its Passion (New York: Simon and Schuster, 1982).
For the background of the Chomskian "revolution" in linguistics and its implications for semantics, see Frederick J. Newmeyer, Linguistic Theory in America: The First Quarter-Century of Transformational Generative Grammar (New York: Academic Press, 1980), pp. 73-81.
For American intellectuals in the Viet Nam era, see Charles Kadushin, The American Intellectual Elite (Boston: Little, Brown and Company, 1974), chapters 5-8. An example of the fate of semanticists in this era is found in the career of S. I. Hayakawa, embattled president of San Francisco State College. He was seen by radical intellectuals as a symbol of establishment oppression whose "intemperate language endeared him to Governor Reagan and the silent majority." William L. O'Neill, Coming Apart: An Informal History of America in the 1960s (Chicago: Quadrangle

Books, 1971), pp. 190-91 (quotation).

1. THE POLISH INTELLECTUAL MILIEU, 1890-1914

1. Alfred Korzybski, "What I Believe," reprinted in Alfred
Korzybski, Manhood of Humanity, 2d ed. Lakeville, Conn.: Institute of
General Semantics, 1950), p. xli, and New York Times, January 18,
1919, 11:2.

2. W. J. Rose, "Russian Poland in the Later Nineteenth Century,"
in W. F. Reddaway, et al., The Cambridge History of Poland: From
Augustus II to Pilsudski, 1697-1935 (London: Cambridge University
Press, 1941), p. 393.

3. Charlotte Schuchardt Read, "Alfred Korzybski: His Contributions
and Their Historical Development," in Lee Thayer, ed., Communication: General Semantics Perspectives (New York: Spartan Books,
1970), pp. 339-40 and "Editor's Note," Manhood of Humanity, p.
vi. See also Anatol Rapoport, "Alfred Korzybski, Biographical
Summary," ETC, 7 (Spring 1950): 163-65. For more detailed (and
anecdotal) biographical accounts, see the memorial essays in
General Semantics Bulletin, no. 3 (Spring 1950): 3-40.

4. Czesław Miłosz, Native Realm: A Search for Self-Definition,
trans. Catherine S. Leach (Garden City, N.Y.: Doubleday and Co.,
Inc., 1968), pp. 15 and 19-20 (quotation). See also Jan
Szczepański, "The Polish Intelligentsia," World Politics, 14
(April 1962): 406-20. Korzybski's name was sometimes spelled de
Skarbek Korzybski in the Western press. See New York Times,
January 18, 1919, 11:2.

5. Read, "Alfred Korzybski," pp. 339-40.

6. Ibid., p. 340.

7. Miłosz, Native Realm, pp. 33-34.

8. Ibid., p. 82.

9. Alex R. Vidler, The Church in an Age of Revolution, 1789 to
the Present Day (Grand Rapids, Mich.: Wm. B. Eerdmans Publishing
Co., 1961), p. 182 (quotation);Czesłow Miłosz, The History of
Polish Literature (London: Collier-Macmillan, Ltd., 1969), chapter
8 and p. 378; Read, "Alfred Korzybski," p. 340.

10. H. Stuart Hughes, Consciousness and Society: The Reorientation
of European Social Thought, 1890-1930 (New York: Alfred A. Knopf,
1958), chapters 2, 4, and 8; Gerhard Masur, Prophets of Yesterday:
Studies in European Culture, 1890-1914 (New York: Macmillan
Co., 1961), chapters 4 and 6; John Weiss, ed., The Origins of
Modern Consciousness (Detroit: Wayne State University Press, 1965).
David F. Lindenfeld has argued that it was not so much a "revolt
against positivism" during this period as it was a transformation

of positivism. See David F. Lindenfeld, The Transformation of
Positivism: Alexius Meinong and European Thought, 1880-1920
(Berkeley: University of California Press, 1981), chapter 6.

11. George Steiner, Language and Silence: Essays on Language,
Literature, and the Inhuman (New York: Atheneum, 1967). Steiner
has argued (1) that a "retreat from the word" has been a characteristic problem of the Western intellectual tradition since the
seventeenth century; (2) that this crisis of language was particularly acute in Central Europe (among German-speaking people)
around the turn of the century; (3) that Nazism showed "what
political bestiality and falsehood can make of a language when the
latter has been severed from the roots of moral and emotional life,
when it has become ossified with clichés, unexamined definitions,
and leftover words" (p. 26); and (4) that once literature and poetry succumb to these tendencies, there is only silence to convey
the ineffable.
12. Miłosz, History of Polish Literature, p. 284. For a literary
evocation of Poland during this period, see Jean Karsavina, White
Eagle, Dark Skies (New York: Charles Scribner's Sons, 1974).

13. John Bowle, Politics and Opinion in the Nineteenth Century:
An Historical Introduction (New York: Oxford University Press,
Galaxy Edition, 1964), chapter 5; D. G. Charlton, Positivist
Thought in France during the Second Empire (London: Oxford Univer-
sity Press, 1959), pp. 24-50, 86-126, and 141-53; Walter M. Simon,
European Positivism in the Nineteenth Century: An Essay in Intell-
ectual History (Ithaca: Cornell University Press, 1963).

14. Terry Nichols Clark, Prophets and Patrons: The French
University and the Emergence of the Social Sciences (Cambridge;
Harvard University Press, 1973), chapters 3 and 6.

15. Józef Chałasiński, "Spencer's Sociology as Assimilated by the
Intellectuals in Britain, Poland, and America at the End of the
Nineteenth Century: A Comparative Study," Polish Sociological
Bulletin, 1 (1962): 32; Miłosz, History of Polish Literature, p.283.

16. Chałasiński, "Spencer's Sociology," pp. 32-33. See also
Andrezej Krasiński, "Polish Positivism," Polish Perspectives, 24
(June-July 1981): 79-81.

17. Chałasiński, "Spencer's Sociology," pp. 35-37 (quotations).
In addition to the positivist historiography of Henry Thomas Buckle,
Polish positivists were sympathetic to the writings of an American
physician-chemist, John William Draper (1811-1882). His History
of the Intellectual Development of Europe (1860) was translated
into French, German, Russian, Polish, and Serbian, (see the preface
to the revised American edition, Harper and Brothers, 1899, p. iv.).
Draper held that "Man is the archetype of society. Individual
development is the model of social progress." Since all phenomena
obey the same natural laws, "groups of men, or nations, . . .
complete the same cycle as the individual." Thus nations go

through the cycle of "Infancy, Childhood, Youth, Manhood, Old Age, and Death respectively." To each stage, there is a corresponding intellectual mode: "1, the Age of Credulity; 2, the Age of Inquiry; 3, the Age of Faith; 4, the Age of Reason; 5, the Age of Decrepitude. . . ." Yet, he held that there was no incompatibility between such determinism and recognition of the "free action of man." The reconciliation of free-will and fate, uncertainty and determinism, was simply a matter of the viewpoint from which one viewed the process. John William Draper, History of the Intellectual Development of Europe, rev. ed. (New York: Harper and Brothers, 1899), pp. 2, 12, 14, 19, and 20-21. For his popularity in Poland, see Alvin Marcus Fountain II, Roman Dmowski: Party, Tactics, Ideology, 1895-1907 (New York: Columbia University Press, 1980), p. 103. For an example of how Anglo-French positivism and German historicism influenced Serbian historiography and philosophy of history during the late nineteenth century, see Božidar Knežević, History, The Anatomy of Time, trans. George Vid Tomashevich (New York: Philosophical Library, 1980).

18. Miłosz, History of Polish Literature, p. 305. See also Joyce Story Kolodziej, "Eliza Orzeszkowa's Feminist and Jewish Works in Polish and Russian Criticism," unpublished Ph.D. dissertation, Indiana University, 1975.

19. Chałasiński, "Spencer's Sociology," p. 38; Ludwig Gumplowicz, The Outlines of Sociology, trans. Frederick W. Moore (Philadelphia: American Academy of Political and Social Science, 1899), pp. 21-33 (the quotation from Comte on methodology is found on p. 23); William M. Johnston, The Austrian Mind: An Intellectual and Social History, 1848-1938 (Berkeley: University of California Press, 1972), pp. 323-26. Gumplowicz blamed the tendency to confuse biological analogies with social realities in part on the nature of the language used to describe both. He noted that Spencer "finds that societies grow as truly as living organisms do; though this comparison holds only because we have but one expression (growth, Wachstum) for two ideas, organic growth and social enlargement. If there were a special expression for each there would be no temptation falsely to compare or identify them. Likewise, nothing but want of verbal precision makes it possible to say that both an organism and a society increase in 'structure' at the same time that they increase in scope. The word 'structure' is biological and should be only metaphorically applied to the development of social classes, departments of government, and the like." Gumplowicz, Outlines of Sociology, p. 30. Johnston notes that Gumplowicz anticipated Lukács's conception of reification and Mannheim's distinction between ideology and utopia. Johnston, Austrian Mind, p. 326.

20. Chałasiński, "Spencer's Sociology," p. 38. See also Gumplowicz, Outlines of Sociology, part 5.

21. Miłosz, History of Polish Literature, p. 289.

22. Johnston, _Austrian Mind_, p. 184. See also Hughes, _Consciousness and Society_, pp. 108-9.

23. Robert Bouvier, _La Pensée d'Ernst Mach_ (Paris, 1923) as quoted by Hughes, _Consciousness and Society_, p. 109. Henry P. Aiken, in _The Age of Ideology_ (New York: Mentor, 1956), chapter 12, argued that Mach's theory of knowledge rested on two methodological principles: (1) empiricism, the belief that sensation alone provides the basis of knowledge; and (2) phenomenalism, the principle that "auxiliary" concepts such as cause, number, and so on may be used in science to organize hypotheses into a coherent order. However, to explain the symbolic function of such nondesignating terms, Mach required a philosophy of language and of logic that was beyond his grasp and that was only later developed by logical positivists and pragmatists. Furthermore, Mach's empiricism rested on the premise that intersubjective observation is the sole and fundamental test of statements of fact. Mach had conceived of the problem of science as being related to the distinction between our perceptions (sensations) and our presentations (awareness or realization of the "objects" of experience). He wrote:

    Now the problem of science can be split into three parts:
1.   The determination of the connexion of presentations. This is psychology.
2.   The discovery of the laws of the connexion of sensations (perceptions). This is physics.
3.   The clear establishment of the laws of the connexion of sensations and presentations. This is psychophysics.

Allan Janik and Stephen Toulmin, _Wittgenstein's Vienna_, (New York: Simon and Schuster, 1973) p. 134. Compare Korzybski's position in the 1920s in chapter 2.

Mach had been influenced by, and corresponded with, the German-American philosopher of science John B. Stallo, whose _Concepts and Theories of Modern Physics_ (1881) applied a critical (Hegelian) understanding of language to the puzzles and paradoxes of physics. Stallo's theory of cognition rested on three premises: (1) "Thought deals, not with things as they are, or are supposed to be, in themselves, but with our mental representations of them. . . . What is present in the mind in the act of thought is never a thing, but always a state of consciousness . . . "; (2) "Objects are known only through their relations to other objects . . . "; and (3) "A particular operation of thought never involves the entire complement of the known or knowable properties of a given object, but only such of them as belong to a definite class of relations." Lloyd D. Easton, _Hegel's First American Followers: The Ohio Hegelians_ (Athens: Ohio University Press, 1966), pp. 77-78 (quotations) and 83.

In short, knowledge is always selective, relational, and symbolic. Since Stallo started from the Hegelian notion of the unity of thought and language (Easton, _Hegel's First American Followers_, p. 216), his third principle could, by implication, be extended to the statement that, since thought never "conceives" of the entire object in all its properties or relations, language can not convey the sense of the entire object. Compare this with Korzybski's

principle that words never say all about anything, in chapter 2.
Stallo's Concepts and Theories of Modern Physics has been reprinted
by the Harvard University Press (1960) with an introduction by P.
W. Bridgmann.

24. Johnston, Austrian Mind pp. 196-99; Janik and Toulmin,
Wittgenstein's Vienna, p. 126 (quotation).
In Russia, A. A. Malinovski, who wrote under the pseudonym A. A.
Bogdanov, attempted to use Avenarius's empirio-criticism to provide
Marxism with a new philosophical foundation. In addition to philosophical positivism, Avenarius held that "scientific concepts ex-
pressing the regularities of natural phenomena are only hypothetical
constructions that the human mind distills from the chaos of experience data" and that "diversified individual experiences are
combined in ordered empirical generalizations and logical concepts
owing to man's basic social, or 'interindividual,' unity; this
operates most effectively through language, which superimposes
discrete verbal labels on a jumble of sense impressions." Alexander
Vucinich, Science in Russian Culture, 1861-1917 (Stanford: Stanford
University Press, 1970), pp. 252-53 (quotation).
Lenin responded with an attack not only on Bogdanov's historicism
but also on the very basis of Mach and Avenarius's empirio-criticism.
According to Louis Althusser, Lenin criticized positivism and empiricism by stressing "the decisive role of scientific abstraction,
or rather, the role of conceptual systematicity, and in a more
general way, the role of theory as such" in actual scientific
practice. The scientists, in practice, were not consistent empiricists. The implication was that just as the proletariat can
spontaneously achieve only a trade-union consciousness and must be
"led" to revolutionary class consciousness by the vanguard of the
proletariat (the Communist party), so the scientists can spontaneously achieve only an empiricist consciousness and must, therefore,
be shown the way to a true scientific consciousness by the inculca-
tion of dialectical materialism, which deals with the true laws of
thought. Louis Althusser, Lenin and Philosophy and Other Essays,
trans. Ben Brewster (New York: Monthly Review Press, 1971), pp.
23-70 (quotation from p. 52). For Lenin's criticism of Mach and
Avenarius, see V. Lenine, Materialisme et Empiriocriticisme
(Moscow: Éditions en Langues Étrangeres, 1952), pp. 96-100, 189-95,
and 404-16. For Lenin's critique of Helmholtz's theory of language,
see pp. 268-73.
See also Robert S. Cohen, "Machists and Marxists: Bogdanov and
Lenin," Boston Studies in the Philosophy of Science, 6 (Dordrecht,
Holland: B. Reidel, 1970): 156-60; and Alexander Vucinich, Social
Thought in Tsarist Russia: The Quest for a General Science of
Society, 1861-1917 (Chicago: University of Chicago Press, 1976),
chapter 8.

25. Janik and Toulmin, Wittgenstein's Vienna, pp. 126-32 (quotations on pp. 127 and 132).
Janik and Toulmin hoped that their study would help "to re-establish
the significance of links between Wittgenstein and the Viennese,
German-language thought and art of his time that have obscured as a
result of his later associations with the English-speaking

philosophers of, for example, Cambridge and Cornell." They particularly assumed that Wittgenstein operated in creative tension
with Karl Kraus and Fritz Mauthner. "Although Wittgenstein explicitly contrasts his own philosophical approach to that of
Mauthner at one central point in the Tractatus," Janik and
Toulmin found "no further evidence that the Tractatus itself was
actually intended as a reply to Mauthner's earlier 'critique of
language'"; however, they admit that this view was somewhat con-
jectural. Janik and Toulmin, Wittgenstein's Vienna, pp. 9-10.
Leonard Linsky and John W. Boyer, in separate reviews, challenged
Janik and Toulmin thesis concerning Wittgenstein's relationship to,
or indebtedness toward, Kraus and Mauthner. Linsky's critique is
primarily philosophical, believing that Wittgenstein does belong
primarily to the British tradition; Boyer's criticism is essentially
historical and disputes the Janik and Toulmin reading of Austrian
social structure and political culture to challenge their thesis
that the central problem of fin-de-siècle Austria was the issue of
communication and language. See Leonard Linsky and John W. Boyer,
reviews of Allan Janik and Stephen Toulmin, Wittgenstein's Vienna,
The Journal of Modern History, 47, no. 4 (December 1975): 699-711.
For another view of the interrelationship of social structure and
cultural movements in Vienna in the 1890s, see Carl E. Schorski,
Fin-de-Siècle Vienna: Politics and Culture (New York: Alfred A.
Knopf, 1980). For Karl Kraus, see J. P. Stern, "Karl Kraus'
Vision of Language," Modern Language Review, 61 (1966): 71-82.

26. Quoted by Lawrence S. Stepelevich, "August von Cieszkowski:
From Theory to Praxis," History and Theory, 13, no. 1 (1974): 44.

27. Ibid., pp. 39-52; Richard J. Bernstein, Praxis and Action: Contemporary Philosophies of Human Activity (Philadelphia: University
of Pennsylvania Press, 1971), pp. xi-xiii.
The case for Cieszkowski's influence on Marx's theory of praxis is
developed in Reinhard Lauth, "Einflüsse slawischer Denker auf die
Genesis der Marxschen Weltanschauung," Orientalia Christiana
Periodica, 21 (1955).
Stepelevich is not convinced that sufficient proof has been presented to prove Marx's indebtedness to Cieszkowski; Bernstein
mentions Cieszkowski's concept of praxis but devotes most of his
attention to proving the uniqueness and importance of Marx's theory
of praxis. See also Nicholas Lobkowicz, Theory and Practice:
History of a Concept from Aristotle to Marx (Notre Dame: University
of Notre Dame Press, 1967), chapter 13. Lobkowicz rejects Lauth's
contention that Cieszkowski influenced Marx (p. 204, n. 136). For
a full intellectual biography of Cieszkowski, see André Liebich,
Between Ideology and Utopia: The Politics and Philosophy of August
Cieszkowski (Boston: D. Reidel, 1979).

28. Miłosz, History of Polish Literature, p. 285. Compare Julian
Krzyżanowski, A History of Polish Literature trans. Doris Ronowicz
(Warsaw: Polish Scientific Publishers, 1978), pp. 366-67 and 369.

29. Miłosz, History of Polish Literature, pp. 291-303 (Prus) and
308-14 (Sienkiewicz); David Welsh, "Sienkiewicz's 'Trilogy': A

Study in Novelistic Techniques," Antemurale (Institutum Historicum Polonicum Romae), 15 (1971): 217-98 (quotation on p. 228). For Sienkiewicz's influence in America see Mieczysław Giergielewicz, "Henryk Sienkiewicz's American Resonance," Antemurale, 10 (1966): 257-354.

30. Miłosz, History of Polish Literature, pp. 325-32 (quotation on p. 327). See also Jeffrey T. Bergner, "Stirner, Nietzsche, and the Critique of Truth," Journal of the History of Philosophy, 11 (1973): 523-34; Max Stirner, The Ego and His Own, ed. John Carroll (New York: Harper & Row, 1971).

31. Miłosz, History of Polish Literature, pp. 322 and 329. Compare Krzyżanowski, A History of Polish Literature, pp. 453-55.

32. Miłosz, History of Polish Literature, pp. 348 (quotation) and 351. On the morphology of the Polish language, see Stanisław Westfal, "The Polish Language," Antemurale, 10 (1966): 74-108. For the development of Polish poetry in this period see Miłosz, History of Polish Literature, pp. 334-47.

33. Frank Joseph Corliss, Jr., "Dimensions of Reality in the Lyrics of Cyprian Norwid," Antemurale, 16 (1972): 114 (poem) and 120 (quotation).
For biographical data on Norwid, see Julian Krzyżanowski, Polish Romantic Literature (New York: E. P. Dutton and Co., 1931), pp. 266-71. Stanisław Brzozowski, the literary historian, devoted some attention to Norwid in his Legenda Młodej Polski (Legend of Young Poland) in 1910 but Zenon Przesmycki (1861-1944) is credited with the rediscovery of Norwid. See Miłosz, History of Polish Literature, p. 333. See also Roman Jakobson, " 'Czułosc' Cypriana Norwida" in Victor Erlich, ed., For Wiktor Weintraub: Essays in Polish Literature, Language, and History (The Hague: Mouton, 1975), pp. 227-37; and Irena Sławińska, "Two Concepts of Time in Dramatic Structure: Turgenev and Norwid," in Erlich, For Wiktor Weintraub, pp. 479-92.

34. Corliss, "Dimensions of Reality," pp. 119 and 125 (quotation).

35. Ibid., pp. 158 (poem) and 160 (quotation).

36. Ibid., p. 160 (poem).

37. Miłosz, History of Polish Literature, pp. 362-64 (quotation on pp. 362-63).

38. Danuta Irena Bieńkowska, "An Analytical Study of the Early Literary Work of Stefan Żeromski, Its Cultural Background and Its Critical Reception in Poland," Antemurale, 16 (1972): 261-62. See also Miłosz, History of Polish Literature, pp. 365-73.

39. Joachim T. Baer, "Wacław Berent, His Life and Work," Antemurale, 18 (1974): 80-90. See also Joachim T. Baer, "Wacław

Berent's Ozimina: An Analysis," in Erlich, For Wiktor Weintraub, pp. 43-57. Nietzsche and Kierkegaard were known in Poland primarily through the work of the Danish literary critic Georg Brandes. Kierkegaard, for instance, was discussed in Brandes's Main Currents in Nineteenth Century Literature, which was published in Poland between 1882 and 1885. Żeromski read all five volumes in 1885. Brandes visited and lectured in Poland in 1886 and published an account of Polish romanticism in literature in 1886. Joachim T. Baer believed that Brandes may have discussed Nietzsche during his visit in 1886. Also, Brandes lectured on Nietzsche in Copenhagen in 1888 and the lecture was published in Poland in 1890. Berent may have read Nietzsche in German during his studies in Munich, 1890-1895; in any case, between 1895 and 1901 Berent published translations from Nietzsche in Young Poland journals. See Bieńkowska, "An Analytical Study," p. 273; George Brandes, Poland, A Study of the Land, People, and Literature (London: William Heinemann, 1903).

40. Miłosz, History of Polish Literature, pp. 373-79 (quotations from pp. 377 and 379).

41. Czesław Miłosz, "A Controversial Polish Writer: Stanisław Brzozowski," California Slavic Studies, 2 (1963): 78. Miłosz has given an apt summary of Brzozowski's philosophy: "The future belonged, in Brzozowski's opinion, to a philosophy that would recognize human struggle through labor against the forces of nature as the basis of freedom." Miłosz, History of Polish Literature, p. 377.

42. Tymon Terlecki, "Stanisław Wyspiański and the Poetics of Symbolist Drama," The Polish Review, 15 (Autumn 1970): 56.

43. Brzozowski as quoted in Miłosz, History of Polish Literature, pp. 352-53.

44. Tymon Terlecki, "Wyspiański in Two Perspectives," Antemurale, 15 (1971); 301-11. For the European reaction to Wyspiański, see Tymon Terlecki, "The Greatness and Ill Fortune of Stanisław Wyspiański," Antemurale, 14 (1970): 259-77.

45. Janusz Degler, " 'Pismo teatralne' Stanisława Wyspiańskiego," Dramat i Teatr: Konferencja Teoretycznoliteracka w Świętej Katarzynie, Jan Trzynadlowski, redaktor (Wrocław: Zakład Narodowy Imienia Ossolińskich, Wydawnictwo, 1967), pp. 74-76 and 78. Translation by Richard Wartman.

46. Terlecki, "Stanisław Wyspiański and the Poetics of Symbolist Drama," p. 62. The protean creativity of Brzozowski and Wyspiański was matched by that of the Hungarian socialist and aesthetician, Georg Lukács (1885-1971). A poet, literary critic, and philosopher, Lukács too "had originally arrived on the { Central European intellectual}scene at a time when it was generally held that the only choice open to one who could accept neither traditional

metaphysics nor religious faith lay between the positivism of
empirical science and the vitalism . . . of irrationalists such
as Nietzsche or Bergson." Where Brzozowski achieved a dialectical
resolution of the subjective world of values and the objective
world of facts in the praxis of human creativity (including literary
or linguistic creativity), Lukács also found his way out of the
dilemma by reviving Hegelian dialectics and unifying it with
literary or aesthetic categories. Lukács saw history as a dialectical process in which the spirit (or soul) of the times was expressed in the literary genre (or forms) that characterized the
history of the essay, novel, and drama. George Lichtheim, George
Lukács (New York: Viking Press, 1970), pp. 15-16 (quotation) and
20. See also Lucien Goldman, "The Early Writings of Georg Lukács,"
trans. Joy N. Humes, in George Gömöri and Charles Newman, eds.,
New Writings of East Europe (Chicago: Quadrangle Books, 1968), pp.
189-205. Lukács had drawn attention to Marx's discussion of the
impact of reification on language and called for a philological
study of language based on historical materialism. Georg Lukács,
History and Class Consciousness, trans. Rodney Livingstone
(Cambridge: MIT Press, 1971), p. 209, n. 16. For further elabora-
tion of this point, see G. H. R. Parkinson, ed., Georg Lukács: The
Man, His Work, and His Ideas (New York: Vintage Books, 1970), pp.
16-17; Peter Hamilton, Knowledge and Social Structure (London:
Routledge and Kegan Paul, 1974), chapter 3; Karl Marx, The
Grundrisse, ed. and trans. David McLellan (New York: Harper & Row,
1971), pp. 71-73.

47. On symbolism in poetry, see Edmund Wilson, Axel's Castle: A
Study in the Imaginative Literature of 1870-1930 (New York: Charles
Scribner's Sons, 1931), chapter 1.

48. Janik and Toulmin, Wittgenstein's Vienna, pp. 88-90, 125-27.

49. Read, "Alfred Korzybski," p. 340. The prohibition against
teaching reading or writing outside of official school buildings
went back to the period of repression following the 1863 insurrection. The dating of the above incident is unclear, but, if after
1904, Korzybski could have benefited in this case from the need of
the Russians to grant concessions in the aftermath of the Russo-
Japanese War and the calling of the Duma. Edward H. Lewinski-Corwin,
The Political History of Poland (New York: Polish Book Importing
Company, 1917), pp. 497 and 546-49.

50. On Wittgenstein's engineering background and philosophical
development for this period, see Janik and Toulmin, Wittgenstein's
Vienna, or William Warren Bartley III, Wittgenstein (Philadelphia:
J. P. Lippincott, 1973).

2. BETWEEN POLAND AND AMERICA, 1914-1933

1. Richard M. Watt, Bitter Glory: Poland and Its Fate, 1918 to
1939 (New York: Simon and Schuster, 1979), pp. 47-48. The text of
the manifesto is reprinted in E. H. Lewinski-Corwin, The Political
History of Poland (New York: Polish Book Importing Company, 1917),

p. 578.

2. Charlotte Schuchardt Read, "Alfred Habdank Skarbek Korzybski:
A Biographical Sketch," General Semantics Bulletin, no. 3 (Spring
1950): 34-35; Charlotte Schuchardt Read, "Alfred Korzybski: His
Contributions and Their Historical Development," in Lee Thayer,
ed., Communication: General Semantics Perspectives (New York:
Spartan Books, 1970), p. 340; New York Times, January 18, 1919,
11:2. The Minister of War, General Sukhomlinov, was removed on
June 26, 1915, and replaced by General Alexis Polivanov. Sukhomlinov was later tried for malfeasance because of Russian munition
shortages at the front. Polivanov advocated raising munitions
output to the maximum, but resigned in March 1916, in another
ministerial shake-up. See New York Times, September 5, 1915, 2,
1:7; March 16, 1916, 3:5; and March 30, 1916, 3:2.
In Canada in January 1916, the Russian government had agreed to
provide working capital for the Canadian Car and Foundry Company
to produce artillery shells and had later extended the order. But
the whole Canadian munitions effort was in a muddle that resulted
in parliamentary investigations and a lawsuit over the Russian
contract. For the Russian munitions deal, see New York Times,
January 6, 1916, 15:5; January 23, 1916, 3, 9:1; and October 6,
1916, 9:1. For the munitions investigations, see New York Times,
January 23, 1916, 2, 10:1; March 30, 1916, 5:5; March 31, 1916,
3:7; and July 22, 1916, 2:7.

3. Hans Roos, A History of Modern Poland, trans. J. R. Foster,
(New York: Alfred A. Knopf, 1966), p. 25. The key figure in these
events was Roman Dmowski, pre-war leader of the Polish National
Democratic party. Dmowski's Polish National Committee had fled
from Warsaw to Petrograd in the summer of 1915. When the Russians
proved perfidious on their promises, Dmowski sailed to London and
then to Paris to bargain with the Allies. It was Dmowski's group
that dominated the government in exile. For background on
Dmowski, see Alvin Marcus Fountain II, Roman Dmowski: Party,
Tactics, Ideology, 1895-1907 (New York: Columbia University Press,
1980) and Watt, Bitter Glory, chapter 2.

4. Read, "Alfred Habdank Skarbek Korzybski," p. 35. For the
French-Polish army and U.S. support of it, see New York Times,
October 7, 1917, 1, 7:3; October 27, 1917, 1:1; and May 7, 1918,
11:6.
The Polish Military Commission arrived in New York in March 1918;
see New York Times, March 24, 1918, 1, 22:1; March 25, 1918, 6:1,
April 8, 1918, 4:1; October 31, 1918, 10:4; and December 23, 1918,
13:2.

5. David M. Kennedy, Over Here: The First World War and American
Society (New York: Oxford University Press, 1980), p. 158.

6. Read, "Alfred Korzybski: His Contributions," p. 341; New York
Times, January 18, 1919, 11:2. Mira Edgerly was born on January
16, 1879, in Aurora, Illinois. Her childhood was spent in Jackson,
Michigan, according to one source, "where her father was a

well-known railroad official." See Helen L. Earle, ed., Biographical Sketches of American Artists, 5th ed., (East Lansing: Michigan
State Library, 1924), p. 106. She had started her career as a
miniaturist but developed a technique of painting portraits on
thin sheets of translucent ivory, an approach that pleased her
wealthy clients. See Lady Mira Edgerly-Korzybska, "The Psychology
of Portraiture," Arts and Decoration," 11 (October 1919): 268-69;
Mira Edgerly-Korzybska, "The Edgerly-Korzybski Technique," exhibit
pamphlet, January 17, 1921, Art Institute of Chicago library. See
also Charlotte Schuchardt Read, "Mira Edgerly Korzybska: A
Biographical Sketch," General Semantics Bulletin, nos. 16-17 (1955):
53-56. Read lists her birth year as 1872 while other sources use
1879.

7. Alfred Korzybski, Manhood of Humanity, 2nd ed. (Lakeville,
Conn.: Institute of General Semantics, 1950), p. 236. For the
details surrounding the origin and writing of Manhood of
Humanity, see Read, "Mira Edgerly Korzybska," 54-55. Dr. Julian
Grove-Korski (or Korski Grove, as he is listed in the National
Union Catalog) was the author of several articles on Polish immigra-
tion and was Polish Consulate General in 1921. See Julian Korski
Grove, "The Polish Group in the United States," Annals of the
American Academy of Political and Social Sciences, 93 (January
1921): 153-56; "Rural Immigrant Colonies," Survey, 44 (September
15, 1920): 713-14; and Szukanie prawdy; zbiór rospraw naukowych
(Toledo, Ohio: A. A. Paryski, 1920).

8. Jacques Loeb (1859-1924) was born in Prussia, the eldest son
of a prosperous Jewish import merchant and "ardent Francophile."
Loeb aspired to be a philosopher but turned to science instead,
earning an M.D. in 1884 at Strausbourg. In 1886 he became an
assistant to Adolf Fick, a pioneer in the application of physics to
biology. "The decisive contact of Loeb's career was his intimate
friendship with Julius von Sachs, from whom he learned of plant
tropisms, obligatory movements elicited by physical stimuli such
as light and gravity." In 1890 he married an American philologist,
Dr. Anne Leonard, and emigrated to the United States in 1891. He
taught at Bryn Mawr, the University of Chicago, and the University
of California. From 1910 to 1924 he served at the Rockefeller
Institute in New York. His most popular work, The Mechanistic
Conception of Life (1912) equated human instincts with tropisms.
"As a materialist in philosophy, a mechanist in science, and a
socialist in politics, he offended against the prevalent American
orthodoxies. But he was correspondingly idolized by the dissenters
and debunkers--including Veblen, Mencken, and Sinclair Lewis--who
increasingly set the intellectual tone" of the 1920s. Donald
Fleming, "Jacques Loeb," in Charles C. Gillispie, ed., Dictionary
of Scientific Biography, vol. 8 (New York: Charles Scribner's
Sons, 1970), pp. 445-47.

9. As quoted by Charlotte Schuchardt Read, "Editor's Note,"
Manhood of Humanity, p. xi. This statement by Korzybski was
written in 1949.

10. Manhood of Humanity was first published by E. P. Dutton
Company. All quotations in this monograph are from the 2d edition
published by the Institute of General Semantics, 1950.
Another such millenialist book, also published in 1921, was James
Harvey Robinson, The Mind in the Making: The Relation of Intelligence to Social Reform (New York: Harper and Brothers Publishers,
1921). His theme was stated boldly on the first page: "If some
magical transformation could be produced in men's ways of looking
at themselves and their fellows, no inconsiderable part of the
evils which now afflict society would vanish away or remedy themselves automatically" (p. 3). Robinson attempted to show that "there
are four historical layers underlying the minds of civilized men--
the animal mind, the child mind, the savage mind, and the traditional civilized mind" (p. 65). The young, said Robinson, "should
early learn that language is not primarily a vehicle of ideas and
information, but an emotional outlet . . ." (p.224).
Robinson noted Korzybski's Manhood of Humanity in a footnote and
concluded: "His aim and outlook are . . . essentially the same as
those of the present writer. His method of approach will appeal
especially to those who are wont to deal with affairs in the spirit
of the mathematician and engineer" (pp. 80-81, n.1).
Korzybski, for his part, based his second chapter on Robinson's An
Outline of the History of the Western European Mind (New York: New
York: New School for Social Research, 1918) and quoted him extensively in the footnotes.
For an interpretation of James Harvey Robinson, see Morton White,
Social Thought in America: The Revolt against Formalism, rev. ed.
(Boston: Beacon Press, 1957), chapter 4. For the post-war
millenialist mood and its origins, see H. Stuart Hughes, Oswald
Spengler: A Critical Estimate (New York: Charles Scribner's Sons,
1952), chapter 6.

11. Korzybski, Manhood of Humanity, pp. 3 and 5 (quotation).

12. Ibid., pp. 58-60. By time-binding he meant "the capacity to
summarize, digest and appropriate the labors and experiences of
the past; I mean the capacity to use the fruits of past labors and
experiences as intellectual or spiritual capital for developments
in the present; I mean the capacity to employ as instruments of
increasing power the accumulated achievements of the all-precious
lives of the past generations spent in trial and error, trial and
success; I mean the capacity of human beings to conduct their lives
in the ever increasing light of inherited wisdom; I mean the
capacity in virtue of which man is at once the heritor of the by-
gone ages and the trustee of posterity" Manhood of Humanity, p. 59.
M. F. Ashley-Montague, the anthropologist, has noted that
Korzybski's concept of time-binding "is virtually identical with
the anthropologist's concept of culture." M. F. Ashley-Montague,
review of Korzybski, Manhood of Humanity, Psychiatry, 14 (1951):
251 as quoted by A. L. Kroelber and Clyde Kluckhorn, Culture (New
York: Vintage Books, 1963), p. 5.
As Mauthner pointed out, language was one way in which culture or
history was passed from one generation to the next. "Language is
only the imperfect means of men to find their bearings in the world

of their memories; to make use of their memory, that is, their own experience and that of their ancestors, with all probability that this world of memory will be like the world of reality." Mauthner, Kritik der Sprache, vol. 3 (Stuttgart, 1901-1902), p. 2, as quoted by William Graham Sumner, Folkways, reprint (New York: Dover Publications, Inc., 1959), p. 134 (emphasis added).

13. Korzybski, Manhood of Humanity, p. 14.

14. Ibid., p. 147. This was what the Polish and Central European philosophers meant when they said it was impossible to have or to describe a scientific basis for ethics; that is, to derive a statement of "ought" from a statement of "is."

15. Ibid., appendix 3, pp. 259-60.

16. Samuel Haber, Efficiency and Uplift: Scientific Management in the Progressive Era, 1890-1920, (Chicago: University of Chicago Press, 1964) p. 43 (quotation) and pp. 143-44; Edwin Layton, "Frederick H. Newell and the Revolt of the Engineers," Journal of the Midcontinent American Studies Association, 3 (Fall 1962): 18-26; Edwin Layton, "Veblen and the Engineers," American Quarterly, 16 (Spring 1962): 64-72; Edwin T. Layton, The Revolt of the Engineers: Social Responsibility and the American Engineering Profession (Cleveland: Press of Case Western Reserve University, 1971), chapters 5-7; and Korzybski, Manhood of Humanity, p. 261. (quotation). See also Bruce Sinclair, A Centennial History of the American Society of Mechanical Engineers, 1880-1980 (Toronto: University of Toronto Press, 1980). Korzybski also thought highly of the engineering views of Walter N. Polakov. Polakov mixed Gantt with modified Marxism, helped the Soviet Union plan its first five-year plan, then joined the technocrats on his return to America. See Haber, Efficiency and Uplift, p. 49, n.41 and p. 159 n.75. The term human engineering had been used by industrial reformers critical of Taylorism as early as 1916. Haber, Efficiency and Uplift, pp. 64-65, n.24.

17. Korzybski, Manhood of Humanity, appendix 2, p. 231 and appendix 1, p. 218. In the preface to the first edition of Manhood of Humanity, Korzybski had acknowledged those who read and criticized the draft manuscript or who had helped him in some way. The list is indicative of his intellectual contacts at the time and can be divided into three groups - the engineering millenialists (discussed above), native American reformers (C. J. Keyser, J. H. Robinson, Burger Johnson, E. A. Ross, and others), and emigré intellectuals.
The emigré intellectuals, who had backgrounds similar to Korzybski, in addition to Loeb and Grove-Korski (discussed above), were: Eliakim Hastings Moore (1862-1932), a German-born mathematician with a Ph.D. from Yale (1885) who taught at the University of Chicago in the early 1900s.
Alexander Petrunkevitch (1875-1964), a Russian-born biologist who served as president of the Connecticut Academy of Arts and Sciences until his retirement in 1946. In addition to his scientific works,

he published essays and books on materialism, free will and deter-
minism, and the role of intellectuals in the Russial revolution.
See Alexander Petrunkevitch, The Russian Revolution (Cambridge:
Harvard University Press, 1918), pp. 3-21.
Walter N. Polakov (1879-), a Russian-born consulting engineer,
was educated at the University of Moscow and the Royal Institute of
Technology at Dresden. He came to the United States in 1906. (For
biographical data, see Daniel A. Wren, "Scientific Management in
the U.S.S.R., with particular reference to the contribution of
Walter N. Polakov," Academy of Management Review, 5 (January 1980):
5-9).
Charles Proteus Steinmetz (1865-1923), a German-born mathematician
and engineer who came to America in 1889 to avoid arrest for socialist activity. It was his book America and the New Epoch (New
York: Harper and Brothers, 1916) that Korzybski cited as "a most
correct engineering picture of the political situation in the world,
with a fine characterization of the psychological peculiarities of
the different races" (Manhood of Humanity, p. 259).
Such men could presumably understand the European background out of
which Korzybski wrote.
The way in which an awareness of Korzybski's European orientation
can add to one's reading of Manhood of Humanity can be illustrated
in Chapter 5 on "Wealth." At one point, Korzybski makes the
puzzling statement: "From an engineer's point of view humanity is
apparently divided into three classes; (1) the intellectuals; (2)
the rich; and (3) the poor. This division would seem to be contrary to all the rules of logic, but it corresponds to facts" (p.
108). In American standard English prose the distinctions are
innocuous. Even the explanations for the categories do not readily
translate into the familiar American sociological categories of
upper class, middle class, and working class. Korzybski continues,
"(1) The intellectuals are the men and women who possess the
knowledge produced by the labor of by-gone generations but do not
possess the material wealth thus produced. . . . (2) The rich are
those who have possession and control of most of the material
wealth produced by the toil of by-gone generations. . . . (3) The
poor are those who have neither the knowledge possessed by the intellectuals nor the material wealth possessed by the rich and who,
moreover, . . . under present conditions are limited to the
struggle for mere existence . . ." (pp. 108-9). Translated back
in European conditions, the distinctions are the familiar ones
between the declassé intelligentsia, the aristocracy and haute
bourgeoisie, and the peasantry and proletariat.
Furthermore, the intellectual figures who are either praised or
criticized in the book--Mill, Spencer, Buckle, and so on--are the
heroes of the positivist generation in Poland. (See comments on
Mill's economics, p. 100; Spencer on energy transformation, pp.
82-83; and Buckle on methodology, pp. 205-6). Korzybski transcends
the capitalist versus socialist rhetoric of the European past,
however, and adopts the "technocracy" of engineering millenialism
instead. (See pages 129-33 and 200-3.)

18. Korzybski, Manhood of Humanity, appendix 2, pp. 250-51.

Donald Flemming has maintained that Jacques Loeb influenced J. B.
Watson, the founder of psychological behaviorism while Watson was
a graduate student at the University of Chicago. Watson's recent
biographer, David Cohen, maintains that Watson was influenced most
by James Angell. Loeb apparently suggested that Watson do his
doctoral dissertation under him, "but Angell felt that Loeb was not
a 'safe' man for a 'green' Ph.D. candidate." David Cohen, J. B.
Watson: The Founder of Behaviorism, A Biography (London: Rothledge
and Kegan Paul, 1979), p. 26; Fleming, Dictionary of Scientific
Biography, p. 446.
Korzybski did not need to dip into Watson to discover behaviorism
as he had already drunk from the wellspring in Jacques Loeb's
mechanistic biology. For the current evaluation of Loeb's contributions in biology, see the comments by Eric R. Kandel, Cellular
Basis of Behavior: An Introduction to Behavioral Neurobiology (San
Francisco: W. H. Freeman and Co., 1976), chapters 1-3.

19. Cassius J. Keyser, The Human Worth of Rigorous Thinking (New
York: Columbia University Press, 1916), pp. 68 and 221. Keyser was
born in Rawson, Ohio, on May 15, 1862. He was a principal and
superintendent of schools in Ohio and Missouri (1885-1890) and
taught mathematics at various places before coming to Columbia in
1905. His early books contained a Darwinist critique of religion.
He also attacked pragmatism and William James's notion that concepts flow out of perceptions. See also Joseph Meyer, "Cassius
Jackson Keyser, 1862-1947," ETC., 5 (August 1947): 19-20. Korzybski
echoes Keyser's distinction between truth and "correctness" (that
is, coherence), Manhood of Humanity, p. 213.

20. Keyser, Human Worth of Rigorous Thinking, p. 161. See also
Cassius J. Keyser, Mathematical Philosophy: A Study of Fate and
Freedom (New York: E. P. Dutton, 1922).

21. Keyser, Human Worth of Rigorous Thinking, p. 78.

22. Korzybski, Manhood of Humanity, p. 217.

23. Alfred Korzybski, "Fate and Freedom," Mathematics Teacher, 16
(1923): 274-75. { emphasis added}

24. Ibid., pp. 279-80 and 275-76.

25. Ibid., p. 277.

26. F. S. C. Northrop, Man, Nature and God: A Quest for Life's
Meaning (New York: Simon and Schuster, 1962), pp. 76-78. The
concept by intuition was similar to Russell's early assumption that
"the meaning of a name is to be identified with the object which it
denotes." A. J. Ayer, Russell and Moore: The Analytical Heritage
(Cambridge: Harvard University Press, 1971), p. 12. Or, conversely,
"a word has a meaning only if it has an unmediated relation to an
object." Such meaningful words were of two kinds: proper names
(particulars) and common words (universals). "When we are speaking
about a proper name we can speak specifically about that word naming

its object," by reference to particular sense data, time, place, and so on. "Common words are those meaningful words that signify or represent universal objects" by reference to attributes, relations, or concepts. Aloysius P. Martinich, "Russell's Theory of Meaning and Descriptions, 1905-1920," Journal of the History of Philosophy, 14 (April 1976): 191-92.
The concept by postulation is a more difficult matter to correlate with Russell's system. Korzybski referred, on concepts by postulation, to Keyser's notion of doctrinal function, Poincaré's definition of logical existence as freedom from contradiction, and Russell's derivation of logical "existence from his theory of propositional function." Russell's conception, according to Korzybski, "is much more fundamental, but for the time being, Poincaré's definition will be sufficient." Korzybski, "Fate and Freedom" pp. 277-78.

27. Korzybski, "Fate and Freedom," p. 277. Technically, the "entity" to which such "incomplete symbols" referred were called logical constructions. In Russell's rather confusing use of terminology in his early works, as incomplete symbol was one that had no meaning in itself or in isolation but that acquired a meaning in use, that is, in a particular context. Thus, ". . . he . . . spoke of himself as having proved that definite descriptions were incomplete symbols which stood for no 'genuine objects' when he should rather have said that the analysis of descriptions had abolished an apparent proof of the existence of objects designated by any and every description, so that one was left to decide on the merits of each case whether a descriptive phrase stood for anything or not." Russell's position reflected his distinction between knowledge by acquaintance and knowledge by description and his insistence that "Every proposition which we can understand must be composed wholly of constituents with which we are acquainted." Subsequently, "the elimination of logical constructions, carried out by replacing in propositions all incomplete symbols by names of possible objects of acquaintance," was called "new-level, or philosophical (as opposed to logical), or directional, or reductive, analysis." Russell's procedure was the basis for distinguishing between the grammatical form and the logical form of a sentence (recasting it into propositions) to determine its meaning. J. O. Urmson, Philosophical Analysis: Its Development between the Two World Wars (London: Oxford University Press, 1956; paperback edition, 1967), pp. 30, 33, and 39 (quotations).
Russell also regarded classes or class symbols as incomplete symbols and, at one point, "decided that the notion of class could be dispensed with in favor of the concept of propositional function." In this so-called substitutional system (which he later abandoned), "the notation which does the work that class notation usually does is syncategorematic; in other words, the linguistic expressions which do duty for classes { called matrices } have no more meaning of themselves than does a single left-hand parenthesis"; that is, they merely help to define a category. He then distinguished "between the determination of a variable { in a propositional function } by a constant, and the substitution of one constant for another"; ruled out determination; and attempted to base the entire

system on the rule of substitution. "Instead of speaking of 'all values of the variable,' the theory will speak of 'all substitutions for the constant.' " From a current perspective, Russell was "reducing classes to propositions, apparently forgetting that propositions are abstract entities, not linguistic entities, like sentences." Douglas P. Lackey, "Russell's Unknown Theory of Classes: The Substitutional System of 1906," Journal of the History of Philosophy, 14 (January 1976): 70, 71-72, and 75 (quotations). In addition to the "meaninglessness" that emerges logically from the presence of incomplete symbols (or syntactically from the use of pseudo-symbols), Korzybski also identified the mistakes in meaning that emerge psychologically from the process of abstracting from sensory experience. He pointed out that "events are recognized and labeled by the objects situated in them. Obviously an object is not the whole of the event, nor does the label which symbolizes the object cover the whole of the object. It is evident that everytime we mistake the object for the event we are making a serious error, and if we further mistake the label for the object, and therefore for an event, our errors become more serious. . . ." Korzybski, "Fate and Freedom," p. 278.

28. Alfred Korzybski, "The Brotherhood of Doctrines," The Builder: A Journal for Freemasonry, 10 (1924): 105-6.

29. Alfred Korzybski, Time-Binding: The General Theory (Second Paper) (Washington, D.C.: Jas. C. Wood, 1926), pp. 12-13. This paper was an expanded version of one given in 1924 at the International Mathematical Congress in Toronto, Canada. This version was presented before the Washington Society for Nervous and Mental Diseases, June 25, 1925, and the Washington Psychopathological Society, March 13, 1926.

30. Ibid., pp. 13-14.

31. Ibid., pp. 16-17.

32. Ibid., pp. 33 and 22.

33. Ibid., pp. 18 and 22.

34. Ibid., p. 40.

35. Ibid., p. 20.

36. Ibid., p. 4.

37. Ibid., p. 12. See also comment on p. 10.

38. Ibid., pp. 7-9.

39. Ibid., p. 54.

40. Korzybski, Manhood of Humanity, appendix 5, p. 283, n.3.

41. H. Stuart Hughes, Consciousness and Society: The Reorientation of European Social Thought, 1890-1930 (New York: Alfred A.
Knopf, 1958), pp. 397-401.

42. Joergen Joergensen, The Development of Logical Empiricism,
Foundations of the Unity of Science: Toward an International
Encyclopedia of Unified Science, 11, no. 9 (Chicago: University of
Chicago Press, 1951), pp. 3 (the first quotation is from Herbert
Feigl) and 4.

43. Ibid., p. 6.

44. Rudolf Carnap, The Logical Structure of the World and Pseudoproblems in Philosophy, trans. Rolf A. George, (Berkeley: University of California Press, 1967), p. 24.

45. Ibid., pp. 175-246 and 325-31. Carnap's terminology referred
to cultural objects, heteropsychological objects, physical objects,
and autopsychological objects. The whole system rested on one
psychological operation as immediately given - the recollection of
similarity - and defined other concepts on this basis. Carnap
later regarded this procedure as too narrow. For his later modifications and emphasis on logical syntax rather than semantics, see
Ernst Nagel, Logic Without Metaphysics (Glencoe: The Free Press,
1956), pp. 220-41, and W. V. Quine, The Ways of Paradox and Other
Essays, rev. and enlarged ed. (Cambridge: Harvard University Press,
1976), pp. 40-43, 107-32, and 203-11.
Carnap had written The Logical Structure of the World during 1922-
1925 and Pseudoproblems in Philosophy in 1927 when he was involved
in the Vienna Circle discussions and was influenced by Wittgenstein's
Tractatus. The similarities between Carnap's and Korzybski's views
during the 1920s relate to their use of common influences: Russell,
Mach, Frege, and Keyser. The differences between them can be
illustrated by comparing their uses of the analogy between maps
and "reality." While both use the analogy to illustrate structural
relationships, their arguments develop in different ways. Carnap
uses the railroad maps of the Eurasian railroad net for his
illustration. If one map gives only a schematic representation of
the connections or order of stations and if it is too difficult to
observe the actual railroad in its entirety, is it logically
possible to establish the correct identity of the "objects" of the
map by using a second map that gives only the names? In other
words, what are the rules of correspondence to plot such points
accurately? Korzybski, on the other hand, is interested more in
the consequences of noncorrespondence between the map and the
territory and in drawing a philosophical conclusion than he is in
the comparison between maps. See Carnap, Logical Structure, pp.
25-26; Korzybski, Science and Sanity: An Introduction to Non-
Aristotelian Systems and General Semantics, 4th ed. (Lakeville,
Conn.: The Institute of General Semantics, 1958), p. 750-51.
According to A. J. Ayer, "it was{ Otto } Neurath who wrongly per-
suaded Carnap that it was metaphysical to talk of comparing propositions with facts, and so led him for a time to abandon a
correspondence theory of truth in favor of a coherence theory, and

it was owing to Neurath also that Carnap was drawn into materialism, to the point of maintaining that propositions apparently about mental states were re-expressible in wholly physical terms." A. J. Ayer, Part of My Life: The Memoirs of a Philosopher (New York: Harcourt Brace Javanovich, 1977), pp. 130-31.

46. Hanno Hardt, "General Semantics and Scientific Ethics," in Lee Thayer, ed., Communication: General Semantics Perspectives (New York: Spartan Books, 1970), p. 17.

47. William M. Johnston, The Austrian Mind: An Intellectual and Social History, 1848-1938 (Berkeley: University of California Press, 1972), pp. 190-91.

48. According to Anatol Rapoport, Moritz Schlick's philosophy of language was very similar to that of Korzybski's general semantics. Hardt, "General Semantics," p. 17, n.10.

49. J. H. Woodger, "Translator's Preface," in Alfred Tarski, Logic, Semantics, Metamathematics: 1923 to 1938 (London: Oxford University Press, 1956), p. vii.

50. Tadeusz Kotarbiński, "Introduction," in Storrs McCall, ed., Polish Logic: 1920-1939 (London: Oxford University Press, 1967), p. 3. See also Henryk Skolimowski, Polish Analytical Philosophy (New York: Humanities Press, 1967), pp. 56-60.

51. Jan Łukasiewicz, "I. On the Notion of Possibility, II. On Three-Valued Logic," "On Determinism," and "Philosophical Remarks on Many-Valued Systems of Propositional Logic," in Storrs McCall, Polish Logic, pp. 15-65.
Łukasiewicz argued that Aristotle had first formulated the law of bivalence (namely that every proposition is either true or false) and had derived from it an argument in support of determinism. He went on dialectically to refute this argument by arguing that sentences concerning future contingent events are neither true nor false at the present time; hence, Łukasiewicz argued, such propositions are indeterminate (or probable). Chrysippus, an outspoken determinist, held that all propositions are determinate, either true or false, and thus laid the base for a system much like modern propositional logic. See especially pages 36-37 and 64-65. Compare Skolimowski, Polish Analytical Philosophy, pp. 65-67. William and Martha Kneale, The Development of Logic (London: Oxford University Press, 1962), pp. 46-47, accepted Łukasiewicz's reading of Aristotle but noted: "That syllogistic { logic } rather than the {propositional} logic of classes was developed at this stage { of Greek thought } is probably to be explained by the fact that Greek, like English, does not have a single expression for each of the class-relationships, so that the class-logic is difficult to develop without an artificial symbolism, a device which did not occur to logicians for many centuries" (p. 40). They had, in short, only words with which to work.

52. Stanisław Leśniewski, "Introductory Remarks to the Continuation of My Article: 'Grundzüge eines neuen Systems der Grundlagen der Mathematik,' " in Storrs McCall, Polish Logic, particularly pp. 118-19, 128-29, and "On Definitions in the So-Called Theory of Deductions," compare p. 173, n.1 and p.175 n.2.

53. Kazimierz Adjukiewicz, "Syntactic Connexion," in Storrs McCall, Polish Logic, pp. 207 and 220 (emphasis added).
Adjukiewicz noted that ordinary language is richer in semantic categories than the artificial language created by Leśniewski's system, and that "the decision to which semantic category a word belongs is rendered difficult by fluctuations in the meaning of words" (p. 211).
The concept of "semantic category" was introduced by Husserl in his Logische Untersuchungen to account for words or expressions that can be substituted for one another without loss of coherence in a given sentence or "context possessing unified meaning." Such words or expressions are said to be of the same semantic category while words or expressions that create incoherence are said to be of different categories. (Adjukiewicz, p. 208).
Leśniewski's system used two basic semantic categories: sentences and names. The category of names was further divided into individual names and universal names. In addition to the basic categories of names and sentences, there were "functor" categories that served as functional signs and created the hierarchy of logical types. "Thus, for example, the functors which form a sentence with one name as argument would represent a distinct semantic category; the functors which form a sentence with two names as arguments would form a different semantic category, and so forth" (Adjukiewicz, p. 210).
Korzybski adopted Leśniewski's system and used as his two semantic categories names for "objects" and names for relations: ". . . . all language can be considered as names either for unspeakable entities on the objective level, be it things or feelings, or as names for relations" (Korzybski, Science and Sanity, 4th ed., p. 20).

54. Skolimowski, Polish Analytical Philosophy, p. 103.

55. Ibid., p. 93.

56. Ibid., pp. 95-96.

57. Ibid., pp. 98 and 106.
Kotarbiński's early work included a study of utilitarianism in Mill's and Spencer's ethics (1915). Kotarbiński served as president of the Polish Academy of Sciences, 1957-1962. His work in methodology and logic has been a continuing critical influence on the development of social science methodology in Poland. See, for example, Stanisław Ossowski, "Two Conceptions of Historical Generalizations," The Polish Sociological Bulletin, No. 1, (1964), pp. 28-33.
It is important to note in considering the work of Kotarbiński and

Łukasiewicz the relative position of Polish philosophy vis-a-vis European intellectual trends. Henryk Skolimowski has noted that Polish analytical philosophy employed the style of analysis that was methodologically meaningful by virtue of the language in which it was carried out. Whereas phenomenology only conceived of analysis as the penetration of "essences," and existenialism utilized analysis to reveal the "existential dimension," in neither of the two was analysis understood as wholly dependent upon nor intimately related to language. These rival movements based their analysis on personal experience. Polish analytical philosophy, in seeking to base analysis on the universality or generality of linguistic structures, was responding to its own definition or understanding of science as a system of deduction. This was different from the Anglo-American empiricist tradition, which tended to define science as the accumulation of inductively tested hypotheses. Polish analytical philosophy regarded language not just as a means to the end of better communication (a container of ideas or transmitter of messages) or clarity of conception but also as an end, an aim of inquiry (a shaper of ideas or a trans- former of ideas). Perhaps it was only in Catholic Poland that the dream of a deductive, coherent summa lingua could last so long. See Henryk Skolimowski, "Analytical-Linguistic Marxism in Poland," Journal of the History of Ideas, 26 (April-June 1965): 236. For more extensive treatment, see his Polish Analytical Philosophy.

58. Zbigniew A. Jordan, "The Development of Mathematical Logic in Poland between the Two Wars," in Storrs McCall, Polish Logic, pp. 352-53.

59. Ibid., pp. 386-87 (quotations) and 388. See also Leon Chwistek, "Antinomies of Formal Logic," in Storrs McCall, Polish Logic, pp. 338-45, and Skolimowski, Polish Analytical Philosophy, pp. 201-5.

60. Korzybski, Science and Sanity, 4th ed., p. 750-51. The material has been arranged in parallel columns and condensed to illustrate the analogy.

61. Ibid., pp. 750-52.

62. Ibid., pp. 752-53. "A { multiordinal } term represents a variable in general, and becomes constant or one-valued in a given context, its value being given by that context. Here we find the main importance of the semantic fact established by Skarżenski { as quoted by Chwistek }, that the 'logical' freedom from contradiction becomes a semantic problem of one- value." Ibid., pp. 753-54.

63. Ibid., pp. 754 (quotation) { emphasis added } and 758 (exten- sional definitions). As F. S. C. Northrop has observed, when Korz- ybski attacked Aristotelian thinking, he was attacking the confused notion "that the relatedness of axiomatically constructed scienti- fic objects is the relatedness of inductively given, concept of intuition, sensed relations." The mathematical world of postulates is related to the experiential world of perception by "rules of

correspondence," which are the epistemological relations between two semantically different worlds of discourse.

64. Ibid., p. 761 and Northrup, Man, Nature and God, p. 86 (quotation) and 88-89.

65. While Polish logicians and analytical philosophers in the inter-war period developed intricate systems of formal semantics, Polish poets continued the tradition of semantic exploration and symbolism that had characterized the Young Poland poets. As Czesław Miłosz has noted in The History of Polish Literature (London: Collier-Macmillan, 1969), Julian Tuwim (1894-1953) was "somewhat akin to Leśmian" in his "sensual, amorous relationship with word stems" and his "pervasive dream of a word so intense that it would be one with the thing it designated" (p. 387). Mieczysław Jastrun (1903-) "was a writer who had an affinity for {Cyprian} Norwid's thought" (p. 408). Stanisław Ignacy Witkiewicz (1885-1939) was a philosopher who was critical of philosophers because they "behaved like the fox who pronounced the grapes to be sour because they were too high. They proceeded to explain away metaphysical problems as illusory notions imposed by the structure of language. Witkiewicz detested Logical Positivists, but he also was an enemy of Bergson, who preferred intuition to intellect, and of the Pragmatists and Marxists because instead of a search for ontological truth they extolled ethics" (p. 415). Witkiewicz turned to drama where his protean creativity was reminiscent of Wyspiański.
For the subsequent career of Julian Tuwim and his struggle with the question of how to preserve the Polish language in wartime, see Madeline G. Levine, "Orpheus in Exile: Some Reflections on Tuwim's Kwiaty Polskie," in Victor Erlich, et al., For Wiktor Weintraub: Essays in Polish Literature, Language, and History (The Hague: Mouton, 1975), pp. 267-75.

3. SCIENCE AND SANITY: A HISTORICAL CRITIQUE

1. Alfred Korzybski, Science and Sanity: An Introduction to Non-Aristotelian Systems and General Semantics, 4th ed. (Lakeville, Conn.: Institute of General Semantics, 1958), pp. 92-94. Korzybski used a series of abbreviations and special punctuation marks that owed much to mathematical and symbolic logic but that were also reminiscent of Wyspiański's experimentation (see Chapter 1). For sake of brevity, these abbreviations have been, in most instances, spelled out in brackets { } within the quotations. For Korzybski's system, see Science and Sanity, pp. 15-16.
The reference to Alfred Tarski and Jan Łukasiewicz in Korzybski's list of accepted premises was to their joint article "Untersuchungen über den Aussagenkalkül (Investigations into the Sentential Calculus)," Comptes Rendus des séances de la Société des Sciences et des Lettres de Varsovie, 23 (1930):30-50. He credited them with the development of a many-valued "logic of probability." But, as Tarski pointed out later, "some scholars mistakenly referred to both authors, Łukasiewicz and Tarski, the many-valued

systems of logic ascribed in the article to Łukasiewicz alone. In
spite of a correction which appeared in 1933 in the Journal of
Philosophy, vol. 30, p. 364, this mistake persists till today."
Alfred Tarski, Logic, Semantics, Metamathematics: Papers from 1923
to 1938, trans. J. H. Woodger, (London: Oxford University Press,
1956), p. 38. The only other reference to Tarski in the bibliography to Science and Sanity was a listing of Tarski's 1930 paper,
"Fundamentale Bergriffe der Methodologie der deduktiven Wissen-
schaften. I (Fundamental Concepts of the Methodology of the
Deductive Sciences)," Monatshefte für Mathematik und Physik, 37
(1930): 361-404. Nonetheless, Korzybski praised Łukasiewicz and
Tarski repeatedly for a many-valued logic that was non-Aristotelian
but still criticized it as "elementalistic." Science and Sanity,
p. 748. Interestingly, Tarski's famous 1931 paper on "The Concept
of Truth in Formalized Languages" developed a semantic theory of
truth. As D. J. O'Connor has summarized his position, Tarski
accepted Aristotle's correspondence theory of truth, but restricted
it to sentences. The sentence is true if what it asserts about
the world is, in fact, the case. "The sentence itself says something
about the world; but to say that the sentence is true is to say
something about the sentence." Furthermore, as to semantics, "the
meaning of sentences for Tarski is not a matter of their content
but rather of their structure. A sentence is meaningful if it has
a place in a formal system in virtue of the fact that it has been
constructed in accordance with the formation rules of the system."
D. J. O'Connor, The Correspondence Theory of Truth (London: Hutch-
inson University Library, 1975), pp. 92 and 105. In Northrop's
terms, Tarski's semantics would be closer to concepts by postulation and would slight concepts by intuition. I believe that this
is the sense of Korzybski's 1947 statement that "Tarski has
nothing to do with my work." Robert P. Pula, "Korzybski's Polish
Matrix," General Semantics Bulletin, no. 47 (1980): 44. Compare
Stuart Mayper, "Tarskian Metalanguages and Korzybskian Abstracting."
General Semantics Bulletin, no. 46 (1979): 26-53.
For Russell's early theory of truth and his concept of semantics,
see A. J. Ayer, Russell and Moore: The Analytical Heritage
(Cambridge: Harvard University Press, 1971), chapters 3 and 4.

2. Korzybski, Science and Sanity, pp. 748-50 and 760 (quotations).

3. William and Martha Kneale, The Development of Logic (London:
Oxford University Press, 1962), pp. 46-47.

4. Jan Łukasiewicz, Aristotle's Syllogistic, 2d ed. (London:
Oxford University Press, 1957), pp. 1-7 (quotation).

5. Ibid., pp. 45 and 47-48 (quotation). { emphasis added }.

6. Ibid., pp. 149 and 151.

7. Ibid., pp. 88-89, for example; and Kneale and Kneale, Development of Logic, pp. 80-91.

8. Korzybski, Science and Sanity, pp. 374-80.

9. Hermann J. Cloeren, "The Neglected Analytical Heritage,"
Journal of the History of Ideas, 36 (July-September 1975): 523-24.
Gruppe was cited favorably by Hans Vaihinger, Philosophy of As If
(New York: Harcourt, Brace and Co., 1924), a work included by
Korzybski in the bibliography to Science and Sanity.   Interestingly,
"Gruppe holds that the period of system-making is the time of the
childhood of philosophy, while { analytical} investigation charac-
terizes its manhood."   Friedrich Ueberweg, History of Philosophy:
From Thales to the Present Time, 4th ed., trans. George S. Morris
(New York: Charles Scribner's Sons, 1901), II: 324.

10. Alfred Korzybski, "The Role of Language in the Perceptual
Process," General Semantics Bulletin, 36 (1969): 15-49.   The essay
was originally published in an anthology in 1951.   Wittgenstein,
too, noted in the Tractatus that{ 3.323 }" in the language of
everyday life it very often happens that the same word signifies
in two different ways - and therefore belongs to two different
symbols - or that two words, which signify in different ways, are
apparently applied in the same way in the proposition.
Thus the word 'is' appears as the copula, as the sign of equality,
and as the expression of existence; . . ."   He concluded{ 3:325 }."
In order to avoid these errors, we must employ a symbolism which
excludes them, by not applying the same sign in different symbols
and by not applying signs in the same way which signify in
different ways. {What we need is } a symbolism . . . which obeys
the rules of logical grammar - of logical syntax. . . ."
In the Notebooks: 1914-1916, Wittgenstein made the Korzybski
sounding observation{ 3.10.14 } that "The name is not a picture of
the thing named!"   The way in which this idea was developed, however, was different, and it is best explained in David Keyt,
"Wittgenstein's Picture Theory of Language," The Philosophical
Review, 73 (1964): 493-511.

11. Korzybski, Science and Sanity, pp.lxxxiv and 194.   Robert P.
Pula has argued that "what Korzybski seems {to be} saying . . . is
that 'identity,' neuro-physiologically and neuro-linguistically,
not only is 'false to facts' if it asserts or implies 'absolute
sameness in all aspects' but that 'identity' is false to facts if it
formulates absolute sameness in any aspect.   All 'samenesses' are
merely formulational - sometimes restrictively useful but 'invar-
iably false to facts.'"   Robert P. Pula, "Knowledge, Uncertainty
and Courage: Heisenberg and Korzybski," Methodology and Science,
10 (1977): 160.   Korzybski also held that the principle (or premise)
that anything was identical with itself was also false to facts.
Science and Sanity, p. 194.   Ladislav Tondl, the Czech semanticist,
has pointed out that "Wittgenstein in his Tractatus { 5.5302 }
claims that Russell's definition of the sign '=' is insufficient,
because in the sense of that definition it cannot be said that two
objects have all properties in common.   In another theorem he adds
that "Von zwei Dingen zu sagen, sie seiden identisch, ist ein Unsinn,
und von Einem zu sagen, es sei identisch mit sich selbst, sagt gar
nichts" (theorem 5.5303). {"To say of two things that they are

identical is nonsense, and to say of one thing that it is identical
with itself is to say nothing." } Ladislav Tondl, Problems of
Semantics, trans. David Short (Boston: D. Reidel Publishing Co.,
1981), p. 376 n.15. Earlier, Frege had described what he called
the "paradox of identity" in his youthful Begriffsschrift (1879).
On the assumption that identity related denoted objects, he concluded that identity sentences of the type a=a and true identity
sentences of the type a=b could not differ in cognitive content;
therefore, the object denoted would stand in relationship to itself,
an obvious paradox since "everything is self-identical." Richard
L. Mendelsohn, "Frege's Begriffsschrift Theory of Identity,"
Journal of the History of Philosophy, 20 (July 1982): 279-99.
Whereas Frege and Wittgenstein rejected self-identity on logical
grounds, Korzybski rejected it on empirio-critical (false to facts)
grounds.

12. Milič Čapek, "Ernst Mach's Biological Theory of Knowledge,"
Boston Studies in the Philosophy of Science, vol. 5 (Dordrecht,
Holland: D. Reidel, 1969), pp. 409 (quotation) and 410-17 (quotation on p. 411). Čapek noted that the Polish author, Zygmunt
Zawirski, in his L'Evolution de la notion du temps (Cracow, 1934)
saw that Poincaré's indeterminism was close to Mach and Bergson in
its assumption that "reality cannot be both successively unfolding
{ becoming} and timelessly complete { being } ." That is, "becoming and indetermination are complementary aspects of the same
basic fact - the temporal incompleteness of the world" (p. 417).
Korzybski's debt to Ernst Mach is evident in the chapter on perception and abstraction in Science and Sanity, chapter 25.   Particularly important was Mach's conception of phenomenalism, which
attempted to avoid the dualism of mind and matter. As Robert S.
Cohen has noted, "the evidence for the material--things or events--
is displayed before us by observation, and the evidence for the
mental likewise." Such observational data is immediate rather
than inferential. Furthermore, "observational evidence for material
events is identical with that for mental events of other persons:
we might talk the sensation language of colors, sounds, smells;
or of the mathematical language of spaces, times, shapes; or of a
thing language of bodies, pressures, temperatures." Science defined entities by a mixture of such languages that stood for the
"colors, sounds, spaces, and times" that constituted the elements
of reality. Thus, "in Mach's well-known phrases, 'bodies do not
produce sensations, but complexes of elements make up bodies . . .
all bodies are but thought-symbols for complexes of elements.' And
in another passage, 'sensations are not signs of things; but, on
the contrary, a thing is a thought-symbol for a compound-sensation
of relative fixedness.' " Robert S. Cohen, "Ernst Mach: Physics,
Perception and the Philosophy of Science," Boston Studies in the
Philosophy of Science, vol. 6 (Dordrecht, Holland: P. Reidel, 1970),
pp. 130-31.

13. Korzybski, Science and Sanity, chapter 28.

14. Ibid., p. 413.

15. L. S. Vygotsky, Thought and Language, trans. Eugenia Hanfmann and Gertrude Vakar (Cambridge: MIT Press, 1962), p. 16.

16. Alfred Korzybski, Time-Binding: The General Theory (Second Paper) (Washington, D.C.: Jas. C. Wood, 1926), pp. 12 and 33. In Science and Sanity, he made extensive reference to S. E. Jelliffe on neurology and child development, pp.(493-99) and to Pavlov on conditioned reflexes, (pp. 315-19). Smith Ely Jelliffe had been a botanist, pharmacologist, neurologist, and an early advocate of Freudian psychoanalysis who, nevertheless, remained skeptical about the emphasis on sex in Freud's theories. In an influencial text book, co-authored with William Alanson White, Jelliffe held that "the nervous system was organized according to evolutionary principles from the older and simpler levels to the newer, more complex and mote integrated. The simplest and oldest system was the 'vegetative' or autonomic and sympathetic nervous system, . . . ; next, was the sensori-motor system of the brain and spinal cord, the traditional province of neurology; finally came the psychic or symbolic level, the province of psychoanalysis. Each level increased integration in the service of broadly defined goals for both the individual and the race." Nathan G. Hale, Jr., Freud and the Americans: The Beginnings of Psychoanalysis in the United States, 1876-1917 (New York: Oxford University Press, 1971), I, pp. 443-44. See also Noland D. C. Lewis, "Smith Ely Jelliffe: The Man and Scientist," Journal of Nervous and Mental Disease, 106 (1947): 234-40.

17. Vygotsky, Thought and Language, p. 5.

18. Ibid., pp. 121 and 124. For Piaget's theory, see Jean Piaget, Six Psychological Studies, trans. Anita Tenzer (New York: Vintage Books, 1968), pp. 88-98.

19. Vygotsky, Thought and Language, p. 151. Vygotsky had concluded that, because of its sociohistorical character, verbal thought was "subject to all the premises of historical materialism." However, he had tread on dangerous ground in his treatment of consciousness; his book was officially suppressed by the Soviet authorities in 1936. See Jerome S. Bruner, "Introduction," Vygotsky, Thought and Language, p. vi; and Michael Cole and Sylvia Scribner "Introduction" in L. S. Vygotsky, Mind in Society: The Development of Higher Psychological Processes (Cambridge: Harvard University Press, 1978), pp. 1-14.

20. A. H. Chapman, Harry Stack Sullivan: His Life and His Work (New York: G. P. Putnam's Sons, 1976), p. 38. For William Alanson White, see S. P. Fullinwider, Technicians of the Finite: The Rise and Decline of the Schizophrenic in American Thought, 1840-1960 (Westport, Conn.: Greenwood Press, 1982), chapter 5.

21. William Alan White, "The Language of Schizophrenia," Archives of Neurology and Psychiatry, 16 (1926): 395-413, as quoted by Harold J. Vetter, Language, Behavior and Psychopathology (Chicago:

Rand McNally and Co., 1969), p.4; and Chapman, Sullivan, pp. 38-39. White had drawn heavily from A. Storch, Das Archaisch-Primitive Erleben und Denken der Schizophrenen { The Primitive Archaic Forms of Inner Experiences and Thought in Schizophrenia } (Berlin: Springer, 1923). Korzybski included both White and Storch in the bibliography to Science and Sanity.

22. Chapman, Sullivan, p. 36. Sullivan's writings from the 1920s are reprinted in Harry Stack Sullivan, Schizophrenia as a Human Process (New York: W. W. Norton and Company, 1962). For Sullivan's background and his relations with White, see Helen Swick Perry, Psychiatrist of America: The Life of Harry Stack Sullivan (Cambridge: Harvard University Press, 1982), chapters 21-22; Fullinwider, Technicians of the Finite, chapter 6.

23. Korzybski, Time Binding, p. 9. Sullivan had "coined the Freudian-like term 'preconcept' (which he later abandoned) to designate structures of thought arising from experience prior to birth to explain some of the phenomena found in the schizophrenic process. . . . Much of this thinking came to be subsumed in Sullivan's later theory of under what he called the prototaxic mode of experience." Helen Swick Perry, "Commentary" in Sullivan, Schizophrenia as a Human Process, p.4. See also pp. 9-10, n.2.

24. Korzybski, Science and Sanity, pp. 184-85. In another passage, Korzybski noted that "the natural survival order is 'senses' first, 'mind' next; object first, label next; description first, inference next. { The unnatural, pathological reversal had symptoms in which } objectivity is ascribed to words, 'mind' projected into 'senses,' inferences evaluated as descriptions . . ." (p.317).

25. Ibid., pp. 358-61. Technically speaking, Korzybski acknowledged that the neurological mechanism behind the therapy, the "delayed reflex," was the discovery of Dr. Zavadzki, a coworker in Pavlov's laboratory.

26. Ibid., p. 387

27. Ibid.

28. The problem of the relationship of the levels of abstraction and the objects contained in them, (rules of correspondence or "epistemic correlations" in Northrops terms) and their meanings, was included in Korzybski's concept of structure. "To 'be' means to be related," he noted. "To be related involves multi-dimensional order and results in structure." Therefore, "if we trace a given doctrine with specific content to its doctrinal function without content, but variable terms, then, only, do we obtain a set of postulates which gives us the linguistic structure." Korzybski; Science and Sanity, pp. 144 and 161. The meaning of a statement was both the objects to which it pointed (which were patterns of stimuli in a particular order or sequence) and the position it occupied in a propositionally determined linguistic structure (its

relationships).
Kazimierz Ajdukiewicz (1890-1963), a Polish logician, argued, on
the other hand, that the formulation of a correct relationship between the expressions of a language and the objects with which these
expressions are concerned seemed to be blocked by the paradox of
the liar and other antimonies. He rejected any denoting theory and
looked for the rules which determine meaningful discourse in any
given language. These rules were of three kinds: (1) axiomatic,
rules that must be accepted in all circumstances; (2) deductive,
rules that connect sentences in such a way that if we accept one
it necessarily implies the acceptance of the other; and (3) empirical, rules that determine in certain situations that we must
use certain expressions in order not to violate the language itself.
Leon Chwistek (1884-1944), another Polish logician-philosopher, also
elaborated an aesthetic hierarchy of realities similar to
Korzybski's levels of abstraction. Chwistek distinguished (1)
everyday reality, (2) physical reality (as constructed by physics),
(3) sensory reality, and (4) visionary reality, including dreams,
hallucinations, and other extrasensory states.
See Henryk Skolimowski, _Polish Analytical Philosophy_ (New York:
Humanities Press, 1967), pp. 139-45 and 201-05.

29. Korzybski, _Science and Sanity_, pp. 389 (quotation) and 392.

30. _Ibid._, p. 392.

31. _Ibid._, p. 399.

32. _Ibid._, pp. 416-18. The emphasis on mime is reminiscent of
Wyspiański's theatrical techniques.

33. _Ibid._, p. 421.

34. _Ibid._, p. 448.

35. Harry Stack Sullivan, "Schizophrenia: Its Conservative and
Malignant Features," _American Journal of Psychiatry_, 81 (1924-1925):
77-91, reprinted in Sullivan, _Schizophrenia as a Human Process_, pp.
7-22. Quotation on p. 13.

36. Harry Stack Sullivan, "Peculiarity of Thought in Schizophrenia,"
American Journal of Psychiatry, 82 (1925-1926): 21-86, reprinted in
Sullivan, _Schizophrenia as a Human Process_, pp. 26-99. Quotation
on p. 32.

37. Sullivan, _Schizophrenia as a Human Process_, p. 89 (quotation).

38. Sullivan, "Schizophrenia: Its Conservative and Malignant
Features," in Sullivan, _Schizophrenia as a Human Process_, pp. 9-10
(quotation).

39. Chapman, _Sullivan_, p. 44. A successful psychoanalytic cure in
the 1930s of a schizophrenic patient by a Freudian psychoanalyst

was reported in M. A. Sechehaye, Symbolic Realization: A New Method of Psychotherapy Applied to a Case of Schizophrenia, trans. Barbo Würsten and Helmut Würsten (New York: International Universities Press, Inc., 1951). Madame Sechehaye started with the assumption that the patient's symbolizations represented a regression to the developmental level of thought and language at the time of trauma (in this case, a very infantile level) and that the therapist must deal with the symptoms and symbols at that level (by "word magic" games) rather than by the usual technique of relating the symbols to a "rational" structure of "logical" explanation. "I could not make her unconsciously understand me except through images," she reported. "I had to speak her language and use her signs" (p. 138). Like Sullivan, Sechehaye also asked, "What is the relation . . . of the illness to the patient's personality?" and treated the persona- lity deficiencies as well as the mental illness (p. 14). For a current professional opinion on the issue of psychoanalysis and schizophrenia, see Dorothy Tennor, Psychotherapy: The Hazardous Cove (New York: Abelard-Schuman, 1975), pp. 108-11. For the re- jection of the regression theory of schizophrenia, see Vetter, Language, Behavior and Psychopathology, p. 5, n.1 and chapter 10.

40. Harry Stack Sullivan, "The Modified Psychoanalytic Treatment of Schizophrenia," American Journal of Psychiatry, 88 (1931-1932): 519-40, reprinted in Sullivan, Schizophrenia as a Human Process, pp. 272-94.

41. Chapman, Sullivan, pp. 45-46.

42. Ibid., pp. 168-69 and 171. On consensual validation, see Harry Stack Sullivan, Conceptions of Modern Psychiatry (New York: W. W. Norton & Company, Inc., 1953), pp. 34-37.

43. C. Wright Mills, Power, Politics and People (New York: Ballan- tine Books, 1963), pp. 426 and 428, 429 (quotations); compare pp. 458-59. See also Perry, Psychiatrist of America, chapters 27-29. Sullivan later refined Mead's "generalized other" into a broader "significant others" theory of personality development. "Now as to the psychic processes whereby these 'significant others' become an actual part of the personality, it may be said that the very sense of 'self' first emerges in connection with anxiety about the attitudes of the most important persons in one's life (initially, the mother, father, and their surrogates . . .), and automatic attempts are set in motion to adjust to these attitudes." Stanley M. Elkins, Slavery: A Problem in American Institutional and In- tellectual Life (New York: Universal Library, 1963), p. 120.

44. Korzybski, Science and Sanity, part 9 and 10. On the issue of the semantic implications of modern physics, see Ernest H. Hutten, The Language of Modern Physics (New York: Macmillan Company, 1956); L. Pearce Williams, ed., Relativity Theory: Its Origins and Impact on Modern Thought (New York: John Wiley and Sons, Inc., 1968), part 4; Peter Havas, "Causality Requirements and the Theory of Relativity," Boston Studies in the Philosophy of Science, 5

(1966-1968): 151-78; and Werner Heisenberg, Physics and Philosophy (New York: Harper and Row, 1958).

45.   Korzybski, Science and Sanity, p. 430.

46.   Ibid., p. 431. To what extent was Korzybski influenced by Wittgenstein's Tractatus Logico-Philosophicus (first published in 1922)? There was no mention of Wittgenstein in either of Korzybski's early essays published in 1923 and 1924. Nor was there any reference to him in the 1931 paper that Korzybski read to the American Mathematical Society (reprinted as an appendix in Science and Sanity). Russell is mentioned frequently, however, and it may have been through Russell that Korzybski encountered Wittgenstein's ideas. The first reference to Wittgenstein in Science and Sanity is a quotation from Russell's introduction to the Tractatus that serves as a prefatory quote for part 2 of Science and Sanity: ". . . every language has, as Mr. Wittgenstein says, a structure concerning which, in the language, nothing can be said, but that there may be another language dealing with the structure of the first language, and having itself a new structure, and that to this hierarchy of languages there may be no limit. Mr. Wittgenstein would of course reply that his whole theory is applicable unchanged to the totality of such languages. The only retort would be to deny that there is any such totality" (Science and Sanity, p. 53).
The ensuing chapter opened with a brief discussion of the concept of structure, and noted: "The term 'structure' is frequently used in modern scientific literature, but, to the best of my knowledge, only Bertrand Russell and Wittgenstein have devoted serious attention to this problem, and much remains to be done." And again: " 'Structure' is analyzed in Principia Mathematica and is also simply explained in Russell's more popular works. The Tractatus of Wittgenstein is built on structural considerations, although not much is explained about structure, for the author apparently assumes the reader's acquaintance with the works of Russell" (Science and Sanity, p. 56).
Only two other quotations by Wittgenstein appeared in Science and Sanity. In the prefatory quotations to book 2, Korzbyski also included Tractatus proposition 4.1212: "What can be shown cannot be said" (Science and Sanity, p. 368). In the chapter on higher order abstractions, Korzybski discussed Russell's theory of types, vicious-circle fallacies, and confusions of orders of abstractions. He concluded: "A set of statements or objects or elements, or the like, and a statement about them belong to different orders of abstractions and should not be confused. . . . In the language of Wittgenstein: 'No proposition can say anything about itself, because the propositional sign cannot be contained in itself (that is the 'whole theory of types')' " {Tractatus 3.332 }(Science and Sanity, p. 431).
These are slim threads on which to weave a web of connections between Wittgenstein's thought and Korzybski's writings. The connecting link is Russell. But as G.E.M. Anscombe and William Warren Bartley III have pointed out, Russell was imbued with British empiricism and read an empiricist epistemology into his

introduction to Wittgenstein's Tractatus. Wittgenstein, on the other hand, was influenced by Schopenhauer's "world as idea" and Frege's logical theories. Thus, Wittgenstein was doubly misunderstood by British empiricists and by Viennese logical positivists. If Korzybski viewed Wittgenstein through lenses ground by Russell (as the quotes from Science and Sanity would seem to indicate), then Korzybski's understanding of Wittgenstein's theories would be incomplete.

See G.E.M. Anscombe, An Introduction to Wittgenstein's Tractatus (Philadelphia: University of Pennsylvania Press, 1971), pp. 12 and 14; William Warren Bartley III, Wittgenstein (Philadelphia: J. B. Lippincott, 1973), pp. 67-68 and 73.

On Korzybski's debt to the Vienna Circle and logical positivism, a similar conclusion is in order. While there are similarities and parallels between the two positions, there is little evidence in Korzybski's writings of direct borrowings or influences. Of the ten members of the Vienna Circle mentioned in Hanno Hardt, "General Semantics and Scientific Ethics" in Lee Thayer, ed., Communication: General Semantics Perspectives (New York: Spartan Books, 1970), pp. 15-21, only three are mentioned in the bibliography to Science and Sanity (Carnap, Menger, and Schlick). Both Korzybski and the Vienna Circle were influenced by the same sources, particularly Ernst Mach, but they developed along separate lines.

47. Korzybski, Science and Sanity, p. 432.

48. Ayer, Russell and Moore, pp. 12-15 and 28 (quotation).

49. Ayer, Russell and Moore, pp. 32 and 33.

50. C. I. Lewis, A Survey of Symbolic Logic (Berkeley: University of California Press, 1918), as quoted by Korzybski, Science and Sanity, p. 173. For Northrop's discussion, see chapter 2.

51. Korzybski, Science and Sanity, p. 174. Korzybski noted: "It seems evident that the extroverted and introverted tendencies have some connection with extensional and intensional types of reaction; but, of course, they are not identical. They influence the individual in the selection of a profession, and in the preference for some special trend of activity" (Science and Sanity, p. 176).

52. Ibid., p. 179.

53. Ayer, Russell and Moore pp. 47-48 (emphasis added).

54. Ibid., chapters 3 and 4; Justus Hartnack, Wittgenstein and Modern Philosophy (Garden City, New York: Doubleday and Company, Inc., 1965), part 4. Otto Friedrich Gruppe in the nineteenth century had also rejected a denoting theory of language. See Cloeren, "The Neglected Analytical Heritage," p. 523.

55. Korzybski, Science and Sanity, p. 561.

56. Korzybski, "The Role of Perception in the Perceptual Process,"

as reprinted in General Semantics Bulletin, no. 36 (1969): 28.
Some of the opacity of Korzybski's prose may also be related to
his Polish background. As Danuta Irena Bieńkowska has pointed out,
generations of Polish writers had to learn how to live with the
impact of censorship. "Writers had to disguise their thoughts in
such a way that they would be palatable to the censors but compre-
hensible to the readers." Danuta Irena Bieńkowska, "An Analytical
Study of the Early Literary Work of Stefan Żeromski, Its Cultural
Background and Its Critical Reception in Poland," Antemurale, 16
(1972): 202. Such habits of caution and circumlocution would have
been quite common in the Polish intellectual milieu of Korzybski's
youth. In addition, there is the question of the structural
differences between linguistic families of languages and culturally
conditioned modes of thought. Robert P. Pula has noted that Frank
B. Hartman, " 'detected' the 'Polish' character of Science and
Sanity after 1956 and wrote about it in a letter to M. Kendig in
1970." Pula, "Korzybski's Polish Matrix," p. 45.

4. IDEOLOGY AND PRAXIS: GENERAL SEMANTICS AND ANALYTICAL PHILOSOPHY
    IN AMERICA AND POLAND, 1930s-1960s

1. Ernest Nagel, "Books in Brief," New Republic, 79 (August 1,
1934): 327; and "Mr. Nagel Answers," 81 (December 26, 1934): 195.

2. Lewis S. Feuer, "From Ideology to Philosophy: Sidney Hook's
Writings on Marxism," In Paul Kurtz, ed., Sidney Hook and the
Contemporary World: Essays on the Pragmatic Intelligence (New York:
John Day Company, 1968), pp. 35-53.

3. Sidney Hook, "The Nature of Discourse," The Saturday Review of
Literature, 10 (March 10, 1934): 546-47. Hook was particularly
critical of Korzybski's affinity for Oswald Spengler: "What appeals
to him is Spengler's conception of morphological determinism, the
view that every culture is organic through and through, and that to
understand anything about a civilization we must understand
everything about it. This notion is a mystical vulgarization of
Hegel's theory of objective Mind. Korzybski holds to an even more
thorough-going morphological cultural determinism than either
Spengler or Hegel, but whereas these latter two were consistent
and postulated a spiritualistic metaphysic as the source of the
pattern of the culture, Korzybski cannot follow them, for this is
precisely what his semantic philosophy forbids."
Korzybski was indeed indebted to Spengler's The Decline of the West
and had summarized Spengler's main contention in Science and Sanity
as follows: ". . . the behaviour of the organisms called humans is
such that, at different periods, they have produced definite
aggregates of achievements, which we dissect and label 'science,'
'mathematics,' 'architecture,' 'sculpture,' 'music,' and that at
any given period all these achievements are interconnected by a
psycho-logical necessity." But while he agreed with Spengler in
general, Korzybski nevertheless felt that there were differences
in detail and in method between them. Spengler had overlooked the
notions that mathematics was a language and that the structures of

language (including mathematics) are also interconnected with the
other expressions of culture. Furthermore, Spengler was an
anthropologist who dealt only with morphology. "Morphology means
'study of forms,' " Korzybski noted, "which carries static
implications. Taken from the dynamic point of view 1933, when we
know that the dynamic unit, out of which the world and ourselves
appear to be built, is found in the dynamic atom of 'action'; his
'form' becomes four-dimensional dynamic structure, the equivalent
of 'function'; and then the whole outlook of Spengler becomes a
structural enquiry into the world of man, including all his
activities." In short, properly understood, Spengler's morphology
of cultural forms was a preface to Korzybski's analysis of the
psycho-logical foundations of semantic reactions.
Alfred Korzybski, Science and Sanity: An Introduction to Non-
Aristotelian Systems and General Semantics, 4th ed. (Lakeville,
Conn.: Institute of General Semantics, 1958), p. 48. In the
preface to the third edition of Science and Sanity published in
1948, Korzybski noted: "Some readers do not like what I said about
Spengler. It is perhaps because they did not read carefully . . . .
In my honest judgment, he gave 'a great description of the child-
hood of humanity,' which he himself did out outgrow." p. xx, n.
The problem, of course, was that by the 1940s Spengler had, in
the minds of Americans, been identified with the rise of Nazism
and blamed for their pathological behavior. See H. Stuart Hughes,
Oswald Spengler: A Critical Estimate (New York: Charles Scribner's
Sons, 1952), chapters 8 and 9.
An English translation of volume one of The Decline of the West
had been published in the United States by Alfred A. Knopf in
1926 and of volume two in 1928. Korzybski included them in the
bibliography of Science and Sanity.

4. Richard J. Bernstein, Praxis and Action: Contemporary
Philosophies of Human Activity (Philadelphia: University of
Pennsylvania Press, 1971), p. 168. On the similarities between
Hook's philosophy and positivism, see Milton R. Konvitz, "Sidney
Hook: Philosopher of Freedom" in Kurtz, Sidney Hook and the
Contemporary World, pp. 17-27. On Dewey and the positivist's
theory of meaning, see Paul Wienpahl, "Dewey's Theory of Language
and Meaning," in Sidney Hook, ed., John Dewey: Philosopher of
Science and Freedom, reprint (New York: Barnes and Noble, Inc.,
1967), pp. 271-88. On the verifiability criterion of meaning in
logical positivism, see Joergen Joergensen, The Development of
Logical Empiricism (Chicago: University of Chicago Press, 1951),
pp. 71-76.
On the criticism of Korzybski's formal ideas that preoccupied his
reviewers, Sidney Hook argued that "Mr. Korzybski's attack on the
law of identity { in Aristotelianism} is an attack on a straw
man...." The law of identity had been variously interpreted
since Aristotle and even Korzybski used it at times. No one
really believed it in the form Korzybski criticized--namely,
absolute identity in all aspects. "Things can never be identical
with each other," Hook noted, "but they can be identical in
respect to their inclusion in the same class or in respect to their

possession of the same property. Science would be impossible if
this were not recognized." Hook, "Nature of Discourse," p. 546.
E. T. Bell, the mathematician, and Cassius Keyser, in separate
reviews, supported Korzybski's position on eliminating the "is" of
identity, at least as far as the foundations of mathematics were
concerned. See Cassius Keyser's review of Science and Sanity in
Scripta Mathematica, 2 (1934): 247-60 and E. T. Bell, in American
Mathematical Monthly, 41 (1934): 571, n.2 and 571-73.
See also E. L. Gates, "Keyser and Korzybski: On Keyser's 'Queries,
Doubts, and Reservations' about Science and Sanity: Identity and
Identification Discussed," General Semantics Bulletin, nos. 26-27
(1960): 105-08; and Oliver L. Reiser, "Modern Science and Non-
Aristotelian Logic," The Monist, 46 (July 1936): 299-317.

5. Korzybski, Science and Sanity, pp. xxv-vi (introduction to
second edition).

6. Vida Ravenscroft Sutton, "The Script of the 'Speaking Press,' "
Education, 57 (September 1936): 21-26.

7. R. Alan Lawson, The Failure of Independent Liberalism, 1930-
1941 (New York: G. P. Putnam's Sons, 1971), p. 221. See also
Richard H. Pells, Radical Visions and American Dreams: Culture and
Social Thought in the Depression Years (New York: Harper and Row,
1973), chapter 7; Donald L. Miller, The New American Radicalism:
Alfred M. Bingham and Non-Marxian Insurgency in the New Deal Era
(Port Washington, N.Y.: Kennikat Press, 1979); and William Barrett,
The Truants: Adventures among the Intellectuals (Garden City, N.Y.:
Doubleday, 1982).

8. Pells, Radical Visions and American Dreams, pp. 322-28. Pells
called attention to the "discovery" of the importance of symbolism,
myths, and the function of emotions in political affairs by social
scientists in the late 1930s, particularly the Lynds, Harold
Lasswell, and Thurmond Arnold. "Divorced from their radical
premises, . . . the fascination with symbolism and propaganda
could have quite conservative implications" (p. 323). For the
original Chase articles and De Voto's rebuttal, see Stuart Chase,
"The Tyranny of Words," Harpers, 175 (November 1937): 561-69;
"Word-Trouble among the Economists," Harpers, 176 (December 1937):
48-58; and "Word-Trouble among the Statesmen," Harpers, 176
(January 1938): 149-57; Bernard De Voto, "Good and Wicked Words,"
Harpers, 176 (January 1938): 221-24.

9. "The Tyranny of Semantics," Christian Century, 55 (March 9,
1938): 296-97. Compare J. M. Gillis, "Craze: Semantics," Catholic
World, 146 (March 9, 1938): 646-49; S. I. Hayakawa, "The Meaning of
Semantics," The New Republic, 99 (August 2, 1939): 354.
10. "General Semantics," Time, 32 (November 21, 1938): 34-35.
The Institute of General Semantics was organized in May 1938 and
was located in an apartment building at 1330 East 56th Street in
Chicago. A year later, the institute moved to 1234 East 56th
Street, a few blocks from the University of Chicago. This site
it occupied until 1946 when the institute moved to Lakeville,

Connecticut. See photos in General Semantics Bulletin, no. 3
(Spring 1950): 28.

11. John P. Diggins, The American Left in the Twentieth Century
(New York: Harcourt, Brace, Jovanovich, Inc., 1973), pp. 110-36;
Pells, Radical Visions and American Dreams, chapters 7 and 8;
Christopher Lasch, The New Radicalism in America: The Intellectual
as a Social Type, 1889-1963 (New York: Alfred A. Knopf, 1965),
chapter 9; Christopher Lasch, The Agony of the American Left (New
York: Vintage Books, 1969), chapter 2; and Ronald Steel, Walter
Lippmann and the American Century (Boston: Little, Brown and Co.,
1980).

12. For the number of the academic professoriate in the 1930s, see
Publication #1142, National Academy of Sciences, Doctorate Production in the United States, 1920-1962, with Baccalaureate Origins
of Doctorates in Sciences, Arts, and Professions (Washington, D.C.:
National Academy of Sciences-National Research Council, 1963),
chapter 1.

13. Samuel I. Hayakawa, "To One Elect," Poetry, 44 (September
1934): 319; "A. E.'s Golden Age," review of A. E.{ George W.
Russell }, Selected Poems (New York: Macmillan Company, 1935) in
Poetry, 48 (August 1936): 290-92; "Japanese Sensibility," Harpers,
174 (December 1936): 98-103; "A Japanese-American Goes to Japan,"
Asia, 37 (April 1937): 269-72; and "My Japanese Father and I,"
Asia, 37 (May 1937): 331-33.
There is some evidence of literary sensitivity and bicultural
awareness of the advantage of knowing a "foreign" language in these
early articles but no evidence of awareness of semantics per se.
Hayakawa portrays himself as a thoroughly acculturated North
American (B.A., University of Manitoba; M.A., McGill University;
and Ph.D., University of Wisconsin) who knew more about English
and American literature than he did about Japanese culture. He
rejected the idea of staying in Japan to teach because there "the
teacher is an instrument of national greatness, and only secondarily a seeker after an abstract or universal truth." Hayakawa,
"My Japanese Father and I," p. 333.

14. Stuart Chase, The Tyranny of Words (New York: Harcourt, Brace
and Company, 1938), pp. 74, 94 (quotation), and 97-103.

15. Hayakawa, "The Meaning of Semantics," pp. 354-57.

16. S. I. Hayakawa, "Problems of Language," The New Republic, 101
(November 15, 1939): 118. This is a review of Karl Britton,
Communication: A Philosophical Study of Language (New York:
Harcourt, Brace and Company, 1939).

17. Hayakawa, "The Meaning of Semantics," pp. 356 (quotation) and
372.

18. Hayakawa, "Problems of Language," p. 117. The first version of Hayakawa's Language in Action was photoprinted and published by the College Typing Company, Madison, Wisconsin, in 1939. The second version, called Language in Action, A Second Draft, was published in Chicago by the Institute of General Semantics in 1940. Harcourt, Brace and Company published a hard-cover text version in 1941 under the title Language in Action: A Guide to Accurate Thinking, Reading, and Writing. This proved to be a popular text, and was reissued in 1943, 1946, 1947, 1948, 1949, and 1952. A comparison of the 1939 and 1940 versions indicates that some material was reordered in sequence; some new material was added on symbols, extensional and intensional meanings, and projecting of abstractions; and, in general, the text was given a more logical ordering. The 1941 version was essentially the same text as the 1940 draft with a longer introduction, additional readings and applications, more headings within chapters and appropriate prefatory quotes. Benjamin Lee Whorf's article on "Science and Linguistics" was added to the readings to round out the idea of linguistic relativism. Korzybski's structural differential diagram had been turned upside down in the 1940 draft and became the "ladder of abstraction," a feature retained in subsequent versions. Language in Action, A Second Draft, p. 54.

19. Korzybski, Science and Sanity, "Introduction to Second Edition," (1941), p. lxv. In what sounded like a plea for government funding or support, Korzybski wrote in 1941: "Counteraction, reconstruction, and/or prevention { of neuro-semantic damage due to propaganda } are impossible unless such mechanisms are utilized constructively under the guidance of governmental specialists in the fields of anthropology, neuro-psychiatry, general semantics, etc., who would understand the language of their fellow workers in related scientific fields, and would be FREE TO DEVOTE THEIR ENTIRE TIME AND EFFORTS TO THIS TASK, AND TO FURTHER INVESTIGATIONS" (p. lxvii, capitals in original).

20. Theodore Longabaugh, General Semantics: An Introduction (New York: Vantage Press, 1957), p. vi.

21. "New Kind of Sense," Time, 38 (August 11, 1941): 32; S. I. Hayakawa, The Use and Misuse of Language (Greenwich, Conn.: Fawcett Publications, 1962), p. x; Longabaugh, General Semantics, p. vii (quotation); and M. Kendig, "Some Institute History," General Semantics Bulletin, no. 32 (1965): 149-51.

22. Alfred Korzybski, "Preface to the Third Edition," Science and Sanity, pp. xxi-xxii.

23. "Always the Etc.?" Time, 53 (February 14, 1949): 68-69; "Always Either-Or," Time, 54 (August 1, 1949): 51; Russell Meyers, "Preface to the Fourth Edition," Science and Sanity (1958), p. xv. Time credited the general semantics movement with societies in twelve cities, connections with fifteen universities, and a mailing list for institute publications of ten thousand.

To judge from the number of articles about semantics and general
semantics listed in the Reader's Guide to Periodical Literature,
publicity about these developments reached a peak during the
period May 1949 to March 1951.

24. Korzybski, "Introduction to Second Edition," Science and
Sanity (1941), pp. xl-xlii. Keyser had chided Korzybski for his
use of either/or logic in a review in 1934, but Korzybski defended
it as pragmatically justified for the sake of clarity. Gates,
"Keyser and Korzybski: On Keyser's "Queries, Doubts, and Reservations . . .," p. 106.

25. This statement is based on twenty years of study, teaching,
and writing in the field of American intellectual history. This
dichotomous tendency, I would argue, has been characteristic of
not only the subject matter of American intellectual history but
also of the historical approaches to that material. The Progressive
historians, in particular, were prone to interpret intellectual
history in two-valued categories. See Robert Allen Skotheim,
American Intellectual Histories and Historians (Princeton:
Princeton University Press, 1966), chapters 2 and 3; Richard
Hofstadter, The Progressive Historians (New York: Alfred A. Knopf,
1968; or Gene Wise, American Historical Explanations: A Strategy
for Grounded Inquiry (Homewood, Ill.: Dorsey Press, 1973), pp.
88-94. This tendency has continued in the recent debates over
consensus and conflict in American historiography.

26. Richard Wayne Lykes, Higher Education and the United States
Office of Education (1867-1953) (Washington, D.C.: Bureau of
Post-Secondary Education, 1975), chapters 4 and 5 (quotation from
p. 159); J. L. Morrill, "Higher Education and the Federal Govern-
ment," The Annals of the American Academy of Political and Social
Science, 301 (September 1955): 41-45.

27. Lasch, The New Radicalism in America, pp. 316-18, 322-23;
Irving Howe, "This Age of Conformity," in Steady Work: Essays in
the Politics of Democratic Radicalism, 1953-1966 (New York:
Harcourt, Brace and World, 1966) pp. 313-45; Richard Hofstadter,
Anti-Intellectualism in American Life (New York: Alfred A. Knopf,
1963), chapter 15; George B. de Huszar, ed., The Intellectuals: A
Controversial Portrait (Glencoe, Ill.: Free Press, 1960), pp.
477-532. Edmund Wilson glimpsed something of the shifting balance
in 1942 when he wrote to Maxwell Geismar: "May it not possibly
turn out to be true that{ social consciousness writers of the late
1930s such as MacLeish and Sherwood} represent merely the beginning
of some awful Collectivist cant which will turn into official
propaganda for a post-war state-socialist bureaucracy? With
MacLeish and Sherwood at the White House as they are now, the whole
thing makes me rather uneasy. It may be necessary for a subsequent
set of writers to lead an attack on phony collectivism in the
interests of the American individualistic tradition." Edmund
Wilson to Maxwell Geismar, May 27, 1942, reprinted in New York
Review of Books (March 17, 1977): 12.
See also V. S. Pritchett, The Tale Bearers: Literary Essays (New

York: Random House, 1980), pp. 141-42. "Wilson was not, in the academic sense, a scholar or historian. He was an enormous reader, one of those readers who are perpetually on the scent from book to book. He was the old-style man of letters, but galvanized and with the iron of purpose in him. He was proud of his journalistic alacrity and of the gift of combining symphonic effects with those of 'no comment.'. . . He is a critic in whom history is broken up into minds. And despite the awkwardness of his prose, he is a coherent artist in the architecture of his subject. I mean that he is an artist . . . in the sense that he is a man possessed."

28. For Chase's reports to the Twentieth Century Fund, see The Road We Are Traveling, 1914-1942 (1942); Goals for America: A Budget of Our Needs and Resources (1943); Where's the Money Coming From? (1943); Democracy under Pressure (1945); and Tomorrow's Trade (1945), all issued under the general title, When the War Ends. For the general issue of planning during World War II and the post-war period, see Otis L. Graham, Jr., Toward a Planned Society: From Roosevelt to Nixon (London: Oxford University Press, 1976), chapters 2 and 3.

29. Stuart Chase, Roads to Agreement: Successful Methods in the Science of Human Relations (New York: Harper and Brothers, 1951), p. ix and chapter 18.

30. Stuart Chase, "Korzybski and Semantics," Saturday Review of Literature, 37 (June 19, 1954): 11.

31. S. I. Hayakawa, Language in Thought and Action, 2d ed. (New York: Harcourt, Brace and World, Inc., 1964), p. ix.

32. Anatol Rapoport, "What Is Semantics?" American Scientist (1952) reprinted in S. I. Hayakawa, The Use and Misuse of Language, pp. 13-14.
In the 1930s and 1940s, the science-fiction "cultists" had dis-covered Korzybski's general semantics. The International Scientific Association, 1935-1936, had as its motto, "Save Humanity with Science and Sanity." It was followed by another organization, the Futurians, which included many pioneering science-fiction writers. Damon Knight, The Futurians: The Story of the Science Fiction "Family" of the 30's That Produced Today's Top SF Writers and Editors, (New York: John Day, 1977), pp. 13-14. In 1945, science-fiction writer A. E. Van Vogt published The World of Ā { Null-A}, a novel based on a future Korzybskian world; reprinted in A. E. Van Vogt, Triad: Three Science Fiction Novels (New York: Simon and Schuster, 1951). Also in 1945-1947 the alienated writers who would later be known as the "beat generation" discovered Korzybski. See Dennis McNally, Desolate Angel: Jack Kerouac, the Beat Generation, and America (New York: Random House, 1979), pp. 74 and 93. In the 1970s, James Blish introduced another generation of cultists--the Star Trek fans--to Korzybski's ideas. See James Blish, Spock Must Die! A Star Trek Novel (New York: Bantam Pathfinder Editions, 1970), p. 24. For background on general semantics and science fiction, see H. L. Drake, "The General Semantics and Science Fiction

of Robert Heinlein and A. E. Van Vogt," General Semantics
Bulletin, nos. 41-43 (1974-1976): 132-49 and "References,"
General Semantics Bulletin, nos. 44-45 (1977-1978): 202-4.

33. For Hayakawa's writings during this period, see the files of
ETC. or the essays reprinted in Language, Meaning and Maturity
(New York: Harper and Brothers, 1954); Our Language and Our World
(New York: Harper and Brothers, 1959); and The Use and Misuse of
Language.
Hayakawa contributed to the "self-help" image of general semantics
in 1953 with an essay on the problem of being a Negro in modern
America in which he utilized the concept of the self-fulfilling
prophecy. "I am not saying that such prophecies always fulfill
themselves," he noted, "because that would be a manifest absurdity.
But { what I am saying is } that your own beliefs about the outcome
of any social situation of which you are a part are a factor in the
outcome." S. I. Hayakawa, "The Self-Image and Intellectual Understanding, or How to Be Sane Though Negro," reprinted in S. I.
Hayakawa, Symbol, Status, and Personality (New York: Harcourt,
Brace and World, Inc., 1963), p. 72 (italics in original).
The step from the self-fulling prophecy to the power of positive
thinking was a short one. See Donald Meyer, The Positive Thinkers:
A Study of the American Quest for Health, Wealth and Personal Power
from Mary Baker Eddy to Norman Vincent Peale (Garden City, N. Y.:
Doubleday and Company, Inc., 1966), pp. 244-49.
For some of the rival attempts at post-Korzybskian popularizations
of general semantics, see Irving J. Lee, How to Talk with People
(New York: Harper Brothers, 1952); Wendell Johnson, Your Most
Enchanted Listener (New York: Harper Brothers, 1956); Longabaugh,
General Semantics; Bess Sondel, The Humanity of Words: A Primer of
Semantics (Cleveland: The World Publishing Company, 1958); or J.
Samuel Bois, Explorations in Awareness (New York: Harper Brothers,
1957); The Art of Awareness: A Textbook in General Semantics
(Dubuque, Iowa: William C. Brown Company, 1966); and Breeds of Men:
Toward the Adulthood of Humankind: Post-Korzybskian General Seman-
tics (New York: Harper and Row, 1969). The activities of the
Institute of General Semantics for this period can be followed in
the General Semantics Bulletin, 1949-1969.

34. Henryk Skolimowski, "Analytical-Linguistic Marxism in Poland,"
Journal of the History of Ideas, 26 (April-June 1965): 241. Also
see Henryk Skolimowski, Polish Analytical Philosophy (New York:
Humanities Press, 1967), chapter 8.

35. Skolimowski, "Analytical-Linguistic Marxism," pp. 241-42.
Compare Z. Jordan, "The Development of Philosophy and Marxism in
Poland since the War," Studies in Soviet Thought, 1 (1961): 92-93.

36. Skolimowski, "Analytical-Linguistic Marxism," p. 243. For an
extensive analysis of Kołakowski's ideas, see the special issue of
Tri-Quarterly, 22 (Fall 1971); George Lichtheim, "A Polish Revisionist," Collected Essays (New York: Viking Press, 1973), pp.
406-10; or Rubem César Fernandes, "The Antinomies of Freedom (on
the Warsaw Circle of Intellectual History)," Ph.D. dissertation,

Columbia University, 1976, part 2.

37. Skolimowski, "Analytical-Linguistic Marxism," p. 244. For
Kołakowski's discussion of determinism and moral responsibility,
see Leszek Kołakowski, Toward a Marxist Humanism: Essays on the
Left Today, trans. Jane Zielonko Peel (New York: Grove Press, 1968),
pp. 188-210.

38. Skolimowski, "Analytical-Linguistic Marxism," p. 249.

39. Skolimowski, Polish Analytical Philosophy, pp. 228-29; Adam
Schaff, Introduction to Semantics, trans. Olgierd Wojtasiewicz
(London: Pergamon Press, 1962), chapter 4 (quotations on 93-4, 97-8,
100, 103-4).
It should be pointed out that Schaff's interpretation of general
semantics encompassed the works of Rapoport, Chase, Wendell
Johnson, and others as well as a close reading of Korzybski. Two
other European works of the 1960s were also critical of general
semantics. Albrecht Neubert, Semantischer Positivismus in den USA:
Ein kritischer Beitrag zum Studium Zusammenhänge zwischen Sprache
und Gesellschaft (Halle: Max Niemeyer Verlag, 1962), pp. 22-30,
complained that society shapes language, not vice versa, and that
general semantics reduced all language experience to subjective
levels. Neubert also included Lee, Johnson, Hayakawa, Rapoport,
Bois, Chase and F. P. Chisholm in his understanding of general
semantics. See the discussion of Neubert in Hanno Hardt, "General
Semantics and Scientific Ethics," in Lee Thayer, ed. Communication:
General Semantics Perspectives (New York: Spartan Books, 1970), pp.
18-19. Ladislav Tondl, Problems of Semantics: A Contribution to the
Analysis of the Language of Science, trans. David Short (Dordrecht,
Holland: D. Reidel Publishing Company, 1981), p. 375 n.15, dismissed Korzybski's views of identity as "an extreme nominalist view."
Tondl, whose work was first published in 1966, included Hayakawa,
Korzybski, H. Walpole, and Chase in the general semantics group
and accused them of producing "popular pseudoscientific writings
drawing eclectically on Freudian psychoanalysis, Pavlovian reflex
theory, psychiatry, linguistics, sociology, etc." Trondl, Problems
of Semantics, p. 5.

40. Adam Schaff, Language and Cognition, trans. Olgierd
Wojtasiewicz, (New York: McGraw-Hill, 1973), pp. 2-3.

41. Ibid., pp. 81-85 and 94-95 (quotations). Schaff also noted
the work of the Cracow school of developmental psychology, particularly the theories of Stefan Szuman on the generalizing function
of words (p. 87).

42. Ibid., pp. 104 and 118. See also Michał Głowinski, "Polish
Structuralism," Books Abroad (Spring 1975): 240-42; and Stanisław
Ossowski, Class Structure in the Social Consciousness, trans. Sheila
Patterson (New York: Free Press, 1963), chapter 11.
In subsequent publications, Schaff attempted to reinterpret Marxism
in the light of the socialist humanism of the young Marx and to
deal with the question of the social conditioning of historical

cognition. See Adam Schaff, Marxism and the Human Individual, trans.
Olgierd Wojtasiewicz (New York: McGraw-Hill, 1970) and History and
Truth (Oxford: Pergamon Press, 1976).

43. Skolimowski, Polish Analytical Philosophy, pp. 232-35 and
259.

44. Czesław Miłosz, The History of Polish Literature (London:
Collier-Macmillan, 1969), pp. 462 (quotation), 469, and 479
(quotation).

45. James Roose-Evans, Experimental Theatre: From Stanislavsky to
Today (New York: Avon Books, 1970), pp. 103 and 107 (quotation).
Grotowski was particularly successful in restaging Wyspiański's
Akropolis as a modern parable of Auschwitz.

46. Miłosz, History of Polish Literature, pp. 479-80.

47. Karol Wojtyla, Easter Vigil and Other Poems, trans. Jerzy
Peterkiewicz (New York: Random House, 1979), pp. xii, xiii, 26, and
30. Wojtyla was also influenced by participation in a clandestine
Rhapsodic Theater during the war (p. ix, n.1). For two "semantic"
poems, see "Thought's resistance to Words" and "Word's Resistance
to Thought" (pp. 19-20).

48. Adam Bromke, Poland's Politics: Idealism vs. Realism (Cambridge:
Harvard University Press, 1967), p. 87.

49. Ibid., p. 134. See also M. K. Dziewanowski, Poland in the
Twentieth Century (New York: Columbia University Press, 1977),
chapter 7.

50. Bromke, Poland's Politics, pp. 155-57. For the mood and
situation of intellectuals in Poland in the early 1960s, see A.
Alvarez, Under Pressure: The Writer in Society: Eastern Europe and
the U.S.A. (Baltimore: Penguin Books, 1965), chapter 1; William
Woods, Poland: Eagle in the East (New York: Hill and Wang, 1968);
Nicholas Bethel, Gomulka: His Poland, His Communism (New York: Holt,
Rinehart and Winston, 1969); and Norman Davies, God's Playground:
A History of Poland: Volume II: 1795 to the Present (New York:
Columbia University Press, 1982), pp. 582-88.
In the 1970s Westerners got a rare glimpse of the semantic nether
world of Polish Communist censorship through the clandestine publi-
cation of "The Black Book of Polish Censorship." According to
Polish dissidents, It's as if censorship as a system brings to its
logical conclusion the post-structuralist principle that reality
is only a message, which can be transformed at will according to
definite rules. Censorship is the most consistent realization of
McLuhan's information theories--for censorship information is not
a true or false image of reality but the sole reality." Furthermore, "censorship as a system does not aim at protecting the
socialist state against open criticism (about this one even fears
to think!). As a semantic system it protects and secures from
criticism not the state and the system, but rather their ideal

models. Censorship is the creation of an ideal image of the state
and the nation." Jan Kott, Czarna Ksiega Cenzury PRL (The Black
Book of Polish Censorship), New York Review of Books (August 17,
1980): 16-17.

51. The similarities in background between Korzybski and Malinowski
were particularly striking. In 1902 Malinowski enrolled in the
Jagiellonian University in Cracow where he studied physics, mathematics, and philosophy. He also attended seminars in psychology
and Polish literature. All of his main teachers had been influenced
by Ernst Mach and Richard Avenarius's empirio-criticism; Malinowski,
however, preferred Mach's version. "The function and genesis of
science cannot, as Avenarius had wanted, be explained just by
psychological laws. These must be taken within the framework of
the relationship man-world, and this relationship is defined by
human biological needs." From this positivistic background,
Malinowski derived two important features of his anthropological
methodology: "(1) an emphasis on functional explanations and (2) a
notion of culture as an instrumental whole." But he was not a
radical empiricist in anthropology who simply wanted to compile
masses of data. Rather, he combined postulational, a priori
categories with direct observations to erect a systematic, theoretical anthropology. Since "concepts determine experience-descrip-
tion of the facts of necessity has to be settled in a proper
theoretical context." Science, therefore, means the investigation
of the relationships between functioning elements of a social
system, of which the concept of culture as an integrated whole is
the highest expression. Andrzej Paluch, "The Polish Background to
Malinowski's Work," MAN: Journal of the Royal Anthropological
Institute, 16 (June 1981): 276-85 (quotations from pp. 279-80).

CONCLUSION

1. Edward Rothstein, review of Douglas R. Hofstadter, Gödel, Escher,
Bach: An Eternal Golden Braid (New York: Basic Books, 1979), in New
York of Books (December 6, 1979): 34. For historical explanation
and simplified "layman's" exposition, see Ernst Nagel and James R.
Newman, Gödel's Proof (New York: New York University Press, 1958).
The dream of a mathematical model for language and thought dies
hard, however. For a recent attempt to base linguistics on
metamathematical foundations, see Richard H. Thomason, ed., Formal
Philosophy: Selected Papers of Richard Montague (New Haven: Yale
University Press, 1974). For an attempt to incorporate Gödel into
the search, see Hofstadter, Gödel, Escher, Bach: An Eternal Golden
Braid. Hofstadter subtitled his book, "a metaphorical fugue on
minds and machines in the spirit of Lewis Carroll." Hofstadter's
use of the concept of self-reflectiveness would have pleased
Korzybski.

2. Quine's logical criticism of Korzybski on the question of
identity, it seems to me, misses the point of Korzybski's psychological reasons for rejecting identity as equality. Quine
noted: ". . . confusion of sign and object is evident in Leibniz
where he explains identity as a relation between the signs, rather

than between the named object and itself: . . . Frege at one time
took a similar line. This confusion is curiously doubled in
Korzybski when he argues that '1 = 1' must be false because the
two sides of the equation are spatially distinct." Willard
Van Orman Quine, Word and Object (Cambridge: MIT Press, 1964), pp.
116-17. Korzybski's rejection was based on the impossibility of
identity of different states of the nervous system not on the
spatial separation of the symbols. Korzybski, Science and Sanity,
pp. 194-95. It is also questionable whether, even in this example,
Korzybski held that identity was a relationship between signs rather
than between the signs and the states of affairs for which they
stood.
On the question of the meaning of "is" as the copula in traditional
Aristotelian logic, see John Malcolm, "A Reconsideration of the
Identity and Inherence Theories of the Copula," Journal of the
History of Philosophy, 17 (October 1979): 383-400.

3. For the evaluations of Freud, see Seymour Fisher and Roger P.
Greenburg, The Scientific Credibility of Freud's Theories and
Therapy (New York: Basic Books, 1977), chapters 7 and 9; Hans J.
Eysenck and Glenn D. Wilson, eds., The Experimental Study of
Freudian Theories (London: Methuen and Co., 1973), Chapter 21;
Stanley Edgar Hyman, The Tangled Bank: Darwin, Marx, Frazer and
Freud as Imaginative Writers (New York: Atheneum, 1962); Murray H.
Sherman, ed., Psychoanalysis and Old Vienna: Freud, Reik,
Schnitzler, Kraus (New York: Humanities Sciences Press, 1978);
Philip Rieff, Freud: The Mind of the Moralist (Garden City, N.Y.:
Doubleday and Co., Inc., 1961); and John Murray Cuddihy, The Ordeal
of Civility: Freud, Marx, Lévi-Strauss and the Jewish Struggle with
Modernity (New York: Basic Books, 1974). Interestingly, "Freud
often thought that 'the future will probably attribute far greater
importance to psychoanalysis as the science of the unconscious
than as a therapeutic procedure." Paul Roazen, Freud and His
Followers (New York: Alfred A. Knopf, 1975), p. 110.
On the current evaluations of the therapeutic techniques of White
and Sullivan, see S. P. Fullinwider, Technicians of the Finite:
The Rise and Decline of the Schizophrenic in American Thought,
1840-1960 (Westport, Connecticut: Greenwood Press, 1982), chapters
5-6. On the status of schizophreniz and linguistic pathologies,
see Richard J. Haler, "The Diagnosis of Schizophrenia: A Review
of Recent Developments," Schizophrenia Bulletin 5 (no. 4, 1979):
1-13; Jason Brown, Mind, Brain, and Consciousness: The Neuropsycho-
logy of Cognition (New York: Academic Press, 1977), chapter 3 and
5; and Harold J. Vetter, Language, Behavior and Psychopathology
(Chicago: Rand McNally and Co., 1969), p. 5, n.1 and chapter 10.
On the presuppositions of psychoanalysis as a therapeutic technique
in the context of its current practice, see Janet Malcolm,
Psychoanalysis: The Impossible Profession (New York: Vintage Books,
1981), chapters 1, 3, 9, and 10.

4. Max Black, "Korzybski's General Semantics" (a lecture delivered
at the State University of Iowa, April 1946), reprinted in Max
Black, Language and Philosophy: Studies in Method (Ithaca: Cornell
University Press, 1949), pp. 223-46. Black did not want to reject

general semantics out of hand but found its theoretical foundations "logically incoherent and in need of thoroughgoing revision" (p. 246). In 1968, Black still separated Korzybski from his disciples' "crass blunder of supposing that language could dispense with the use of abstractions," but did criticize Korzybski for his "unnecessary . . . rejection of 'two-valued' conventional logic." Max Black, The Labyrinth of Language (New York: Frederick A. Praeger, Publishers, 1968), p. 118, n.9. See chapter 7 for Black's discussion of meaning.

5. Barbara Herrnstein Smith, "The New Imagism," Midway, 9 (Winter 1969): 35.

6. For the early logical positivist position on verification and meaning, see Victor Kraft, The Vienna Circle: The Origin of Neo-Positivism (New York: Greenwood Press, 1953), pp. 34-36. For a critique, see Ralburne S. Heimbeck, Theology and Meaning: A Critique of Methodological Scepticism (Stanford: Stanford University Press, 1969), chapter 2. For the counterfactual argument, see George Steiner, After Babel: Aspects of Language and Translation (London: Oxford University Press, 1975), chapter 3.
It was the postulational ability of Korzybski's general semantics to envision alternate psychosemantic systems, its recognition of the role of convenient fictions in scientific theories, and its notion of what might be called "metaconsciousness" (conciousness of abstracting) that made it more congenial to science fiction writers and fans than logical positivism. In short, general semantics could countenance the counterfactual whereas logical positivism could not.

7. Frederick J. Newmeyer, Linguistic Theory in America: The First Quarter-Century of Transformational Generative Grammar (New York: Academic Press, 1980), chapters 1 and 2; Geoffrey Sampson, Schools of Linguistics (Stanford: Stanford University Press, 1980), chapters 3 and 6. Bloomfield's classic text, Language, was published in 1933, the same year as Korzybski's Science and Sanity. "In semantics, Bloomfield's reasoning led him to conclude that the statement of meanings was in practice impossible, and would remain so 'until human knowledge advances very far beyond its present state' {Bloomfield, Language, p. 140} --for instance, science would have to lay bare the 'obscure internal stimuli' that impinge on a man just before he utters a sentence such as I hear that applies will be cheaper next year. Bloomfield was mistaken in supposing that such stimuli exist; but . . . even a behaviourist . . . must agree that the observable data are in practice insufficient to permit the construction of models of the interaction between observable speech and unobservable mind." Sampson, Schools of Linguistics, p. 69.

8. William Labov, "Preface" to Uriel Weinreich, On Semantics (Philadelphia: University of Pennsylvania Press, 1980), p. vii.

9. According to Stephen Ullmann, in Europe "the 1920's brought a sudden and unexpected quickening in semantic research." Given the

diversity of philosophical movements in Europe, there was a good
bit of cross-fertilization in semantic theory. Thus, Hans Sperber
introduced Freudian insights into semantics; Weisgerber and Trier
combined de Saussurean structuralism with Husserl's phenomenology;
and Ogden and Richards combined analytical insights with traditional
"individualistic" linguistics. Stephen Ullman, The Principles of
Semantics (Glasgow: Jackson, Son and Co., 1951), pp. 2 and 72.
For background on the changing status of positivism, see David
Lindenfeld, The Transformation of Positivism: Alexius Meinong and
European Thought, 1880-1920 (Berkeley: University of California
Press, 1981).
For the development of socialist humanism, see Erick Fromm, Socialist
Humanism: An International Symposium (Garden City, N.Y.: Doubleday,
1966), or Donald Clark Hodges, Socialist Humanism: The Outcome of
Classical European Morality (St. Louis: W. H. Green, 1974).
For the issue of language in Hegel's phenomenology, see Daniel J.
Cook, Language in the Philosophy of Hegel (The Hague: Mouton,
1973).

10. See chapter 4, pages 75-9 above.

11. Of the 600 members of the Institute of General Semantics as
of the end of the year 1949, the following occupations were represented:

Medicine (including psychiatry)		46
Psychology		23
Dentistry		10
Speech and Hearing		10
Teachers		
Elementary and high school	29 }	
College	30 }	59
College and university students(undergraduate and graduate)		98
Engineering		27
Homemaking		28
Government service (federal, including armed forces)		24
Law		17
Social work		9
Fine and applied arts		15
Writing and editing		15
English language and literature		15
Business and industry		108
including advertising and promotion	14}	
Banking, investment, brokerage	9}	
Agriculture	6}	
Accountancy	6}	
Insurance	5}	
Steel Products	5}	
Newspapers	6}	
Unclassified	45}	

See the report on membership, General Semantics Bulletin, nos. 1-2 (1949-1950): ii.

For the relations between the Institute of General Semantics and the International Society for General Semantics, on the one hand, and academia, on the other, see M. Kendig, "The Old Order Changeth . . .'," General Semantics Bulletin, nos. 30 and 31 (1963-1964): 5; and M. Kendig, "Some Institute History . . .," General Semantics Bulletin, no. 32 (1965): 149-51.

12.   The modern European version of freedom as the recognition of necessity owes much to Kant's formulation of ethics. As Nicholas Lobkowicz has pointed out: "Just as the distinction between the possible and the actual has no foundation in the things themselves but is due only to the fact that the human intellect cannot intuit and therefore grasps as a possible object whatever sense intuition represents as actual . . . so 'it is owing to the subjective constitution of our practical faculty that the moral laws must be represented as commands and the actions conforming to them as duties, and that reason represents this necessity not by an is (as an actual event) but by an ought-to-be.'" Nicholas Lobkowicz, Theory and Practice: History of a Concept from Aristotle to Marx (Notre Dame: University of Notre Dame Press, 1967), pp. 130-31 (emphasis added). Significantly, it was Comte, the founder of positivism, who insisted on the recognition of natural law in the social realm as the sine qua non of freedom. Ernst Cassirer, The Problem of Knowledge: Philosophy, Science, and History Since Hegel, trans. William H. Woglom and Charles W. Hendel (New Haven: Yale University Press, 1950), p. 244.

It is precisely this aspect of the European tradition in Freud's psychoanalysis that Americans find so hard to accept. See Malcolm, Psychoanalysis: The Impossible Profession, pp. 156-63.

For an example of a European thinker trying to explain to Americans the semantics of freedom, see Bronislaw Malinowski, Freedom and Civilization (New York: Roy Publishers, 1944).

For a comparative attempt to ground cultural freedom in sociological conditions, see Jeffrey C. Goldfarb, On Cultural Freedom: An Exploration of Public Life in Poland and America (Chicago: University of Chicago Press, 1982).

13.   Conservative intellectuals were quick to detect the liberal bias in general semantic advocates. As a historian of conservatism has noted: "Like { Richard } Weaver in Ideas Have Consequences, { Gordon Keith } Chalmers { in The Republic and the Person (Chicago, 1952)} criticized this new science which Alfred Korzybski and S. I. Hayakawa had developed." George H. Nash, The Conservative Intellectual Movement in America, since 1945 (New York: Basic Books, 1976), p. 44.

14.   Hence the popular mistrust of the phrase, "it is just a matter of semantics" and the misuse of Korzybski's ideas by dianetics and scientology.

15.   An attempt to maintain a viable synthesis of some of Korzybski's ideas in a biological, anthropological, and cybernetic model is

found in the work of Gregory Bateson. See Gregory Bateson, <u>Mind</u> <u>and</u> <u>Nature</u>: <u>A</u> <u>Necessary</u> <u>Unity</u> (New York: E. P. Dutton, 1979) and John Brockman, ed., <u>About</u> <u>Bateson</u>: <u>Essays</u> <u>on</u> <u>Gregory</u> <u>Bateson</u> (New York: E. P. Dutton, 1977).

16. On the charge of scientism, see Lee Thayer, "Editor's Preface," <u>Communication</u>: <u>General</u> <u>Semantics</u> <u>Perspectives</u> (New York: Spartan Books, 1970), pp. viii-xii.

17. George Steiner, <u>Language</u> <u>and</u> <u>Silence</u>: <u>Essays</u> <u>on</u> <u>Language</u>, <u>Literature</u>, <u>and</u> <u>the</u> <u>Inhuman</u> (New York: Atheneum, 1967), pp. 21-25.

BIBLIOGRAPHIC ESSAY _____

To approach the subject of semantics (particularly the possibility
of a general science of meaning) from a comparative historical,
rather than a comprehensive theoretical, perspective, the most
fruitful framework for this study was George Steiner, Language and
Silence: Essays on Language, Literature, and the Inhuman (New York:
Atheneum, 1967), After Babel: Aspects of Language and Translation
(London: Oxford University Press, 1975), and On Difficulty and
Other Essays (London: Oxford University Press, 1979). Not all
critics agree with Steiner on his geographic and temporal arguments,
however. Isaiah Berlin surveyed the same period from a different
philosophical perspective in Vico and Herder (New York: Vintage
Books, 1976) and Against the Current: Essays in the History of
Ideas, ed. Henry Hardy (New York: Penguin Books, 1982). Edward
Rothstein provided a succinct summary in his review of Gödel,
Escher, Bach: An Eternal Golden Braid by Douglas R. Hofstadter
(New York: Basic Books, 1979) in the New York Review of Books
(December 6, 1979): 34-35.
In addition to Steiner, this study was influenced by the work of
H. Stuart Hughes on recent European intellectual history: Oswald
Spengler: A Critical Estimate (New York: Charles Scribner's Sons,
1952), Consciousness and Society: The Reorientation of European
Social Thought, 1890-1930 (New York: Alfred A. Knopf, 1958), and
The Sea Change: The Migration of Social Thought, 1930-1965 (New
York: Harper and Row, 1975). Hughes's thesis of a "revolt against
positivism" in European thought in the 1890s has been challenged
recently by David F. Lindenfeld, The Transformation of Positivism:
Alexius Meinong and European Thought, 1880-1920 (Berkeley:
University of California Press, 1981). Lindenfeld's work is useful
for understanding the complexity of European intellectual influences;
however, for shaping a comparative framework uniting European and
American thought, I found Hughes to be more useful.

Helpful supplements to Hughes on European intellectual history
were William M. Johnston, The Austrian Mind: An Intellectual and
Social History, 1898-1938 (Berkeley: University of California
Press, 1972); Allan Janik and Stephen Toulmin, Wittgenstein's
Vienna (New York: Simon and Schuster, 1973); and Carl E. Schorski,
Fin-de-Siècle Vienna: Politics and Culture (New York: Alfred A.
Knopf, 1980). Leonard Linsky and John W. Boyer challenged the
Janik and Toulmin thesis in separate reviews in The Journal of
Modern History, 47 (December 1975): 699-711. The connection between
Vienna and the development of psychoanalysis has been explored in
Murray H. Sherman, ed., Psychoanalysis and Old Vienna: Freud, Reik,
Schnitzler, Kraus (New York: Humanities Sciences Press, 1978).
See also J. P. Stern, "Karl Kraus' Vision of Language," Modern
Language Review,6 (1966): 71-82; and Thomas Szasz, Karl Kraus and
the Soul-Doctors: A Pioneer Critic and His Criticism of Psychiatry
and Psychoanalysis (Baton Rouge: Louisiana State University Press,
1976).

To survey the general background of the several separate disciplines
which became involved in the attempt to unite philosophical (or
mathematico-logical) theory with psychological (or psychoanalytical)
therapy in a generalized science of meaning required works of wide-
ranging scope as well as highly specialized monographs and articles
in linguistics, mathematical logic, philosophy, psychology, and
semantics.

For linguistics, Geoffrey Sampson, Schools of Linguistics (Stanford:
Stanford University Press, 1980) was particularly valuable in
setting a framework for the detailed articles in Dell Hymes, ed.,
Studies in the History of Linguistics: Traditions and Paradigms
(Bloomington: Indiana University Press, 1974). Ferdinand de
Saussure, Course in General Linguistics, trans. Wade Baskin (New
York: Philosophical Library, 1959) was essential for understanding
structuralism in European linguistics. Jacques Ehrmann, ed.,
Structuralism (Garden City, N. Y.: Doubleday and Co., 1970) was a
useful supplement as were the essays in the special edition of
Books Abroad, 49 (Spring 1975) on European structuralism. For the
Chomskian "revolution" in linguistics, there is a convenient summary
in Frederick J. Newmeyer, Linguistic Theory in America: The First
Quarter-Century of Transformational Generative Grammar (New York:
Academic Press, 1980).

For the interaction of mathematics and logic, the following works
were helpful in sorting out trends: William and Martha Kneale, The
Development of Logic (London: Oxford University Press, 1962);
William Warren Bartley III, Lewis Carroll's Symbolic Logic (New
York: Clarkson N. Potter, 1977); Jean van Heijenoort, From Frege to
Gödel: A Source Book in Mathematical Logic, 1879-1931 (Cambridge:
Harvard University Press, 1967); and N. I. Styazhkin, History of
Mathematical Logic from Leibniz to Peano (Cambridge: MIT Press,
1969). An older work, Men of Mathematics by E. T. Bell, first
published in 1937, was useful more for the attitudes and inter-
pretations exhibited in it than for the historical information it
contained. Ernst Nagel and James R. Newman, Gödel's Proof, 2d ed.

(New York: New York University Press, 1973) was invaluable in putting Gödel's contribution in proper perspective.

On the philosophical innovations intertwined with the above developments, I limited my scope primarily to Russell, Wittgenstein, and the Vienna Circle. J. O. Urmson, Philosophical Analysis: Its Development between the Two World Wars (London: Oxford University Press, 1956) proved to be an indispensible starting point, especially when supplemented by A. J. Ayer, Russell and Moore: The Analytical Heritage (Cambridge: Harvard University Press, 1971), and Bertrand Russell (New York: Viking Press, 1972). Two specialized articles were essential for an historical understanding of Russell: Aloysius P. Martinich, "Russell's Theory of Meaning and Descriptions, 1905-1920," Journal of the History of Philosophy, 14 (April 1976): 183-201, and Douglas P. Lackey, "Russell's Unknown Theory of Classes: The Substitutional System of 1906," Journal of the History of Philosophy, 14 (January 1976): 69-78. A somewhat humorous light was thrown on Russell the social reformer by Barry Feinberg and Ronald Kasrils, Bertrand Russell's America: vol. 1 1896-1945, (New York: Viking Press, 1973).

For getting through the tangled thickets of Wittgensteinia, I relied on the aforementioned Wittgenstein's Vienna by Janik and Toulmin; on William Warren Bartley III, Wittgenstein (Philadelphia: J. P. Lippincott, 1973); G.E.M. Anscombe, An Introduction to Wittgenstein's Tractatus (Philadelphia: University of Pennsylvania Press, 1971); and Justus Hartnack, Wittgenstein and Modern Philosophy, trans. Maurice Cranston (Garden City, N. Y.: Doubleday and Company, Anchor Books, 1965). Of course, everyone must ultimately struggle through the Tractatus Logico-Philosophicus on their own. Wittgenstein's Philosophical Remarks, ed. Rush Rhees, trans. Raymond Hargreaves and Roger White (New York: Barnes and Noble, 1975) were helpful as were two articles: David Keyt, "Wittgenstein's Picture Theory of Language," The Philosophical Review, 73 (1964): 493-511 and Ian Hacking, "Wittgenstein the Psychologist," New York Review of Books (April 1, 1982): 42-44.

For material for the history of the Vienna Circle see Joergen Joergensen, The Development of Logical Empiricism, Foundations of the Unity of Science: Toward An International Encyclopedia of Unified Science, vol. II, no. 9. (Chicago University of Chicago Press, 1951); Victor Kraft, The Vienna Circle: The Origin of Neo-Positivism (New York: Greenwood Press, 1953); the aforementioned The Austrian Mind by William M. Johnston; and Hanno Hardt, "General Semantics and Scientific Ethics," in Lee Thayer, ed., Communication: General Semantics Perspectives (New York: Spartan Books, 1970), pp. 15-21. See also Rudolf Carnap, The Logical Structure of the World and Pseudoproblems in Philosophy, trans. Rolf A. George (Berkeley: University of California Press, 1967). Additional insight was provided by comments on Carnap in Hilary Putnam, "Foreword" to Thomas Reid's Inquiry: The Geometry of Visibles and the Case for Realism, by Norman Daniels (New York: Burt Franklin & Co., 1974) and A. J. Ayer, Part of My Life: The

Memoirs of a Philosopher (New York: Harcourt, Brace, Jovanovich, 1977), pp. 130-69. See also Brian McGuinness, ed., Wittgenstein and the Vienna Circle: Conversations Recorded by Friedrich Waismann, trans. Brian McGuinness and Joachim Schulte (New York: Barnes and Noble, 1979).

On the philosophy of science, relativity theory, and the neo-positivism of Ernst Mach, the following works provided a general introduction: L. Pearce Williams, ed., Relativity Theory: Its Origins and Impact on Modern Thought (New York: John Wiley and Sons, Inc., 1968); Henry P. Aiken, The Age of Ideology (New York: Mentor Books, 1956); and Johnston, The Austrian Mind. Specialized sources included Martin J. Klein, "Planck, Entropy, and Quanta, 1901-1906, "The Natural Philosopher, 1 (1963): 83-108; Milič Capek, "Ernst Mach's Biological Theory of Knowledge," Boston Studies in the Philosophy of Science, 5 (1969): 400-20; and Robert S. Cohen, "Ernst Mach: Physics, Perception and the Philosophy of Science," Boston Studies in the Philosophy of Science, 6 (1970): 126-64.

The subject of therapeutic psychology and the emergence of psychoanalysis in the European tradition is a complicated one, some of the dimensions of which are indicated in the following general works: Pedro Laín Entralgo, The Therapy of the Word in Classical Antiquity, trans. L. J. Rather and John M. Sharp (New Haven: Yale University Press, 1970); Stefan Zweig, Mental Healers: Franz Anton Mesmer, Mary Baker Eddy, Sigmund Freud, 1932, reprint, trans. Eden and Cedar Paul, (New York: Viking Press, 1962); Philip Rieff, Freud: The Mind of the Moralist (Garden City, N. Y.: Doubleday and Co., Anchor Books, 1961); and Paul Roazen, Freud and His Followers (New York: Alfred A. Knopf, 1975). George Steiner's essay "Language and Gnosis" in After Babel is also pertinent to this topic. For criticism of Freud's therapy, see Hans J. Eysenck and Glenn D. Wilson, The Experimental Study of Freudian Theories (London: Methuen, 1973) and Seymour Fisher and Roger P. Greenberg, The Scientific Credibility of Freud's Theories and Therapy (New York: Basic Books, 1977).

The possibility of a therapy of the word had to compete in European intellectual history with the promise of a theory of action, the doctrine of praxis, which informed the socialist humanist movement. The background of praxis was outlined in Nicholas Lobkowicz, Theory and Practice: History of a Concept from Aristotle to Marx (Notre Dame: University of Notre Dame Press, 1967) and in Richard J. Bernstein, Praxis and Action: Contemporary Philosophies of Human Activity (Philadelphia: University of Pennsylvania Press, 1971). The notion of a primary "linguistic" alienation in Hegel (which is overcome in praxis) was explored by Daniel J. Cook, Language in the Philosophy of Hegel (The Hague: Mouton, 1973). A significant critique of "reified" language and alienation and a hope for a revolutionary praxis was developed by Georg Lukács, the Hungarian Marxist revisionist, in History and Class Consciousness, trans. Rodney Livingstone, 1921, reprint

(Cambridge: MIT Press, 1971). On Lukács, see George Lichtheim, Georg Lukács (New York: Viking Press, 1970); G.H.R. Parkinson, ed., Georg Lukács: The Man, His Work, and His Ideas (New York: Vintage Books, 1970); and E. San Juan, Jr., ed., Marxism and Human Liberation: Essays on History, Culture and Revolution by Georg Lukács New York: Delta Books, 1973). See also Erick Fromm, Socialist Humanism: An International Symposium (Garden City, N. Y.: Doubleday and Co., 1966) or Donald Clark Hodges, Socialist Humanism: The Outcome of Classical European Morality (St. Louis: W. H. Green, 1974). Equally important is Louis Althusser, Lenin and Philosophy and Other Essays, trans. Ben Brewster (New York: Monthly Review Press, 1971).

For the study of a science of semantics per se, there is a growing body of literature but no recent comprehensive history. Stephen K. Land, From Signs to Propositions: The Concept of Form in Eighteenth-Century Semantic Theory (London: Longman Group, 1974) provides a suitable foundation. Richard D. Loewenberg, "George C. Lichtenberg: An Eighteenth Century Pioneer of Semantics," ETC., 1 (1943-1944): 99-104 and Herman J. Cloeren, "The Neglected Analytical Heritage," Journal of the History of Ideas, 36 (July-September 1975): 513-29 provide important information. Charles S. Hartwick, ed., Semiotics and Significs: The Correspondence between Charles S. Peirce and Lady Victoria Welby (Bloomington: Indiana University Press, 1977) and Michel Bréal, Semantics: Studies in the Science of Meaning, 1900, reprint, trans. Mrs. Henry Cust (New York: Dover Books, 1964), illustrate the claims of rival "founders" of modern semantics. Stephen Ullman, The Principles of Semantics (Glasgow: Jackson, Son and Co., 1951) provided a comprehensive survey of the field with a strong emphasis on European influences but should be supplemented with Uriel Weinreich, Explorations in Semantic Theory (The Hague: Mouton, 1972); M. J. Cresswell, Logics and Languages (London: Methuen & Co., 1973); Geoffrey Leech, Semantics (Middlesex, England: Penguin Books, 1974); and Uriel Weinreich, On Semantics (Philadelphia: University of Pennsylvania Press, 1980).

On the emergence of formal systems of semantics within the "revolt against positivism," the creation of modern consciousness, and the debates over the nature of language in Poland during the period 1890 to 1914, the best introductions, in English, are the works of Nobel laureate Czesław Miłosz, particularly Native Realm: A Search for Self-Definition, trans. Catherine S. Leach (Garden City, N. Y.: Doubleday and Co., 1968) and his monumental The History of Polish Literature (London: Collier-Macmillan, 1969). Mieczysław Giergielewicz, ed., Polish Civilization: Essays and Studies (New York: New York University Press, 1979) also contains some useful essays. On the unique role of the intelligentsia, see Jan Szczepański, "The Polish Intelligentsia," World Politics, 14 (April 1962): 406-20; A. Alvarez, Under Pressure: The Writer in Society, Eastern Europe and the U.S.A. (Baltimore: Penguin Books, 1965); Rubem César Fernandes, "The Antinomies of Freedom (on the Warsaw Circle of Intellectual History)," Ph.D. dissertation, Columbia University, 1976; and Jeffrey C. Goldfarb, On Cultural Freedom: An Exploration of Public Life in Poland and America (Chicago:

University of Chicago Press, 1982).

For the unfolding drama of Polish political history, the following sources proved invaluable: Edward H. Lewinski-Corwin, The Political History of Poland (New York: Polish Book Importing Company, 1917); Hans Roos, A History of Modern Poland, trans. J. R. Foster (New York: Alfred A. Knopf, 1966); W. F. Reddaway et al, The Cambridge History of Poland: From Augustus II to Piłsudski, 1697-1935 (London: Cambridge University Press, 1941); Adam Brooke, Poland's Politics: Idealism vs. Realism (Cambridge: Harvard University Press, 1967); Alexander Solzhenitsyn, August 1914, trans. Michael Glenny (New York: Farrar, Straus and Giroux, 1972); M. K. Dziewanowski, Poland in the Twentieth Century (New York: Columbia University Press, 1977); Richard M. Watt, Bitter Glory: Poland and Its Fate, 1918 to 1939 (New York: Simon and Schuster, 1979); R. F. Leslie et al., The History of Poland since 1863 (London: Cambridge University Press, 1980); Norman Davies, God's Playground: A History of Poland, Vol. II: 1795 to the Present (New York: Columbia University Press, 1982); and Lawrence Weschler, Solidarity: Poland in the Season of its Passion (New York: Simon and Schuster, 1982). Especially valuable for the period 1895 to 1905 was Alvin Marcus Fountain II, Roman Dmowski: Party, Tactics, Ideology, 1895-1907 (New York: Columbia University Press, 1980).

For background on Polish intellectual developments, particularly praxis, positivism, and sociology, see Lawrence S. Stepelevich, "August von Cieszkowski: From Theory to Praxis," History and Theory, 13 (1974): 39-52; Andrzej Krasiński, "Polish Positivism," Polish Perspectives, 24 (June-July 1981): 79-81; Józef Chałasiński, "Spencer's Sociology as Assimilated by the Intellectuals in Britain, Poland, and America at the End of the Nineteenth Century: A Comparative Study," Polish Sociological Bulletin, 1 (1962): 29-44; and Andrzej K. Paluch, "The Polish Background to Malinowski's Work," Man: Journal of the Royal Anthropological Institute, 16 (June, 1981): 276-85.

On Polish literature (which played a crucial role in intellectual developments), the basic sources were the aforementioned History of Polish Literature by Miłosz; some of the articles in Victor Erlich, ed., For Wiktor Weintraub: Essays in Polish Literature, Language, and History (The Hague: Mouton, 1975); and relevant portions of Julian Krzyżanowski, A History of Polish Literature, trans. Doris Ronowicz (Warsaw: Polish Scientific Publishers, 1978). The articles and dissertations in Antemurale (Institutum Historicum Polonicum Romae) proved invaluable, especially Danuta Irena Bieńkowska, "An Analytical Study of the Early Literary Work of Stefan Żeromski, Its Cultural Background and Its Critical Reception in Poland," Antemurale, 16 (1972): 187-316; Frank Joseph Corliss, Jr., "Dimensions of Reality in the Lyrics of Cyprian Norwid," Antemurale, 16 (1972): 95-186; David Welsh, "Sienkiewicz's 'Trilogy': A Study in Novelistic Techniques," Antemurale, 15 (1971): 217-81; and Tymon Terlecki, "Wyspiański in Two Perspectives," Antemurale, 15 (1971): 299-315. Other important articles were Czesław Miłosz,

"A Controversial Polish Writer: Stanisław Brzozowski," California Slavic Studies, 2 (1963): 53-95; Michał Głowinski, "Polish Structuralism," Books Abroad (Spring 1975): 239-43; George Lichtheim, "A Polish Revisionist { Leszek Kołakowski}, in George Lichtheim, Collected Essays (New York: Viking Press, 1973); and Tymon Terlecki, "Stanisław Wyspiański and the Poetics of Symbolist Drama," The Polish Review, 15 (Autumn 1970): 55-63.

For Polish mathematics, logic, and philosophy in the twentieth century, the basic sources used were Henryk Skolimowski, Polish Analytical Philosophy (New York: Humanities Press, 1967); Storrs McCall, ed., Polish Logic: 1920-1939 (London: Oxford University Press, 1967); Jan Łukasiewicz, Aristotle's Syllogistic, 2d ed. (London: Oxford University Press, 1957); and Alfred Tarski, Logic, Semantics, Metamathematics: 1923 to 1938, trans. J. H. Woodger (London: Oxford University Press, 1956). On Marxism and semantics, useful articles included Z. Jordan, "The Development of Philosophy and Marxism in Poland since the War," Studies in Soviet Thought, 1 (1961): 88-99 and Henryk Skolimowski," Analytical-Linguistic Marxism in Poland," Journal of the History of Ideas, 26 (April-June, 1965): 235-58. The works of Adam Schaff, the key figure in the Marxist reevaluation of semantics, are available in translations by Olgierd Wojtasiewicz and include Introduction to Semantics (London: Pergamon Press, 1962), Marxism and the Human Individual (New York: McGraw Hill, 1970), and Language and Cognition (New York: McGraw-Hill, 1973). Important for understanding this debate were the works of the Russian psychologist L. S. Vygotsky, Thought and Language, trans. Eugenia Hanfmann and Gertrude Vakar (Cambridge; MIT Press, 1962) and Mind in Society: The Development of Higher Psychological Processes, trans. Michael Cole and Sylvia Scribner (Cambridge: Harvard University Press, 1978).

Shifting the focus from Europe in general and Poland in particular to the United States in the period of World War I and the 1920s, the following general works were essential for setting the stage for the American reception of European ideas: David M. Kennedy, Over Here: The First World War and American Society (New York: Oxford University Press, 1980); F.S.C. Northrup, Man, Nature and God: A Quest for Life's Meaning (New York: Simon and Schuster, 1962); Natan G. Hale, Jr., Freud in America, vol. I Freud and the Americans: The Beginnings of Psychoanalysis in the United States, 1876-1917 (New York: Oxford University Press, 1971); Edward A. Purcell, Jr., The Crisis of Democratic Theory: Scientific Naturalism and the Problem of Value (Lexington: University Press of Kentucky, 1973); and Morton White, Social Thought in America: The Revolt against Formalism, rev. ed. (Boston: Beacon Press, 1957). Three developments in this period deserved detailed examination: engineering millenialism, mechanistic biology and behavioristic psychology, and mathematical philosophy. On engineering millenialism, Samuel Haber, Efficiency and Uplift: Scientific Management in the Progressive Era, 1890-1920 (Chicago: University of Chicago Press, 1964) provided basic information while the specialized articles and studies by Edwin T. Layton filled in details: "Frederick H. Newell and the Revolt of the Engineers," Journal of the Midcontinent

American Studies Association, 3 (Fall 1962): 18-26; "Veblen and
the Engineers," American Quarterly, 16 (Spring 1962): 64-72; and
The Revolt of the Engineers: Social Responsibility and the American
Engineering Profession (Cleveland: Press of Case Western Reserve
University, 1971). On mechanistic biology and behaviorism in
psychology, Donald Fleming's essay on Jacques Loeb in the Dictionary
of Scientific Biography, vol. 8, ed. Charles Gillispie (New York:
Charles Scribner's Sons, 1970), pp. 445-47, was concise and
fruitful as was John C. Burnham, "The New Psychology: From Narcissism
to Social Control," in John Braeman, Robert H. Bremner, and David
Brody, eds., Change and Continuity in Twentieth-Century America:
The 1920's (Columbus: Ohio State University Press, 1968), pp.
351-97. David Cohen, J. B. Watson: The Founder of Behaviorism, A
Biography (London: Routledge and Kegan Paul, 1979) corrected a
number of misconceptions about behaviorism in the 1920s as did
B. F. Skinner, Particulars of My Life (New York: Alfred A. Knopf,
1976). On American mathematical philosophy in the 1920s, see the
chapter on non-Euclideanism in Edward A. Purcell, Jr., Crisis of
Democratic Theory: Scientific Naturalism and the Problem of Value
(Lexington: University Press of Kentucky, 1973); and Cassius J.
Keyser, The Human Worth of Rigorous Thinking (New York: Columbia
University Press, 1916) or Mathematical Philosophy: A Study of
Fate and Freedom (New York: E. P. Dutton & Co., 1922). On Keyser,
see Joseph Meyer, "Cassius J. Keyser, 1862-1947," ETC., 5 (August
1947): 56-57; Elton S. Carter, "On Keyser's 'Queries, Doubts, and
Reservations,' " General Semantics Bulletin, nos. 16-17 (1955):
66-7 and E. L. Gates, "Keyser and Korzybski: On Keyser's 'Queries,
Doubts, and Reservations' about Science and Sanity: Identity and
Identification Discussed," General Semantics Bulletin, nos. 26-27
(1960): 105-8. For additional details, see Keyser's review of
Korzybski in Scripta Mathematica, 2 (1934): 247-60 and Oliver L.
Reiser, "Modern Science and Non-Aristotelian Logic," The Monist,
46 (July 1936): 312-17.

On the question of the role of language in American psychiatry in
the 1920s, Harold J. Vetter, Language, Behavior and Psychopathology
(Chicago: Rand McNally and Co., 1969) surveys the field. For the
contributions of H. S. Sullivan, the following were useful: Harry
Stack Sullivan, Schizophrenia as a Human Process (New York: W. W.
Norton and Company, 1962); A. H. Chapman, Harry Stack Sullivan:
His Life and His Work (New York: G. P. Putnam's Sons, 1976); Helen
Swick Perry, Psychiatrist of America: The Life of Harry Stack
Sullivan (Cambridge: Harvard University Press, 1982); and S. P.
Fullinwider, Technicians of the Finite: The Rise and Decline of the
Schizophrenic in American Thought, 1840-1960 (Westport, Conn.:
Greenwood Press, 1982). For other developments concerning language
theories in the 1920s, the following works indicate some of the
parameters: Edward Sapir, Language: An Introduction to the Study of
Speech,1921, reprint (New York: Harcourt, Brace and Co., 1949);
Theodora Kroeber, Alfred Kroeber (Berkeley: University of California
Press, 1970); and Reuben Brower, Helen Vendler, and John Hollander,
eds., I. A. Richards: Essays in His Honor (New York: Oxford University Press, 1973). Developments in the study of language in the

early 1930s are represented by Leonard Bloomfield, Language (New York: Holt, Rinehart, and Winston, 1933) and are summarized in Harry deVeltheym Velten, "The Science of Language and the Language of Science," PMLA, 48 (June 1933): 608-22.

On American radicalism and independent reform thought in the 1930s, basic works included: R. Alan Lawson, The Failure of Independent Liberalism, 1930-1941 (New York: G. P. Putnams, Sons, 1971); Richard H. Pells, Radical Visions and American Dreams: Culture and Social Thought in the Depression Years (New York: Harper and Row, 1973); Otis L. Graham, Jr., Toward a Planned Society: From Roosevelt to Nixon (London: Oxford University Press, 1976); Donald L. Miller, The New American Radicalism: Alfred M. Bingham and Non-Marxian Insurgency in the New Deal Era (Port Washington, N. Y.: Kennikat Press, 1979); and Ronald Steel, Walter Lippman and the American Century (Boston: Little, Brown and Co., 1980).

Against this background of intellectual trends in Europe, 1890-1920, and America, 1920s-1930s, it was necessary to reconstruct the evolving thought of Alfred Korzybski. The published biographical accounts of Korzybski's life by his colleagues were based on comments and reminiscences during his American career. Few documents survived from his pre-war years in Poland. The basic sources for his life include: M. Kendig, "A Memoir: Alfred Korzybski and His Work," General Semantics Bulletin, no. 3 (1950): 3-11 { reprinted in Alfred Korzybski, Manhood of Humanity, 2d ed. (Lakeville, Conn.: Institute of General Semantics, 1950), pp. xvii-xl }; photo essay on his career, General Semantics Bulletin, no. 3 (1950): 23-32; Charlotte Schuchardt Read, "Alfred Habdank Skarbek Korzybski: A Biographical Sketch," General Semantics Bulletin, no. 3 (Spring 1950): 33-40 { reprinted in part as "Alfred Korzybski: His Contributions and Their Historical Development," in Lee Thayer, ed., Communication: General Semantics Perspectives (New York: Spartan Books, 1970), pp. 339-47. }; Charlotte Schuchardt Read, "The Korzybski Archives, circa 1914-1938," General Semantics Bulletin, nos. 24-25 (1959): 134; and Anatol Rapoport, "Alfred Korzybski, Biographical Summary," ETC., 7 (Spring 1950): 163-65. Autobiographical material is found in the so-called Keyes interview of 1947, excerpts of which are included in Robert P. Pula, "Korzybski's Polish Matrix," General Semantics Bulletin, no. 47 (1980): 38-54. Biographical material on Mira Edgerly, Korzybski's American-born wife, was found in the following sources: New York Times, January 18, 1919, 11:2 (marriage noted); Lady Mira Edgerly-Korzybska, "The Psychology of Portraiture," Arts and Decoration, 11 (October 1919): 268-69; Mira Edgerly-Korzybska, "The Edgerly-Korzybski Technique," exhibit pamphlet (January 17, 1921), Art Institute of Chicago Library; Helen L. Earle, ed., Biographical Sketches of American Artists, 5th ed. (East Lansing: Michigan State Library, 1924), p. 106; Vida Ravenscroft Sutton, "The Script of the 'Speaking Press,' " Education, 57 (September 1936): 21-6; and Charlotte Schuchardt Read, "Mira Edgerly Korzybska: A Biographical Sketch," General Semantics Bulletin, nos. 16-17 (1955): 53-6.

To reconstruct Korzybski's system as it evolved, the following
published works by Korzybski were used: Manhood of Humanity, 2d ed.
(Lakeville, Conn.: Institute of General Semantics, 1950); "Fate
and Freedom," Mathematics Teacher, 16 (1923): 274-90; "The Brotherhood of Doctrines," The Builder: A Journal of Freemasonry, 10
(1924): 105-7; Time-Binding: The General Theory (Second Paper)
(Washington, D.C.: Jas. C. Wood, 1926) {also reprinted in Time-
Binding: The General Theory: Two Papers, 1924-1926 (Lakeville,
Conn.: Institute of General Semantics, 1949)}; Science and Sanity:
An Introduction to Non-Aristotelian Systems and General Semantics,
4th ed. (Lakeville, Conn.: Institute of General Semantics, 1958);
and "The Role of Language in the Perceptual Processes," in
Perception: An Approach to Personality, ed. Robert R. Blake and
Glenn V. Ramsey (New York: Ronald Press, 1951) { reprinted in
General Semantics Bulletin, no. 36 (1969): 15-49 }.

For the background on Samuel Ichiyé Hayakawa, the following
selections by Hayakawa were invaluable: "To One Elect," Poetry, 44
(September 1934): 319; "A. E.'s Golden Age," Poetry, 48 (August
1936): 290-92; "Japanese Sensibility," Harpers, 174 (December 1936):
98-103; "A Japanese-American Goes to Japan," Asia, 37 (April 1937):
269-72; and "My Japanese Father and I," Asia, 37 (May 1937): 331-33.
Hayakawa's contributions to general semantics were traced through
the following: "The Meaning of Semantics," The New Republic, 99
(August 2, 1939): 354; Language in Action (Madison, Wisc.:
College Typing Company, 1939); Language in Action, A Second Draft
(Chicago: Institute of General Semantics, 1940); Language in Action:
A Guide to Accurate Thinking, Reading, and Writing (New York:
Harcourt, Brace and Company, 1941); Language in Thought and Action,
with Basil H. Pillard (New York: Harcourt, Brace and Co., 1949);
Language, Meaning and Maturity (New York: Harper and Brothers, 1954);
Our Language and Our World (New York: Harper and Brothers, 1959);
The Use and Misuse of Language (Greenwich, Conn.: Fawcett Publica-
tions, 1962); Symbol, Status, and Personality (New York: Harcourt,
Brace and World, 1963); and Language in Thought and Action, 4th ed.,
with Arthur Asa Berger and Arthur Chandler (New York: Harcourt,
Brace, Jovanovich, 1978).

For Stuart Chase, the important primary sources were Chase's articles
in Harpers magazine in 1937-1938, which became The Tyranny of Words
(New York: Harcourt, Brace and Company, 1938), his reports for the
Twentieth Century Fund, 1942-1945, issued under the general title,
When the War Ends, and Roads to Agreement: Successful Methods in
the Science of Human Relations (New York: Harper and Brothers, 1951).
Particularly revealing was his article, "Korzybski and Semantics,"
Saturday Review of Literature, 37 (June 19, 1954): 11-12.

For the post-World War II struggle between free intellectuals and
academics in the American scene, the following works provided basic
concepts for historical interpretation: George B. de Huszar, ed.,
The Intellectuals: A Controversial Portrait (Glencoe, Ill.: Free
Press, 1960); Christopher Lasch, The New Radicalism in America:
The Intellectual as a Social Type, 1889-1963 (New York: Alfred A.
Knopf, 1965); Richard Hofstadter, Anti-Intellectualism in American

Life (New York: Alfred A. Knopf, 1963); Irving Howe, Steady Work:
Essays in the Politics of Democratic Radicalism, 1953-1966. (New
York: Harcourt, Brace and World, 1966); Donald B. Meyer, The
Positive Thinkers: A Study of the American Quest for Health,
Wealth, and Personal Power from Mary Baker Eddy to Norman Vincent
Peale (Garden City, N.Y.: Doubleday, 1965); Charles Kadushin, The
American Intellectual Elite (Boston: Little, Brown and Co., 1974);
and William Barrett, The Truants: Adventures among the Intellectuals
(Garden City, N.Y.: Doubleday, 1982). The lines of division and
influences among the followers of Korzybski in the 1940s and 1950s
can be found in the General Semantics Bulletin and the issues of
ETC. See especially Irving J. Lee, "On the Varieties of Research
in General Semantics," General Semantics Bulletin, nos. 1-2
(1949-1950): 10-16; Dean C. Barnland, "Is There Any New Business?"
ETC., 20 (May 1963): 82-83; and M. Kendig, "Some Institute History,"
General Semantics Bulletin, nos. 32-33 (1965-1966): 151.

Some of the rival attempts at popularization of post-Korzybskian
general semantics were Irvin J. Lee, How to Talk with People (New
York: Harper Brothers, 1952); Wendell Johnson, Your Most Enchanted
Listener (New York: Harper Brothers, 1956); Theodore Longabaugh,
General Semantics: An Introduction (New York: Vantage Press, 1957);
J. Samuel Bois, Explorations in Awareness (New York: Harper Brothers,
1957), J. Samuel Bois The Art of Awareness: A Textbook in General
Semantics (Dubuque, Iowa: William C. Brown Co., 1958); Bess Sondel,
The Humanity of Words: A Primer of Semantics (Cleveland: World
Publishing Co., 1958); Harry L. Weinberg, Levels of Knowing and
Existence: Studies in General Semantics (New York: Harper Brothers,
1959); and J. Samuel Bois, Breeds of Men: Toward the Adulthood of
Humankind: Post-Korzybskian General Semantics (New York: Harper and
Row, 1969). Some evidence of the influence of, and evaluations of,
Korzybski's system can be found in Hanno Hardt, "General Semantics
and Scientific Ethics," in Lee Thayer, ed., Communication: General
Semantics Perspectives (New York: Spartan Books, 1970); in Robert
P. Pula, "Knowledge, Uncertainty and Courage: Heisenberg and
Korzybski," Methodology and Science, 10, no.2 (1977): 140-66, and
in H. L. Drake, "The General Semantics and Science Fiction of
Robert Heinlein and A. E. Van Vogt," General Semantics Bulletin,
nos. 41-43 (1974-1976): 139-49, and nos. 44-45 (1977-1978): 202-4.

The reaction of some of Korzybski's contempories resulted in multi-
faceted criticism of his ideas, as was the case with the philosopher
Max Black in Language and Philosophy: Studies in Method (Ithaca:
Cornell University Press, 1949). Neo-conservative intellectuals
such as Gordon Keith Chalmers and Richard Weaver also found reason
to criticize the notion of a "liberal" science of semantics. See
George H. Nash, The Conservative Intellectual Movement in America,
since 1945 (New York: Basic Books, 1976). In Poland, Marxist
critic Adam Schaff in Introduction to Semantics (1962) criticized
Korzybski's ideas as being too American but attempted to rescue
Korzybski from the crude stereotypes of orthodox Marxist polemics
and to subsume portions of Korzybski's general semantics once
again into the European tradition. Albrecht Neubert, Semantischer

<u>Positivismus</u> <u>in</u> <u>den</u> <u>USA</u> (Halle: Max Niemeyer Verlag, 1962),
compared general semantics and semantics but was also critical.
The Czeck semanticist Ladislav Tondl, in his <u>Problems</u> <u>of</u> <u>Semantics</u>:
<u>A Contribution to the Analysis of the Language of Science</u>, trans.
David Short (Dordrecht, Holland: D. Reidel, 1981) gave a balanced
and evenhanded account while still maintaining critical distance.

The ghost of Korzybski's system still lingered in international
intellectual circles, however, through his influence on Gregory
Bateson, the anthropologist. See Gregory Bateson, <u>Mind</u> <u>and</u> <u>Nature</u>:
<u>A Necessary Unity</u> (New York: E. P. Dutton and Co., 1979). See
also John Brockman, ed., <u>About</u> <u>Bateson</u>: <u>Essays</u> <u>on</u> <u>Gregory</u> <u>Bateson</u>
(New York: E. P. Dutton and Co., 1977).

INDEX _____

Abstraction: consciousness of, 51, 52, 87; Korzybski and, 35, 56, 58, 83, 86, 90, 113n; orders of, 35, 46, 54, 60, 123n, 126n

Academicians, academics, 65, 69, 72, 73, 79, 89

Ajdukiewicz, Kazimierz, 75, 88, 116n, 124n

Analytical philosophy. See Philosophy, analytical

Aristotle: law of bivalance, 115n; law of identity, 49, 57, 85, 129n; logic of, 33, 39-50 passim, 63, 71, 72, 85, 129n; metaphysics, 45, 47; syllogistic, 49-52 passim; mentioned, 35, 48, 69, 84, 119n

Avenarius, Richard, 16, 37, 81, 100n, 138n

Berent, Wacław, 20, 22, 35, 82, 104n

Biology. See Mechanistic biology

Bivalance, law of, 39, 48, 84, 115n

Black, Max, 140n

Bloomfield, Leonard, 87, 94n, 140n

Boole, George, 33; mentioned, 3, 49

Brandes, Georg, 104n

Brzozowski, Stanisław, 20-22, 34, 36, 104n, 105n; mentioned, 82

Carnap, Rudolf, 37, 73, 114n, 115n

Chase, Stuart: general semantics, 6, 69, 73, 90; The Tyranny of Words, 6, 7, 68; mentioned, 88, 89, 136n

Chwistek, Leon, 40, 124n; mentioned, 42, 43, 62, 83, 117n

Cieszkowski, August von, 17-19, 33, 81, 102n

Circle, the Vienna See Vienna Circle

Class of life, 27, 28, 30. See also Time-binding

Comte, Auguste, 14, 15, 142n; mentioned, 33, 37

Concept by intuition: Korzybski's, 48, 61, 83, 87, 111n; Northrop's, 32, 42, 55, 83; Tarski's, 119n

Concept by postulation: Korzybski's, 61, 83, 87, 112n; Northrop's, 32, 55, 83; Tarski's, 119n

Contradiction: law of, 40, 47, 48, 75

Depression, the Great, 6, 65, 69, 84

Determinisim, 27, 30, 31, 39, 48, 75, 115n

Dewey, John, 5, 65, 66

Edgerly-Korzybska, Mira, 26, 66, 67, 106n, 107n

Einstein, Albert, mentioned, 32, 37, 59, 69, 85

Empirio-criticism: and Avenarius, 81, 100n; and Korzybski, 42, 47, 59, 62, 87; Mach's, 16, 20, 32, 49, 51, 63, 66, 83, 101n, 138n; mentioned, 84, 88, 91

Empiricism, 37, 42, 50, 100n, 126n

Engineering millenialism, 29, 37, 62, 82, 109n, 110n. See also Millenialism

Epistemology, 17, 21, 66, 70, 81, 83, 126n

ETC.: A Review of General Semantics, 7, 71, 74, 88, 90

Excluded middle (third), law of, 47-49, 84, 85

Form of representation, 34, 35

Free intellectual: American, 69, 72, 79, 85, 89; Chase as a, 73; European, 12; Korzybski as a, 13, 30; Polish, 88

Frege, Gottlieb: and identity, 121n, 139n; and logical theories, 127n; and mathematics, 3; mentioned, 37, 60, 114n

Freud, Sigmund: literary analysis, 5; psychoanalysis, 30, 58, 86, 142n; mentioned, 4, 43, 53, 85, 122n

Gantt, Henry L., mentioned, 82

General semantics: article in Time, 69, 132n; and Black, 140n, and Chase, 67-69, 73; First Am. Congress on, 66; and Hayakawa, 70, 73, 74; Institute of, 7, 69-71, 74, 89, 90, 130n; International Society for, 71; Korsybski's, 7, 9, 36, 40-43, 60, 66-79 passim, 84, 87; movement, 8, 72-74, 79, 87; movement after 1950, 88, 90, 91, 133n; and Northrop, 56; and Schaff, 136n; Second Am. Congress on, 71; Third Congress on 71; and science fiction, 134n, 140n: See also Semantics

Gödel, Kurt, 85, 89

Grove-Korski, Dr. Julian, 27, 107n

Gruppe, Otto Friedrich, 50, 120n, 127n; mentioned, 85

Gumplowicz, Ludwig, 14, 15, 17, 35, 81, 99n

Hayakawa, Samuel Ichiyé: background, 70; editor of ETC., 74, 90; and general semantics, 70, 73, 131n, 135n; Language in Action, 70, 73, 132n; Pres. of San Francisco State College 96n; mentioned, 89, 136n

Hegel, George Wilhelm,17, 128n; mentioned, 21, 88

Hook, Sidney, 65, 66, 128n, 129n

Human engineering, 29, 31, 33. See also Time-binding

Identity, laws of, 47-52, passim, 57, 60, 63, 84, 85, 121n. See also Aristotle: Korzybski; Łukasiewicz

Institute of General Semantics. See General semantics

Intellectuals: American, 5, 6, 8, 30, 37, 71, 72, 90; Central European, 23, 37, 79, 82, 88, 110n, 117n; Polish, 13, 15, 33, 74, 78, 79, 81, 83, 128n. See also Free intellectual

Intelligentsia, 11, 12, 36, 72, 81

Intuition, concepts by. See Concepts by intuition

Irzykowski, Karol, 20-23, 34, 35; mentioned, 82

Janik, Allan: and Stephen Toulmin, 100-102n

Jelliffe, Smith Ely, 52, 53, 63, 86, 122n

Keyser, Cassius J.: background, 111n; criticism of Korsybski, 133n; on doctrinal function, 112n; law of identity, 130n; on logical fate, 82; on mathematical philosophy, 30,

31, 37, 43, 62; mentioned, 27, 34, 46, 109n, 114n

Kierkegaard,Søren, 18, 20, 104n

Kołakowski, Leszek, 75, 78

Korzybska, Mira Edgerly. See Edgerly-Korzybska

Korzybski, Alfred: articles and papers of 1920's, 31-33, 36, 52, 82, 126n; article of 1931, 40, 43, 126n; criticism by Keyser, 133n; critique of Aristotelian logic, 8, 42, 49, 71, 72, 85; education and training, 12, 33; governmental appeal, 70, 132n; identity laws, 49, 52, 57, 85, 120n, 129n, 130n, 138n, 139n; Keyes document, 96n; logic of, 32, 36, 118n; Manhood of Humanity, 27-32 passim, 82-90, 96n, 109n, 110n; map analogy, 40, 41, 114n; military duty, 25, 26; morphology, 128n, 129n; Polish background, 7, 8, 11, 81, 89, 96n, 105n, 128n; Science and Sanity, 6, 7, 36, 43, 45, 52-76 passim, 83, 84, 91, 96n, 121n, 122n, 128n; speeches by, 13, 36, 66, 71, 79; theory of language, 7, 47, 53, 60, 63, 82, 84; therapy of language, 7, 47-63 passim, 82, 84, 86; Time-Binding: The General Theory (Second Paper), 54, 113n; in U.S., 26, 27, 36, 37, 96n; in 1890-1914, 22, 23; in 1920's, 83, 114n; and Wittgenstein, 126n; and WWII, 70; mentioned, 38, 119n, 121n, 136n, 138n, 142n. See also Abstraction; Class of life; Empirio-criticism; General Semantics; Human engineering; Language; Leap of negation; Meaning, theory of; Positivists; Semantics; Structural differential; Time-binding

Kotarbiński, Tadeusz, 38–40, 116n; mentioned, 42, 43, 62, 81, 83

Krzywicki, Ludwik, 14–15; mentioned, 35

Language: development, 53, 59, 63; elementalistic, 41; and logic, 3–5, 31, 34, 35, 40–42, 60; nature of, 5, 33, 42, 81; and society, 16; structure of, 40, 41, 71, 76, 126n; theory of, 4, 5, 16, 50, 127n; therapy of, 4, 5, 54. See also Korzybski

Leap of negation, 45–49, 63, 84, 85

Leśmian, Bolesław, 18, 20, 22, 23, 34, 81; mentioned, 82, 118n

Leśniewski, Stanisław, 38–40, 116n; mentioned 42, 43, 62

Linguistics, 8, 59, 75

Loeb, Jacques, 27, 30, 43, 82, 107n, 111n

Logic: laws of, 59; mathematical, 4, 31–47, 62, 82–85, 91, 118n; modern propositional, 39; Stoic, 39. See also Aristotle; Korzybski; Language; Logical systems

Logical empiricism. See Empiricism

Logical positivism. See Positivism

Logical systems: two-valued, 45, 47; three-valued, 32, 71, 83; multi-valued, 49, 76, 83, 85, 118n, 119n; infinitely-valued, 71; Mill's, 39

Logos, 4, 17, 19, 84

Lukács, Georg, 99n, 104n, 105n

Łukasiewicz, Jan: bakcground, 38, 39; critique of Aristotelian logic, 86, 89, 115n, 119n; laws of identity, 48–52, 63, 85; mentioned, 42, 43, 46, 62, 76, 83, 117n

Mach, Ernst: background, 15, 16; phenomenalism, 121n; theory of knowledge, 100n; mentioned, 42, 43, 46, 62, 76, 81, 114n, 127n. See also Empirio-criticism

Malinowski, Bronisław, 79, 138n

Marx, Karl, 102n, 105n; mentioned 18, 21, 37, 65

Marxism, Marxists, 18, 21, 37, 65, 84, 85, 88

Mathematical philosophy, 29, 30, 37

Mauthner, Fritz, 16, 17, 23, 83, 102n, 108n; mentioned, 32, 34, 35, 81, 86

Mead, George Herbert, 59, 125n

Meaning, theory of, 42, 46, 71, 84, 95n

Mechanistic biology, 29–31, 37, 62, 82, 111n

Mill, John Stuart: system of logic, 39; mentioned, 14, 37, 116n

Millenialism, 27, 66. See also Engineering millenialism

Miłosz, Czesław, 11, 12, 21, 104n, 110n, 118n

Multiordinality: of symbols, 76; of terms, 42, 46, 117n

Natural law, 27-29, 36, 38, 82, 90, 142n

Negation, leap of. See Leap of negation

New Deal, 67-69, 72

Nietzsche, Friedrich, 18, 20, 22, 104n; mentioned, 105n

Northrop, F. S. C., 32, 42, 55, 61

Norwid, Cyprian, 19, 78; mentioned, 20, 22, 36, 81, 118n

Ogden, C. K.: theory of meaning, 95n; and Richards, 5, 70, 74, 95n, 114n

Ontology, 39, 40, 83

Orzeszkowa, Eliza, 14, 15; mentioned, 35, 81

Pavlov, Ivan, 86; mentioned, 43, 52, 53, 55, 63, 76

Philosophy: analytical, 8, 50, 66, 74, 75, 77, 79, 87, 88; Polish analytical, 77, 84, 117n, 118n

Piaget, Jean, 52, 53, 76

Poincaré, Jules Henri, 112n, 121n; mentioned, 32, 37, 51, 88

Polakov, Walter N., 109n, 110n

Poland: 1890-1914, 8; WWI, 25, 26; post-WWI, 26, 38, 43; post-WWII, 77; reform 1957, 78; 1960's, 75; 1960-70's, 8

Poland, Young. See Young Poland

Positivisim: American, 89: Austrian, 16, 81; and Avenarius, 101n; and Comte, 142n; European, 13-15, 47,

62, 81, 88, 89; and Korzybski, 28, 32; logical, 37, 66, 87, 140n; Polish, 17, 18, 62, 63, 66, 79, 81; scientific, 22

Positivists: and Korzybski, 82, 89; logical, 38, 100n, 118n, 127n; Polish, 13-21 passim, 27-36 passim, 79-82, 88, 98n, 110n

Postulation, concept by. See Concept by postulation

Pragmatism, 65, 66, 88, 118n

Praxis, theory of, 17-19, 23, 81, 102n

Prus, Bolesław, 17, 35, 81

Psychology: associational, 31, 53; developmental, 76, 77, 89; and mathematics, 31, 33

Pula, Robert P., I, 96n, 120n, 128n

Rapoport, Anatol, 73, 74, 115n; mentioned, 136n

Reification, 16, 34, 81, 83, 86, 99n, 105n

Reism: somatic, 39, 40; semantic, 40

Representation, form of. See Form of representation

Reymont, W. S., 20, 22, 35

Richards, I.A., 70, 95n. See also Ogden

Robinson, James Harvey, 108n, 109n

Russell, Bertrand: influence on Korzybski, 126n; logical atomism, 62; logical system, 39, 43, 82, 83, 112n; theory of descriptions, 61, 111n; theory of language, 60, 62,

63; theory of types, 36, 60, 63, 76, 113n, 126n; mentioned, 3, 5, 37, 46, 73, 88, 114n, 120n

Schaff, Adam, 75-77, 79 , 88, 136n

Schizophrenia, 53, 57-60, 63, 123-125n

Schlick, Moritz, 37, 38, 115n

Semantics: analysis, 32, 39, 53, 83; categories, 39, 42, 51, 85, 86, 116n; and Chase, 6; and Chwistek, 40; and Korzybski, 36, 42, 71, 83; logistic, 79; and Mach, 20: and positivism, 68; in Polish thought, 77; as psycho-social therapy, 8; reactions, 51, 52, 54, 56; and Schaff, 75; science of, 4, 68, 69, 73, 84, 87; systems of, 42, 83; theory of, 46, 59, 87. See also General semantics

Semantic reism. See Reism

Sienkiewicz, Henryk, 17, 35: mentioned 81

Skolimowski, Henryk, 74, 75, 77, 117n

Social evolution, 14, 15, 35, 89

Sociology: in France, 14; Gumplowicz's theory of, 15; of knowledge, 21; in Poland, 14; positivistic, 14, 15, 37

Somatic reism. See Reism

Spencer, Herbert, 14, 15, 99n, 116n; mentioned, 28, 37, 110n

Spengler, Oswald, 128n, 129n

Stallo, John B., 100n

Structural differential, 55-59, 69, 86, 132n

Sullivan, Harry Stack: and abstractions, 58; idea of preconcept, 36, 123n, theory of semantics, 59; treatment of schizoprenia, 54, 57-59, 63, 86, 125n; mentioned, 82

Tarski, Alfred, mentioned, 46, 73, 79, 96n, 118n, 119n

Three-valued logical systems. See Logical systems

Time-binding: theory of, 30, 33, 36, 82, 108n. See also Class of life; Korzybski

Toulmin, Stephen. See Janik, Allan

Tropism, 30, mentioned, 43

Types, theory of, 60, 63, 126n

Vienna Circle, 37, 38, 40, 114n, 127n

Vygotshy, Lev Semenovich: language research and development, 52, 53, 63, 89, 122n; critique of Piaget, 76, 86; mentioned, 59

White, William Alanson, 53, 54, 57, 59; mentioned, 82, 86, 122n

Whitehead, Alfred North: logical system, 39: and Russell, 31, 35; mentioned, 34, 37, 73

Wittgenstein, Ludwig: ingluence on Korzybski, 126n, 127n; Tractatus, 5, 62, 102n, 114n, 120n; Vienna, 101n; mentioned, 23, 37, 56, 60, 212n

Wyspiański, Stanisław, 21-33, 36, 82, 104n; mentioned 118n

Young Poland, 13, 18, 20–23, 27,
    33, 35, 36, 79, 81, 82, 88,
    104n, 118n

Żeromski, Stefan, 20, 22, 104n;
    mentioned, 35, 82

About the Author

Ross Evans Paulson is Professor of History at Augustana College in Rock Island, Illinois. Among his earlier publications are *Radicalism and Reform: The Vrooman Family and American Social Thought, 1837-1937*, which was awarded the 1967 Frederick Jackson Turner Award by the Organization of American Historians, and *Women's Suffrage and Prohibition: A Comparative Study of Equality and Social Control*.